Maharal of Prague

Nesivos Olam
Nesiv HaAvodah

The Philosophy and Practice of Prayer

Chapter 18 - Kos Shel Bracha, Zimun, Birchas HaMazon, Mayim Acharonim

A translation with commentary, including a beginner's guide to studying Maharal

Eliakim Willner

For permission requests, write to the author/publisher at the address below.

Eliakim Willner
1510 East 4th Street
Brooklyn, NY 11230

eli@eliwillner.com

Ordering Information:
Quantity sales. Special discounts are available on quantity purchases by corporations, associations, and others. For details, contact the author/publisher at the address above. Orders by U.S. trade bookstores and wholesalers, contact the author/publisher at the address above..

Printed in the United States of America

ISBN 978-0-9974596-0-9 (print)
   978-0-9974596-1-6 (eBook)

First Edition (Preview), April 2016

Nesiv HaAvodah

18

The Blessing After Meals

Chapter Sections

Foreword

I am grateful to Hashem for providing me the opportunity to continue my *avodas HaKodesh* in presenting the works of the Maharal, and in particular *Nesivos Olam*, to the English-speaking Torah world.

Adapting *Nesiv HaAvodah* into English presents challenges beyond those encountered in the adaptation of *Nesiv HaTorah*, my first venture into bringing the works of the Maharal to a wider audience. *Nesiv HaAvodah* deals with *Tefillah*, prayer. The Maharal first covers very fundamental issues regarding prayer, such as: Why does Hashem need prayer? Why does it work? Why does it have to be spoken? These are issues that our Sages have continually grappled with and they have taken varied approaches taken to dealing with them over the centuries. The commentators that preceded the Maharal formed a context for the Maharal's approach. The ones that followed him provided different perspectives on it. I felt that it would not be fair to the student to ignore either the contexts or the perspectives, thus, many of them appear either in the footnotes, the end notes (themselves an innovation in this volume) or in separate chapters (in the full version of this work).

After discussing the philosophy of prayer the Maharal treats select prayers individually, and since prayer by definition is wide-ranging the Maharal's discussion dips into different topics that bear little direct relationship to prayer. Thus the scope of topics covered in *Nesiv HaAvodah* is more diverse than in *Nesiv HaTorah*. For example the second *bracha* of *Birchas HaMazon* speaks of the land of Israel, of *Bris Milah* and of Torah. In order to explain the relationship of these topics to *Birchas HaMazon* the Maharal has to elaborate on them and in our commentary we must do them justice as well.

There are also myriad *halachic* issues that pertain to prayer and the Maharal discusses many of them, either peripherally or directly. At times the position of the Maharal is at variance with common practice today. Although this adaptation is not a work of *halacha* we felt that it would be inappropriate to gloss over the halachic issues. We therefore provide guidance primarily in the form of marginal callouts that provide references to the issues discussed in *Shulchan Aruch* and *Mishna Brurah*, along with brief summaries. The student is urged to consult the references or a competent authority for practical *halachic* guidance.

We also used callouts as "signposts" to show where the Maharal is holding in his discussion of an extended prayer, such as *Birchas HaMazon*.

Chapters are preceded by chapter tables of content. Some of the chapters have many sections and the tables of content make it easier to find particular topics of interest. Chapters are followed by summaries that conform to the section numberings within the chapters. These can serve as reviews, to firm up the student's understanding of the chapter content and as a way of viewing how the sections fit together into a coherent whole.

A further innovation in the current work is inclusion of the full Hebrew text of *Nesiv HaAvodah* at the end of the volume. We urge students to consult it either in conjunction with study of the English text and annotations, or afterwards. No translation can possibly convey every nuance intended by the original author. By studying both the English adaptation and the original Hebrew the student can have the best of both worlds.

While working on this volume I often thought to myself, wryly, that this *Nesiv* is aptly named *Nesiv HaAvodah*. *Avodah* in the context the Maharal uses it means prayer but the word also means "labor" and indeed much labor was invested into this work – which for me, was and is a labor of love. I hope that my labor investment repays the student by clearing the way to understanding the Maharal's words with much less of an investment of the student's own labor.

Our adaptation of *Nesiv HaTorah* (Artscroll, 1994) has an extended Foreword and Introduction with much valuable information that is equally applicable here. It seems redundant to repeat it; the interested student is referred there.

This "preview" edition contains chapter 18 of *Nesiv HaAvodah* – by far the largest chapter, it deals with *Kos Shel Bracha, Zimun, Birchas HaMazon* and *Mayim Acharonim* although, as mentioned earlier, many other topics not directly related to those are also covered. Since we changed our approach somewhat from that used on *Nesiv HaTorah*, we are releasing this chapter to a limited audience prior to a release of the entire *Nesiv*. We solicit feedback on content, presentation, style and every other aspect of the work. All comments are welcome; please email them to eli@eliwillner.com. (The suggestion to do this came from my good friend Rabbi Moshe Wiener, an accomplished *talmid chochom*, a noted *mechaber seforim*, and an overall wise man. We will attempt to thank him properly in the Acknowledgements!)

Dedication and Acknowledgements

This work is dedicated to the memory of my mother *a'h*, Brana Esther (Bronnie) (*bas* R' Dovid) Willner, may her *neshomo* have an *aliyah*, and as a *zechus* for my father, *y'blchtv*, Rav Yisroel (Eric) Willner (*ben* Mirel) *shlita*, may he have a *refuah shlaimo b'korov, b'soch shaar cholei Yisroel.* Thanks are inadequate for what parents provide their children and my parents went above and beyond for myself and my siblings. May they, and my in-laws *a'h*, Reb Froim and Chaja Kenigsberg, to whom we are also deeply grateful, derive continued *nachas* from us.

My parents launched us and kept us on our trajectories but, for me at least, the fuel that kept me going and the trajectories themselves were supplied by my Yeshiva of nearly half a century, Yeshiva Rabbeinu Chaim Berlin, and its *Roshei Yeshiva*, especially Rav Yitzchok Hutner *zt'l*, who recognized my writing abilities before I myself did and put me to work using them, and *y'blchtv*, Rav Aharon Schechter, *shlita*, who guided me directly and behind-the-scenes in my learning, my *hashkofo* development and my maturity, as fathers guide their sons. Rav Yosef Fruchthandler, *shlita*, with whom I developed and maintain a close *kesher*, did the same, and also had a major personal impact on my life in his role as my mentor, my advisor – and my *shadchan*.

Chazal tell us that a person's *chaburah* has a major influence on his life and I can testify that this is true from personal experience. Our *chaburah* from our Yeshiva years is mostly intact, and in touch, and its positive influence is evident in this work.

I have the great satisfaction and *nachas* of seeing our sons traveling on the same path, in the same Yeshiva, and *shtaiging* to the maximum of their abilities thanks to the Yeshiva and the *Roshei Yeshiva*. May the *Roshei Yeshiva* be *zoche* to be *megadel talmidim bnai Torah v'yisrai shomayim ad meah v'esrim shana, b'nachas u'b'brius.*

The impetus to resume my work on *Nesivos Olam* after a long hiatus came from Rav Shlomo Mandel *shlita*, who invited me to give an evening *shiur* in Maharal for *baalei batim* in his Yeshiva, the Yeshiva of Brooklyn, and who encouraged me to keep at it over the years. Thank you, Rav Shlomo, and may you continue to see *nachas* from all your *talmidim* and *talmidos* in all your *mosdos!* (This is perhaps not the proper venue for expressing *hakoras hatov* to YOB and to Rav Manis Mandel *zt'l*, for the incredible *chinuch* they gave our daughters but I do so anyway. *Im lo achshav aimosai!*)

Thanks are due as well to the stalwarts who manage to make it to the Maharal *shiur* almost every week, week in and week out, no matter the weather and often in spite of other engagements. Reb Yosef Liberman, Reb Menachem Sperling and Reb Aharon Ausfresser, thank you for being the sounding board for many of the concepts that made it into this *chibur*.

I would like to thank Rabbi Pinchos Lipschutz, editor and publisher of Yated Neeman, for graciously agreeing to publish several articles based on this work in his excellent weekly newspaper.

Our summer home for the past twenty-five years has been Camp Bais Yaakov in Ferndale, NY. I have found both the *gashmius'dike* and *ruchnius'dike* atmosphere there very conducive to doing concentrated learning and writing and I would like to thank the Newhouse family, *b'roshom* Reb Shimon Newhouse, *zt'l,* for creating and nurturing that atmosphere.

I mentioned earlier that Rabbi Moshe Wiener encouraged me to produce this "preview" edition of *Nesiv HaAvodah.* In fact Reb Moshe has provided all manner of advice, encouragement and *chizuk* to me over the more than thirty years I have been privileged to know him. He has also treated me to many *divrei Torah* and assisted me with *mareh mekomos* relevant to this work, particularly with respect to *Toras HaChassidus,* thereby enriching the final result. (I would be remiss if I did not also take this opportunity to express *hakoras hatov* to him for the assistance he has provided me over the years in a professional capacity.) Reb Moshe, may you see much *nachas* from your family, your *kehilla* and your incredible *chesed* machine, the Jewish Community Council of Greater Coney Island.

We were *zoche* to wonderful children, children-in-law, grandchildren and *mechutanim* who continue to be a source of great *nachas* and inspiration to us. We thank Hashem for this *brocha* and *daven* to Him that it should continue and extend into all future *doros.*

Acharon acharon chaviv, I thank my *ezer k'negdo,* Gittle, for our home, our family, the "soil" that nurtured our children as well as ourselves and the environment that makes our *avodas hakodesh* possible. What is mine is hers. May we see continued *nachas* from our children, grandchildren and (*i''yH*) great-grandchildren – and from each other – *ad bias goel tzedek, b'korov.*

Eliakim Willner
18 Adar II, 5776
Brooklyn, NY

Introduction: A Beginner's Guide to Studying Maharal

Basic Concepts and Advice to Facilitate Understanding the Torah of the Maharal

The Maharal of Prague is one of the most influential of the early *acharonim*.[1] Many concepts that are today considered mainstream foundations of Jewish thought were originally elucidated by him. He had a major impact on a wide spectrum of the Jewish world, spanning the *Litvishe* Yeshivos, diverse Chassidic courts and other streams of Jewish thought and practice. His influence can found, either explicitly or implicitly, in the teachings of Rav Yitzchok Hutner, Rav Shimon Schwab, Rav Eliyahu Dessler, Rav Chaim Friedlander, Rav Avraham Yitzchok Kook, the *Shem MiShmuel, Avnei Nezer, Chidushei HaRim, Klei Chemda, Rav Tzadkok HaKohen* and many other renowned Jewish thinkers who followed him.

Nonetheless, and despite the fact that his known works are all in print and readily available, study of the Maharal today is not proportional to his stature and his influence. True, the Maharal is not an easy *limud* but most of the impediments that discourage people from studying his works in depth can be cleared away with some pre-study orientation, which we aim to provide in this introduction, and from a work such as this one.

Not Alone

We will begin by observing that almost everyone encounters at least some of the issues we will be discussing when they begin studying the Maharal. Not knowing that these issues are common, some students may think, "it's me", conclude that they are not equipped to understand the Maharal, and give up. But as we will explain, not only are the issues common, they are surmountable with the right approach and with perseverance. Everyone who today swims with assurance in the sea of the Maharal's Torah has had the same learning curve. Persistence is rewarded by entre into the rich, fertile and profound world of the Maharal's Torah, and by an in-depth understanding of many of the most fundamental principles of Judaism. It is well-worth the effort.

Toras HaNistar

At root of several issues that may make the Maharal difficult to approach is his frequent use of *Toras HaNistar*, the "hidden Torah", based on *Kabbalah* and accessible only to a select few, to explain concepts in or answer questions about *Toras Nigleh*, the "revealed" Torah that is commonly studied by the masses. It has been said that the Maharal presents *Toras HaNistar* garbed in the clothing of *Toras Nigleh* – that is, the Maharal couches *Kabbalistic* concepts in terminology familiar to those whose experience has only been with the "revealed" Torah.[2] In this way limited aspects of the "hidden" concept are exposed and brought to bear to solve a problem in the revealed Torah.

In reality there is only one Torah and "hidden" and "revealed" are complimentary components of the same unified entity. Thus it is perfectly natural for a hidden Torah

---

[1] Sages that lived from, roughly, the 16th century to the present day.

[2] As stated by Rabbi Moshe Shlomo Kasher in his introduction to *Nishmas Chaim*, a commentary on the Maharal's *Derech Chaim* by Rabbi Eliyahu Sarason. Rabbi Kasher illustrates his point by citing several ideas from the works of the *Arizal*, which are presented in the typical terse and veiled *Kabbalistic* style, and then citing the same ideas presented by the Maharal in his more verbose and accessible style. The Maharal has adapted the hidden Torah concept to a context and terminology base that are familiar to his audience, who are largely unversed in hidden Torah.

concept to be brought to bear on a discussion that focuses primarily on a revealed Torah issue. The challenge for someone on the level of the Maharal, who is equally comfortable in both realms, but who is addressing an audience that is largely unfamiliar with hidden Torah, is to couch the hidden Torah concept in language the audience can understand. The Maharal does not shy from the challenge.

In turn, we, as members of the Maharal's audience, should not shy from our own challenge, which is to work to overcome the impediments to understanding the concepts the Maharal is carefully laying out for us. After all, most of us will never formally study hidden Torah and the glimpses the Maharal and those who followed in his footsteps provide us may very well be our sole connection to this rarefied aspect of Torah wisdom.

What are some of the hurdles presented by the Maharal's use of *Toras HaNistar* in his works, and how can we overcome them? That is the subject of the following sections.

Apparent Redundancies

First, since the Maharal is using borrowed revealed-Torah terminology to express hidden Torah concepts, direct and concise wording is often impossible. Thus the Maharal attempts to refine his explanation by repeating the concept in subtly different ways, each perhaps slightly off the exact mark, but in combination, forming as accurate a picture of the concept as revealed Torah terminology permits.

Without careful study this repetition can appear to be unnecessarily redundant. But with careful study the sophisticated student may pick up on the intent of the different nuances and gain a refined composite picture of the concept the Maharal is attempting to convey. Unfortunately, though, many if not most students will miss many if not most of the nuances and for them the seemingly unnecessary repetitions can be frustrating. The solution is to understand what is happening and to realize that even without being able to plumb the full depths of the concept the Maharal is attempting to convey a reasonably clear understanding can be achieved.[3]

Super-Rationality

Most students will be unfamiliar with the hidden Torah concepts the Maharal introduces. It is natural, when exposed to new concepts, to attempt to understand them on rational grounds. Yet, without a foundation in hidden Torah the concept itself may seem arbitrary, ill-defined and at times inconsistent, and therefore not amenable to rational analysis. Students will of course find this frustrating.

For example in *Gur Aryeh* on *Parshas Chukas*[4] and elsewhere the Maharal writes that the number three has a particular association with Yisroel[5] because three represents a separation from the physical and an association with the intellectual.[6] Why does the number three have

---

[3] In this translation we attempt to bring out, wherever possible, what we perceive as the intent behind the "repetitions" but we certainly do not claim to have discerned exactly what the Maharal actually had in mind with any particular "repetition". Students capable of doing so are urged to carefully study the Maharal's original language and arrive at their own conclusions. For this reason the full Hebrew text of the relevant chapters in *Nesiv HaAvodah* are included at the back of the volume.

[4] *Bamidbar* 21:35.

[5] The Maharal treats letters, numbers and names as highly significant. This is discussed in more detail in the next section.

[6] In the Maharal's terminology "intellectual and not physical" is identified with "spiritual".

that property? Imagine, says the Maharal, a center point with two end-points emanating from it in different directions. The two endpoints, which are distant from the central point, represent the material plane, since they have extent. Two alone thus cannot represent the non-physical. But the central point does not extend and therefore does not have dimension. It exists conceptually but not physically. The number three thus describes Yisroel, whose strength is intellect-based and not material-based.

Now, while this concept, once digested, strikes an intuitive chord, it is hard to see that it is essential. Yet the Maharal is clearly treating it as definitively true. Also no information is provided as to the parameters of the concept – is every grouping of three inherently associated with the intellect? If not, when does this concept apply and when does it not? The Maharal cited does not share this information with us.

Moreover in his *Drasha al HaTorah* the Maharal writes that the number three is associated with being unconstrained by time; as representing a continual "present". Is this a corollary of the Maharal's association of the number three with the intellect or is it a separate and unrelated interpretation of the number three? If it is a corollary, how so? If a separate interpretation, what rules determine which interpretation to apply and in which circumstances?

Not knowing how to deal with these kinds of questions as they continually arise when the Maharal introduces new hidden-Torah-based concepts can discourage students from proceeding with their Maharal studies.

The "Black Box" Solution – An Approach to Dealing with the Maharal's Hidden Torah References

We would like to suggest an approach to this particular issue which we call "the black box solution" – a term borrowed from the world of technology. A black box is a device, system or object which can be viewed in terms of its behavior, without any knowledge of its internal workings. Those are "opaque" (black).

To lay the groundwork for our black box solution we view the concept presented – say, that the number three represents the non-physical – as axiomatic; as a proposition that is assumed to be true without proof for the sake of studying the consequences that follow from it.[7] This enables us to focus on the concept without being distracted by the question, "But how does the Maharal **know** that…?". Instead we are able to focus on the outcomes – that is, on the points that the Maharal is trying to make, based on the concept.

It is reasonable to assume that the concept is axiomatic because even though its truth may not be intuitively obvious, it is grounded in the Torah and its veracity comes along as part of the package, with our acceptance of the truth of the Torah, whether or not we understand the basis for this or that individual Torah concept. However we are not being asked to avoid attempting to understand the concept, merely to prioritize understanding what the Maharal wants from the concept over attempting to understand the concept itself. Paradoxically, this

---

[7] An example of a mathematical axiom is, "Things which are equal to the same thing are also equal to one another". This statement cannot be proven but if accepted as true it can be used, along with other axioms, to prove useful derivative theorems.

Some axioms, such as this one, are intuitively obvious. Others, less so, but treating them as axiomatic nonetheless allows the process of deriving new knowledge from them to proceed – and as we explain in the text, that process itself can help make the truth of the axiom become self-evident.

approach will not only enable us to understand the Maharal, it will also gradually lead to a better if not complete understanding of the concept itself.[8]

This is because many fundamental concepts of this nature recur frequently in the works of the Maharal and as the student encounters them again and again, in different contexts, they gradually shift into clearer focus. After reviewing some of the earlier encounters the student will find that what might previously have been muddy, and accepted only begrudgingly as axiomatic, has, in retrospect, become clear.

Having accepted the concept as true, we now employ our "black box" technique by observing the "behavior" of the concept in different settings and gradually building a fleshed out composite picture that displays the concept in all its depth and with all its ramifications.

An Example Application of the Black Box Solution

Returning to our example,[9] the Maharal in *Chukas,* as mentioned above, states the principle that three represents the non-physical based on the three-point analogy. That principle becomes our black box. We now set out to see how it "behaves". The Maharal immediately provides some instant applications. Yaakov, the third of the forefathers, is particularly identified with sanctity. Moshe, the third child born to his parents, is referred to as a G-dly man. From these applications we observe the behavior that sanctity equates to non-physical. We observe the behavior that people who are holy have an affinity to the number three.

Still in *Chukas,* the Maharal cites a *Gemara* in *Shabbos[10]* that associates, among other things, the Torah with three and the nation Yisroel in its entirety with three. From this *Gemara* we are able to add some additional behaviors to our growing collection: non-animate things that are holy are also associated with three. Aggregate groups that are holy are also associated with three.

In *Drush al HaTorah* the Maharal writes that the Torah, which is pure intellect, is not subject to the constraints of time that afflict physical things. Our picture of the "three" principle now includes the behavior that the stronger the association with holiness, the weaker the association with the limits of time.

In *Derech Chaim* 1:2 the Maharal writes that the Torah was given in the merit of Yaakov, the third of the forefathers, who is referred to as *Yeshurun* – the "straight-shooter". We are now getting a glimpse of the depth inherent in the "three" principle we have been studying: the third, central point that is intellect-only, and that signifies removal from the physical and holiness, also signifies *yashrus* absolute fairness, a hallmark of the Torah. We begin to appreciate the depth of meaning that lies behind this and the other nuggets of hidden-Torah-in-revealed-Torah-clothing that the Maharal divulges to us.

---

[8] It is important to realize that the Maharal has sources for the *Kabbalistic* concepts that he utilizes but he almost never cites them, for the same reason he clothes them in revealed-Torah terminology – most of his intended audience is unfamiliar with hidden Torah and would therefore be unable to make sense of the sources. One exception is his mention, in *Be'er HaChamishi* of *Be'er HaGolah,* of the *Midrash* on *Sefer HaZohar* and the *Midrash HaBahir* by Rabbi Nechunya ben Hakanah. In his third introduction to *Gevuros Hashem* he references the *Sefer HaYetzira.* So we know that those are some of the Maharal's *Kabbalistic* sources but doubtless there are others.

[9] We are not doing justice to the number three principle here since our point is to use it to illustrate the "black box" approach to studying the Maharal, not to study it in its own right, though it certainly deserves that kind of study. We treat the subject in more detail in Chapter 18, Section 24.

[10] 88a.

There is much more to the "three" principle than we have discussed here but this is sufficient to illustrate our suggested approach to dealing with the apparently impenetrable hidden Torah references in the Maharal.

Letters, Numbers and Names

Perhaps the most common context in which the Maharal calls on the hidden Torah to establish a point is with respect to letters, numbers and names. In hidden Torah the letters that comprise words, and their letter-shapes, are significant, and teach important lessons (as an illustration, it is significant that the letter *hai*, ה, is open at the bottom and has a "window" at the top).[11] Counts (such as, there are exactly three forefathers, not less and not more) and positions-in-sequence (for example, that Shabbos is, specifically, the seventh day) also have meaning.[12] Even proper names are meaningful.[13] Indeed, examples of such are cited by earlier commentators in revealed Torah works as well.

Our approach to understanding these references should follow the process described in the previous section on *Toras HaNistar* – assume the specifics to be axiomatic and build a gradual picture of each reference by systematically gathering its behaviors, black-box style.

Dealing with the Maharal's Scope

Now, notice that we built our illustrative composite picture of the "three" principle from the Maharal's writings in *Gur Aryeh*, *Drush al HaTorah* and *Derech Chaim*. It might be asked, does the student have to traverse the entire corpus of the Maharal's works to understand each hidden Torah usage presented by the Maharal? It seems an insurmountable task! The answer is, yes and no. Yes, in theory, to fully understand the Maharal one must have a very broad knowledge of his writings. But no, because each of the sources presents a satisfying look at the "three" principle that, while not complete, is sufficient to establish the point the Maharal is focused on, in context. And it is gratifying to encounter familiar concepts when learning the Maharal over time, and adding additional dimensions to one's understanding of them.[14]

The Maharal's Writing Style

We have already explained that the Maharal uses the technique of repetition with variations to convey hidden-Torah concepts using familiar, revealed Torah terminology. Another feature of the Maharal's style is to utilize complex sentence and paragraph structures to bring home the sometimes complex points he is trying to make. Sentences and paragraphs must sometimes be re-read several times before understanding what those points are and why the Maharal chose that way to express them.

There is sometimes a tendency for students to "skim", in a rush to get the gist of the message without investing a great deal of effort. This approach does not work with the Maharal and will only lead to frustration. Neither the concepts presented by the Maharal nor

---

[11] See *Rashi* and the *Gur Aryeh* on *Beraishis* 2:4.

[12] See *Chidushei Aggados* on *Chulin* 91b where the Maharal writes, "Every number… has an independent existence…".

[13] In *Ohr Chodosh* (London edition, p. 110) the Maharal writes that, "Names are always indicative of the essence of a thing". See Also *Gur Aryeh* on *Beraishis* 14:14 where the Maharal relates the name and *Gematria* of Eliezer (Avrohom's servant) to his attributes.

[14] In this translation we attempt to provide a short-cut to this process by supplying references to other places in the works of the Maharal where the concept is also discussed. When studying the Maharal in the original Hebrew the editions of Rabbi Yehoshua Hartman are invaluable in that they provide in-context cross-references for the concept under the discussion as well as detailed topical indexes.

their mode of presentation lend themselves to this tactic. Patient effort is required and the student should be prepared to re-read certain sections multiple times in order to fully grasp the Maharal's message.[15]

The Maharal often builds his concepts sectionally, first constructing and presenting one component, then another, then another, and finally putting them together into a complex but coherent structure. Since he may not state up-front what his final objective is going to be, it is only at the end when this is visible to the student. Therefore the student must focus on the train of thought the Maharal is developing and not jump to the conclusion that he "gets it" before reaching the end of the current section. And once the structure has become clear it is advisable to re-read the section to reinforce understanding of the component pieces and how they fit together.[16]

Multiple Explanations of Increasing Depth

The Maharal often quotes a *Gemara* or other *ma'amar chazal*, presents a list of questions on it, then presents his novel understanding of the quoted text, which answers the questions. There is nothing unusual in that, but then the Maharal presents one or more other ways of understanding the quoted text which answer the questions in a different way. The discerning student will notice that the first explanation is usually straightforward, and successive explanations become deeper and often more hidden-Torah oriented as they progress, and will be left wondering which is the "real" way of understanding the text.

Sometimes the Maharal will indicate which one he views as primary but often he does not. In that case they are all valid, even though they may logically be mutually exclusive, following the principle that "there are seventy facets to the Torah".

Grammar

The Maharal is an expert grammarian and he often uses fine grammatical distinctions to make significant points with major ramifications. Unfortunately many today are not well-versed in grammar and these discussions are therefore often difficult to follow. Access to a text on Hebrew grammar to research the issue is helpful.[17]

Our Sages point out that Hebrew is a holy tongue of divine origin; the language used by Hashem to create the world. It did not evolve over time as did other "natural" languages. While other languages have words with two unrelated meanings (homonyms/homographs), Hebrew does not. If a Hebrew word has two meanings, there is a significant relationship between the two meanings, with practical implications. The Maharal frequently takes pains to explain what that relationship is and what the practical implications are.

Other languages have two words with the same meaning (synonyms) but this too is impossible in Hebrew. There must be a subtle difference in meaning between the two words

---

[15] We attempt to mitigate these issues in this translation by restructuring sentences to increase readability, by adding "bridge" phrases to telegraph to the student where the Maharal is headed with a concept, and by adding commentary in the footnotes to provide background, to explain and to compare and contrast with similar concepts developed in other writings of the Maharal and others who deal with similar concepts. Nonetheless, even in translation, the Maharal should be studied slowly and carefully, and with reference to the original Hebrew whenever possible.

[16] Here too we attempt to lay out the Maharal's roadmap in advance, in such cases, to ease the process of understanding.

[17] In our footnotes we provide a quick course in the relevant grammatical principles – sufficient to understand the Maharal's discussion – but access to a good text on Hebrew grammar is still going to be helpful!

or one of the words would not exist. Here as well the Maharal labors to bring out that subtle difference in meaning and describes the practical implications.

Get a Rebbi

The best way to learn Maharal, and most other complex studies, especially those having to do with *Kabbalah*, is from a pious and learned teacher who is an expert in the subject matter and who studied it himself from a teacher who was the same. Unfortunately such teachers are few and far between. It is our hope that this translation and commentary will provide students with the next best thing, and open the door to the Torah of the Maharal to a wide audience of sincere Jews who hunger for the depth of thought, the focus on basic principles of Judaism, the beauty and the intellectual satisfaction inherent in the Torah of the Maharal.

Section 1 – The Importance of the Blessing After Meals

הברכה שהוא עיקר בברכות הוא ברכת המזון...

*B*irchas HaMazon[1] is the most important of all the blessings.[2] A person must be meticulous about blessing Hashem, who provides him with his sustenance – the need that stands above all others. As the *Gemara* states in chapter *Arvei Pesachim*,[3] "Providing man's sustenance is more difficult than [bringing about] the redemption. Regarding redemption the verse states,[4] 'The angel that redeems me from all evil' while regarding sustenance the verse states,[5] 'G-d Who sustained me as long as I am alive'."[6]

[Why is sustenance more difficult than redemption?] Redemption is the repatriation of a person who is under the domination of another, to a state of self-determination. This is something than an angel is capable of doing since an angel himself is not under anyone's dominion. True, he is under the dominion of Hashem but this does not constitute being under someone else's dominion because everything is under the dominion of Hashem, this is the way the universe was set up; it is not a weakness but a natural state of affairs.[7]

Now when a person is under someone else's control he requires redemption. An

———————————— פירוש בנתיבות לב ————————————

[1] ברכת המזון, *Birchas HaMazon*, also known as *"Bentching"*, which is Yiddish for "blessing", is the term commonly used to refer the series of four blessings and other prayers that are recited after meals. It literally means, "the blessing for food". We will refer to it heretofore as "the blessing after meals" or "the after-meals blessing", to distinguish it from the blessings made prior to eating food.

[2] It is the only blessing that is biblically mandated.

[3] *Pesachim* 118a.

[4] *Beraishis* 48:16. The context of both this and the next verse cited is a blessing that Yaakov was bestowing on his grandsons Ephraim and Menashe. He calls upon Hashem, who has been his own stalwart guardian, to confer the blessings, and in so doing he refers to the **angel**, or messenger of Hashem, who **redeems** him from evil, as well as to **Hashem**, who has provided him with **sustenance**. It is clear that to provide redemption it is sufficient for Hashem to send a messenger, but to provide sustenance requires Hashem's direct intervention, as it were. This demonstrates the *Gemara's* point that providing sustenance is more difficult. It is therefore, as the Maharal says, a need that stands above all others.

Since, from the standpoint of Hashem, who is omnipotent, there is no such thing as "difficulty" there is also no such thing as relative difficulty – nothing can be said to be more "difficult" to Hashem than anything else. However since the ability of angels is limited, as the Maharal will detail, there is, for them, a concept of relative difficulty and from that standpoint sustenance is more difficult than redemption since the angels can perform the latter but not the former.

[5] *Beraishis* 48:15.

[6] In *Gevuros Hashem* chapter 65 the Maharal explains the sequence of praises to Hashem found in *"Hallel HaGadol"*, *Tehillim* 136. This chapter culminates in the verse, "Who gives bread to all flesh, for His kindness is eternal" and the Maharal, citing the same *Gemara* in *Pesachim* that is cited here, explains that the fact that Hashem provides sustenance to all is the most significant of His kindnesses and miracles, superseding even redemption, and therefore appears last in the list. (See footnote 173 for an alternative understanding of the verse in *Tehillim*.)

Therefore, during the *Pesach seder*, after we relate the events of the *Pesach* redemption itself, we recite *Hallel HaGadol* to praise Hashem for his ultimate kindness – He sustains us.

[7] So a lack of independence from Hashem is not a "weakness" since it is shared universally and is absolute – being a subject of Hashem is not amenable to "redemption". Thus no one can claim superiority in this respect – it is a level playing field. The point the Maharal is driving at is that a being cannot free someone else from a flaw the he himself is susceptible to. The Maharal is now establishing that an angel is not susceptible to being dominated and thus he is equipped to save humans from domination – and the fact that he is dominated by Hashem does not impede that ability since being dominated by Hashem is universal and "incurable" and therefore does not suggest a "weakness".

angel, [as we said,] cannot be dominated and so never needs redemption. Thus an angel is capable of providing redemption [to others] since he himself is never subject to the weakness of being dominated.

On the other hand sustenance is the fuel that keeps a person going; a person was created in such a way that he needs continual upkeep, and sustenance is the means of providing that upkeep. The same is true, however, of ethereal creatures such as angels. They also require and receive sustenance from Hashem. So how can an angel, who himself depends on others for his own sustenance, provide other beings with sustenance? How can he redress a need in others when he requires an outside force to redress the same need in himself?

This is why [Yaakov said regarding sustenance,] "**G-d** Who sustained me" while with regard to redemption he said, "**The angel** that redeems me from all evil".

Now, realize and understand that just as the heart, by itself, sustains all the body's organs – they all receive their vitality from it – in the same way all creatures receive their vitality from Hashem. The same point is brought out in the *Gemara* in the first chapter of *Brachos*,[8] which states, "Just as Hashem sustains the entire world, so does the soul sustain all the body's organs".[9]

In the same vein the *Gemara* in *Pesachim* cited earlier provides numerous additional analogies, which we will not detail here,[10] for the difficulty of providing sustenance. [And yet Hashem surmounts these difficulties and provides our sustenance nonetheless.]

Halacha הלכה

See the discussion of the various points of view on the complex subject of the blessing-cup in the *Shulchan Aruch* section cited below.

Shulchan Aruch Orach Chaim 182 and 183.

Therefore our Sages were very particular that the blessing after meals be as complete as possible, just as Hashem "completes" us with food. [For this reason] it is appropriate to accompany the recitation of the blessing after meals with a cup of wine[11] and even those who hold that this is not required agree that it is meritorious to have available a blessing-cup of wine [for the blessing after meals].

A cup of wine, [in particular,] is most appropriate for the blessing-cup[i] because it indicates the extent of the bounty we enjoy from Hashem – which is why, in fact, it

──────── פירוש בנתיבות לב ────────

[8] *Brachos* 10a.

[9] The Maharal is emphasizing in these two comparisons the point he made in the previous paragraph – Hashem "Himself", provides sustenance to all earthly and heavenly creatures alike. The heart provides physical vitality universally to all the organs of the body and Hashem provides physical vitality to all creatures in the world. The soul provides the spiritual spark of life that animates all the organs of the body and Hashem provides the spiritual spark of life that animates the world. In sum, all forms of sustenance to all beings come directly from Hashem.

In *Gevuros Hashem* chapter 65 the Maharal elaborates on this point, writing that just as there is no organ in the body that gets its sustenance "second hand", through another organ that connects to the heart and not through the heart directly, so also there is no being that gets its sustenance through intermediaries – it all comes from Hashem directly.

[10] To list two examples, "Man's sustenance involves twice as much suffering as [that of] a woman in childbirth", "A man's sustenance is as difficult [to provide] as the dividing of the Red Sea".

[11] In Hebrew, כוס של ברכה, *kos shel bracha*, which we translate as "blessing-cup". The phrase originates in the Gemara (*Brachos* 51a, discussed in the next section). As the Maharal explains in Chapter 8 the word ברכה, *bracha*, which is commonly translated as "blessing", actually means "wellspring" and denotes a gushing flow of abundance. A "blessing" to Hashem is an acknowledgement that he is the source of that abundant flow. The blessing-cup is a metaphorical representation of that abundant flow as the Maharal is in the process of explaining, and that is why it is appropriate to use it during the blessing after meals.

is called "blessing-cup".[12] When blessing Hashem [after meals] on the bounty He has bestowed upon us it is appropriate for the blessing cup of wine to come first, and to take its place at the start [of the blessing]. When wine, the expression of the abundance of our bounty, is in front of us we are motivated to praise and bless Hashem on the full gamut of blessing we enjoy from Him. This is why it is important to accompany the blessing after meals with a blessing-cup.

Section 2 – Wine and the Blessing-Cup

ובפרק שלשה שאכלו אין מברכין על היין...

Halacha הלכה

See the discussion of the various points of view on the complex subject of the need to dilute the wine in the blessing-cup in the *Shulchan Aruch* section cited below.

Shulchan Aruch Orach Chaim 183:2 (and Mishna Brurah)

From chapter *Shlosha She'achlu*.[13] "One may not recite a blessing[14] on wine until water is added to it: This is the opinion of Rabbi Eliezer.[15] The Sages hold that one may make a blessing [without the addition of water]."

From a related *Gemara*.[16] "Rabbi Yosi bar Chanina said that the Sages concede to the view of Rabbi Eliezer in the case of a blessing-cup and agree that one may not recite a blessing on it until water is added. The reason, Rabbi Oshia explains, is that the blessing-cup requirement must be satisfied in an optimal manner."[17]

It appears to me that there is no difference in this regard between the wines of Israel [as they were in the times of the Gemara] and other wines in the countries we live in today; water must be added regardless. This is because the wines of Israel are the primary wines[18] and therefore the nature of all wine is such that they are not fit for

───────── פירוש בנתיבות לב ─────────

[12] Wine in particular represents abundance because it is a luxury. When we showcase our wine in the blessing-cup as we bless Hashem after meals we are stating that Hashem has given us not only our basic food requirements but even items of luxury, like wine, and we express our profound gratitude to Him for doing so.

On a deeper level, as explained in end note i, "On Wine", wine is a primarily spiritual substance and is thus suitable for accompanying the spiritual statement we make when we bless Hashem for providing our sustenance.

[13] *Brachos* 50a, in the *Mishna*.

[14] The pre-blessing prescribed for wine, "*Borei pri hagefen*".

[15] The custom in the time of the Gemara was to dilute wine to 25% of its full strength by mixing three parts water to one part wine, because undiluted wine was too strong to drink straight. Wine was also given its own pre-blessing, different from the pre-blessing of grapes, because, although wine is a derivative of grapes, it is fundamentally different from, and superior to, grapes. Rabbi Eliezer holds that since uncut wine is undrinkable it cannot be called superior and thus does not merit its own pre-blessing; a person drinking uncut wine recites the same *borei pri hoeitz* pre-blessing that is recited on grapes.

The Sages hold that since drinks could be made from straight wine by adding other ingredients, such as honey, peppers, aromatic oils and the like, the wine itself can be called superior, even without the addition of water, thus meriting the special pre-blessing specified for wine.

[16] *Brachos* 50b.

[17] That is, even though wine retains its distinct and superior identity from grapes without water dilution, thus meriting its unique pre-blessing regardless of dilution, it is still superior when diluted as described in footnote 15 and therefore when optimality is called for, such as for wine used in a blessing-cup, the wine must be diluted.

There are opinions that hold that dilution is irrelevant even for a blessing-cup nowadays since our wine is considerably weaker than the wine used in the times of the *Gemara* and is drinkable straight. However the Maharal rules that the addition of water to a blessing-cup applies even today, as he will explain.

[18] And they thus set the standard for other wines. The characteristics of wine are defined by the characteristics of the wine of Israel. The wines of Israel are primary because grape and grape products are one of the seven species that Israel is renowned for, as enumerated in *Devarim* 8:8.

a blessing unless diluted. Nonetheless it is not necessary [in order to satisfy this requirement] that the wine be diluted entirely;[19] the implication [of the *Gemara*] is that [the requirement is satisfied] as long as some water is added, be that a large or small amount. The Gemara states only that water be added, not that [the wine] be diluted.[20]

Moreover, on the contrary, it is preferred that the wine be undiluted as this is one of the ten characteristics that are attributed to a blessing-cup.[21] Thus it is clear that the wine [in the blessing-cup] must be *chai* and not fully diluted and the requirement is to merely add some water since water has a beneficial effect on wine, but a small amount is sufficient. Diluting the wine [fully] is detrimental since diluted wine is not full-fledged wine. Water in small amounts is beneficial, however, so one should limit himself to that.

There is another reason why water [in small amounts] is beneficial that is rooted in hidden wisdom. Wine in pure form [in the blessing-cup] is not optimal because wine brought lamentation to the world[22] and our Sages said several things about wine that are the antithesis of blessing. Moreover the *Gemara* in chapter *Ben Sorer U'Moreh*[23] describes the thirteen instance of the letter *vov* that appear in the Torah's description of the wine-related events that occurred to Noach after he exited the ark.[24]

Therefore one does not recite a blessing on wine until water is added; only after that it is suitable for a blessing. Once the wine has been adulterated with water it no longer brings lamentation to the world. Once it is joined with water it is suitable for blessing.[25] This and not some of the other prevalent customs is the proper practice.[26]

פירוש בנתיבות לב

[19] Using the 3:1 ratio common in the times of the *Gemara*, which was called מזוג, *mazug*, or diluted.

[20] The word *mazug* is not used, implying that the addition of water need not be to the then-commonly accepted dilution ratio.

[21] *Brachos* 51a. The Maharal will discuss this *Gemara* at length in the next section. One of the ten characteristics is that the wine in the blessing cup must be חי, *chai*, which literally means "raw". What it means in this context is a matter of dispute among the commentaries but the Maharal understands it to mean "undiluted". If this is in fact the meaning though, the *Gemara* apparently contradicts the previously cited *Mishna* which states that the wine in the blessing-cup must contain water! The resolution, the Maharal explains, is that the wine not be diluted in the 3:1 ratio but must contain a small measure of water.

[22] *Sanhedrin* 70b. See also *Yoma* 76b. *Rashi* comments there that through wine much immorality and suffering is brought into the world. See *Vayikra Rabbah* 10:4, "Wine leads both men and women to adultery" and *Eruvin* 65a, "Enter wine, exit the secret".

[23] *Sanhedrin* 70a.

[24] The *vov's* onomatopoeically represent the sound of a cry of dismay: *vay*! See end note i "On Wine" for a discussion of the meaning of this *Gemara* and its significance.

[25] Apparently the Maharal is saying that once water is added to the wine its spiritual characteristics are diminished to the point where, although it retains some level of spirituality, its ability to generate lamentation has been neutralized. See end note i "On Wine" for a full discussion of the spiritual nature of wine and its implications.

[26] The Maharal apparently is taking issue with the *Ramah* in *Shulchan Aruch Orach Chaim* 183:2 who writes that no water need be added to modern wines since they are not as strong as the wines prevalent in the times of the *Gemara*.

The *Bais Yosef* on *Orach Chaim* 183 writes that it was the custom in his part of the world to add some water to the wine in the blessing-cup for Kabbalistic reasons, even though their wines were not strong, and the *Eshel Avraham* comments that the *Bais Yosef* is referring to the reason the Maharal presents here: that the negative aspects of wine which create lamentation are neutralized once any amount of water is added to the wine. See end note i "On Wine" for background information.

Section 3 – The Blessings of the Blessing Cup – Part 1

ובפרק שלשה שאכלו תנא עשרה דברים...

From chapter *Shlosha SheAchlu:*[27]

"We learned in a *Braiso:* Ten requirements were specified for a blessing-cup: (1) It requires הדחה, *hadacha*[28] (2) שטיפה, *shtifa*[29] (3) חי, *chai*[30] (4) מלא, *maleh* (5) עיטור, *itur*[31] (6) עיטוף, *ituf*[32] (7) נוטלו בשתי ידיו, *notlo b'shtei yadav*[33] and (8) נותנו ביד ימין, *nosno b'yad yemin*[34] (8) מגביהו מן הקרקע תפח, *magbiho min hakarka tefach*[35] (9) נותן עיניו בו, *nosein eniav bo.*[36] [There are those who add] that (10) he must also present it to his household.[37]

"Rabbi Yochanan said, our custom is to observe only four of these requirements: (1) הדחה, *hadacha* (2) שטיפה, *shtifa* (3) חי, *chai* (4) מלא, *maleh.*

"We learned in a *Braiso* that (1) *hadacha* means to wash the inside [of the cup] while (2) *shtifa* means to wash the outside.

"Rabbi Yochanan said, whoever makes a blessing on a full cup ((4) *maleh*) is granted an unbounded inheritance, as the verse says,[38] '...and full (*maleh*) of Hashem's blessing. Take possession of the [west] sea and the south'.[39] Rabbi Yosi bar Chaninah said, he merits and inherits both worlds, this world and the world-to-come.[40]

——————————— פירוש בנתיבות לב ———————————

[27] *Brachos* 51a-b.

[28] A kind of washing; the *Gemara* will discuss the meaning of each of these ten requirements in detail after they are enumerated.

[29] Another variety of washing.

[30] As discussed previously there are a variety of different understandings of this word; the Maharal understands it to mean undiluted.

[31] Adornment.

[32] *Ituf* literally means "to wrap oneself". The *Gemara* will discuss what the blessing-cup *ituf* requirement is shortly.

[33] He uses both hands to lift the blessing cup.

[34] He transfers it to his right hand.

[35] He lifts it a *tefach* from the ground. A *tefach* is between 3-4 inches.

[36] He gazes at it.

[37] The reference is to his wife.

The numbering scheme given is that of the Maharal, though others have a different numbering scheme that counts "uses both hands to life the blessing-cup" and "transfers it to his right hand" as separate items and omits "he must also present it to his household" from the list of ten. The difference between the two numbering schemes depends on whether one's edition of the Talmud has the words, "there are those who add" before "he must also present it to his household". This will be fully explained in section 7.

[38] *Devarim* 33:23.

[39] Homiletically the verse is saying that if the blessing [-cup] of Hashem is full, the way is clear for taking possession of the west and the south. The *Maharsha* on the *Gemara* explains that the sea is free of habitation so it has no borders and similarly the land south of Israel is desolate desert and is also free of habitation and of borders. Thus in this context "west and south" is tantamount to unbounded.

[40] One way of understanding Rabbi Yosi bar Chaninah is suggested by the commentary of *Tosfos*, who says that it is based on the same verse cited by Rabbi Yochanan. In particular, in the phrase, "Take possession of..." the word ירשה, *yerasha*, is used for "take possession" when the simpler form of the word, רש, *rash*, would have suited as well. The additional two letters are a *yud* and a *hey*. Now, the *Gemara*

"[What is] (5) *itur?* Rabbi Yehudah would surround his blessing-cup with students.[41] Rav Chisda would surround the blessing-cup with "satellite" cups filled with wine. Rabbi Chanan said[42] that [the wine in the satellite cups] should be undiluted. Rabbi Sheshes said that *itur* should be done by the blessing of the land.[43]

(6) *ituf:* "Rav Pappa would wrap himself in his cloak and sit [when he used the blessing-cup]. Rav Assi would don his head-covering.[44]

(7) "He takes the blessing-cup in both his hands": Rabbi Chininah bar Pappa said, where is this alluded to in scripture? [In the verse,][45] "Lift your hands[46] in the holy place and bless the Lord".

"And he transfers it to his right hand": Rabbi Chiya bar Abba said in the name of Rabbi Yochanan, earlier Sages questioned whether it was permissible for the left hand to assist the right [in holding the blessing-cup]. Rav Ashi said, since earlier Sages posed the question without answering it we will adopt a stringent position.

(8) "And he lifts it a *tefach*[47] from the ground": Rav Acha son of Rabbi Chaninah said, where is this alluded to in scripture? [In the verse,][48] "I will lift up a cup of salvations, and I will call out in the name of Hashem".

(9) "And he gazes at it": So that his attention should not wander from it.[49]

(10) "He must also present it to his household": So that his wife should

---

פירוש בנתיבות לב

in *Menachos* 29b states that this world was created using the letter *hey* and the next world, with the letter *yud* (see the *Gemara* for the reason). Those letters are often used as references to each of the worlds. Their seeming superfluous addition to the word meaning "take possession" in the verse is to teach us, Rabbi Yosi says, that one whose cup is *maleh* inherits (takes possession of) the worlds created with each of those letter.

The *Maharsha* adds an additional explanation. He writes that "sea" is a reference to this world, based on a *Gemara* that associates mercantile exchange with the sea and that "south" is a reference to the world-to-come based on a *Gemara* that states that one who wishes to acquire the wisdom of the Torah – which is other-worldly – should face south. One who makes a blessing on a full cup merits the ability to attain both these sometimes contradictory acquisitions, simultaneously.

[41] In honor of the blessing his students would surround him in a circle when he held the blessing-cup thereby symbolizing mastery, as will be explained in the next section.

[42] The version of the *Gemara* the Maharal cites in this section leaves out the requirement of Rav Chanan. However, the Maharal includes it in the upcoming section that discusses the *itur* requirement in detail so the omission here is evidently a transcriber error. We have therefore restored it.

[43] The second blessing in the blessings after a meal.

[44] G-d fearing people observe *ituf* nowadays by wearing a hat (and according to some a jacket as well) when reciting the blessings after meals, even when reciting the blessings alone and without a blessing-cup. See *Mishna Brurah* 183:11.

[45] *Tehillim* 134:2.

[46] "Hands" plural.

[47] A *tefach* is approximately 3-4 inches.

[48] *Tehillim* 116:13. Before "calling out in the name of Hashem" – a homiletical reference to the blessings after meals – I will "lift up a cup"; a homiletical reference to the blessing-cup.

[49] Or, as the *Mishna Brurah* understands it, so that his attention should not wander from the blessing itself.

also benefit from the blessing.[50]

Without a doubt the fact that there are ten requirements specified for a blessing-cup is no coincidence; it did not just happen to work out to that number. [Rather,] these ten items correspond[51] to the ten [*v'yiten l'cha*[52]] blessings that Yitzchok bestowed on Yaakov.[53] [We will go through them one by one.]

"May Hashem bestow upon you dew from the skies and moisture from the earth." The [blessing-cup] practices that correspond to [these, first two of Yitzchok's blessings] are *hadacha*, interior-of-cup washing and *shtifa*, exterior-of-cup washing. [The blessing is that] dew will bathe the surface of the earth until it is awash with life-giving wetness. Our parallel action [to invoke this blessing] is to wash the exterior of the blessing-cup. We also do interior-cup washing to parallel the [blessing for] interior moisture of the earth since [the blessing includes] "fatness", not dryness, beneath the surface of the earth as well. This accounts for the requirements of *shtifa* and *hadacha*.

Chai, undiluted, corresponds to the "abundance of wine" blessing. *Chai* denotes wine at full strength, unmixed with anything else. In that state it accurately reflects Yitzchok's blessing for wine. But if it is adulterated with water it does not accurately reflect the blessing, since as we said earlier,[54] "wine" implies wine in pure form.[55]

───────────────────── פירוש בנתיבות לב ─────────────────────

[50] Drinking from the blessing-cup brings blessing. See footnote 51.

[51] The Maharal is saying that we observe these ten practices in order to invoke the ten blessings of Yitzchok onto ourselves and by extension, onto all of Yisroel. His source is likely a *Gemara* which appears in *Horios* 12a and *Krisos* 5b: "Our Rabbis taught that kings may only be anointed next to a well-spring so that their rulership should endure. [Just as the well-spring flows continually, so should the new king's rule endure continually.]... *Abaye* said, now that it has been said that symbolism is significant [and can affect actual events], people should make a regular habit of eating pumpkin, fenugreek, leek, beets and dates [because the Aramaic names of these foods are evocative of various different blessings]." It is indeed common custom to eat these foods on *Rosh HaShanah* to invoke the power of their blessing.

The Maharal is saying that the ten blessing cup practices are evocative of the blessings of Yitzchok and therefore they have the power to bring those blessings to those who observe the practices and by extension, onto all of Yisroel.

[52] The verses containing the blessings begin with the words *v'yiten l'cha*, "May Hashem bestow up on you", and the blessings are often referred to as the *v'yiten l'cha* blessings.

[53] The verses containing the blessings appear in *Beraishis* 27:28. They are broken down into ten separate blessings in *Pirkei d'Rabbi Eliezer* 32. The Maharal will now explain how each of the ten requirements for a blessing cup corresponds to one of the ten blessings.

For clarity in the following sections, and for reference, we include this table of the correspondences.

	Yitzchok's Blessing – וְיִתֶּן לְךָ הָאֱלֹקִים		Blessing-cup Requirement	
1	מִטַּל הַשָּׁמַיִם	From the dew of the skies	שטיפה	Wash (exterior)
2	וּמִשְׁמַנֵּי הָאָרֶץ	The moisture of the earth	הדחה	Wash (interior)
3	וְרֹב דָּגָן	An abundance of grain	מלא	Full
4	וְתִירֹש	Wine	חי	Undiluted
5	יַעַבְדוּךָ עַמִּים	Nations shall serve you	עיטור	Surrounded
6	וְיִשְׁתַּחֲווּ לְךָ לְאֻמִּים	And bow to you	עיטוף	Enrobed
7	הֱוֵה גְּבִיר לְאַחֶיךָ	Be dominant over your brothers	ומקבלו בשתי ידיו ונותנו בימינו	Take with both hands and place into right hand
8	וְיִשְׁתַּחֲווּ לְךָ בְּנֵי אִמֶּךָ	Your mother's sons will bow to you	ומגביה מן הקרקע טפח	Hold it a *tefach* off the ground
9	אֹרְרֶיךָ אָרוּר	Those who curse you shall be cursed	ונותן עיניו בו	Gaze at it
10	וּמְבָרֲכֶיךָ בָּרוּךְ	Those who bless you shall be blessed	ומשגר לאשתו ולבניו ולביתו	Present to wife, children and household members

[54] In the previous section.

[55] Albeit it should contain a modicum of water for reasons described in the previous section.

Maleh, full, corresponds to an abundance of grain. Abundance does not apply to wine since the primary distinction of wine is its strength, which is characteristic of the wines of Israel. Abundance does, however, apply uniquely to grain, so [to instantiate that blessing] we fill the blessing-cup until it overflows. Filling [symbolizes abundance and] is applicable to granaries as we see in the verse,[56] "And the granaries shall be filled with grain". Moreover grain is satiating and makes a person feel full. Thus "abundance" is apropos to grain. [This applies on a macro level as well;] when the world has an abundance of grain it is in an overall state of satisfaction and fullness.[57]

Really, [to keep the symbolisms of the blessing-cup in the same the order as Yitzchok's blessings,] *maleh* should have preceded *chai* [in the list of blessing-cup requirements,] except that the wine obtained to fill the blessing-cup must be *chai* and only then [when wine that is *chai* is at hand] can the blessing-cup be filled.[58] Thus *chai* precedes *maleh* [in the list of blessing-cup requirements].

The *Gemara* adds[59] that whoever makes a blessing on a full cup is granted an unbounded inheritance.[60] This follows from the fact that a full cup also signifies completeness[61] which means that the attribute of completeness is added to the blessings that ensue from the blessing-cup. Completeness in the context of blessing implies boundlessness.[62] That one who makes a blessing on a full cup also merits both this world and the world-to-come[63] takes the concept a step further by extending the boundlessness that ensues from a full blessing-cup beyond the realm of this world into, even, the world-to-come.

Section 4 – The Blessings of the Blessing Cup – Part 2

עיטור ועיטוף, עיטור כמו ויהיו עוטרים את דוד...

tur and *ituf*: *Itur* is used in the sense that it is used in the verse,[64] "[…but Shaul and his men] were encircling[65] Dovid"; in other words, they were surrounding him. The *Gemara* states that Rabbi Yehudah would observe the *itur* requirement using his students, which Rashi explains to mean that his students encircled him

———————————— פירוש בנתיבות לב ————————————

[56] *Yoel* 2:24. The prophecy describes the blessings of the end of days.

[57] The Maharal has presented three reasons to explain why the blessing for abundant grain is expressed by fullness (of the blessing-up): 1) the verse that associates full granaries with blessing, 2) grain has the capacity to make a person feel full, 3) the world is satiated and "full" when there is an abundance of grain. These reasons apply only to grain, and not to wine or other foods, which is why it is uniquely appropriate to represent the blessing of abundant grain with a full-to-overflowing cup.

[58] In other words, chronologically, obtaining *chai* for the blessing-cup must precede actually filling the blessing-cup, therefore *chai* appears first in the list of blessing cup requirements.

[59] In the name of Rabbi Yochanan.

[60] This blessing seems to go beyond Yitzchok's blessing of abundant grain, which the Maharal associates with the full-cup requirement. This could call into question the basis for the association of the blessing-cup requirements and Yitzchok's blessings but the Maharal is explaining that boundlessness is a "bonus" byproduct of "full". We fill the cup to invoke the blessing of an abundance of grain and we gain the further blessing of boundlessness as a byproduct.

[61] In addition to abundance, as the Maharal had previously stated.

[62] If the blessing had bounds there would be a "beyond-the-bounds" area that would not be covered by the blessing. Thus it would not be complete. See also the Maharal's *Chidushei Aggados* on *Bava Metzia* 42a where he writes, "blessing is by definition boundless; this is part of the essence of blessing."

[63] As stated by Rabbi Yosi bar Chaninah.

[64] *Shmuel* I 23:26.

[65] The Hebrew word used is עֹטְרִים, *otrim*, from the same root as *itur*. The context of the verse is that King Shaul is in pursuit of Dovid and attempting to trap him, thus it is clear that the root means to encircle.

when he recited the after-meal blessing, while Rav Chisda would surround the blessing-cup with "satellite" cups filled with wine. The reason for these customs is that *itur* corresponds to "nations shall serve you" [in Yitzchok's blessings] and servants accompany their master, walking beside him, blazing the trail in front of him and bringing up the rear. [To enact this symbolically Rabbi Yehudah] surrounded himself with students, since students minister to their Rabbi.[66] This triggers the blessing that other nations shall serve you.

[Similarly] the satellite cups surrounding the blessing-cup are a metaphor for the nations who will encircle Yisroel as servants encircle their master. The requirement of Rav Chanan to use undiluted wine for the satellite cups is to be consistent with the wine in the blessing-cup itself, which must be undiluted. This is to avoid the appearance of using diluted wine for the blessing-cup itself.[67] The requirement of Rav Sheshes to add the satellite cups by the blessing of the land[68] is to avoid the appearance of using multiple blessing-cups, which might be assumed to be the case if the satellite cups were present at the beginning of the after-meal blessing.

Another possible reason for requiring the use of undiluted wine in the satellite cups is to allude to the nations that will be subjugated to Yisroel – [since that is the blessing of Yitzchok corresponding to *itur*]. There are seventy such nations[69] and that is the numerical value of יין, [the Hebrew word for wine]. If the wine were diluted it would no longer be pure wine with a numerical value of seventy. In any event, *itur* was instituted to symbolize the blessing of Yitzchok, "and nations shall serve you.

To correspond to "and nations shall bow to you" [in the blessings of Yitzchok] the *ituf* requirement was instituted. Being enrobed is a sign of distinction; respected people generally present themselves enrobed as a symbol of their status [and are therefore accorded respect by others,] who bow to them, as we see from the words of Rabbi Yochanan, who called his garments "My honorers".[70] This is self-evident. *Ituf*, then, was instituted to symbolize the blessing of Yitzchok, "and nations shall bow to you" since bowing is a term used to describe bestowing of honor on distinguished individuals.[71]

Section 5 – The Blessings of the Blessing Cup – Part 3

ואמר ומקבלו בשתי ידיו ומגביהו מן הקרקע טפח...

The *Gemara* continues, "He takes [the blessing-cup] with both hands and he transfer it to right hand". This corresponds to [the blessing of] "be dominant over your brothers". Grasping something with both hands [represents power and] invokes a blessing of power. [This is because] hands typify power, as in the

---

פירוש בנתיבות לב

[66] Thus, although students are not servants *per se*, their relationship to their Rabbi includes elements of service so they can be used to enact the servitude symbolism.

[67] If the satellite cups were diluted a casual observer might mistakenly conclude that the blessing-cup itself was being diluted.

[68] The second of the blessings in the after-meal blessings.

[69] See the endnote "Bil'am's Erroneous Rationale" in chapter 1 for a full discussion of the significance of the seventy nations.

[70] See *Shabbos* 113a. He referred to them in this way because garments dignify the person.

[71] The Maharal is saying that the blessing of Yitzchok is not limited to literal bowing but rather is a term to describe the accordance of respect due to distinguished individuals.

verse,[72] "…his hand will be upon all". The usage of "hand" to typify power and dominion is common. Therefore he takes [the blessing cup] with both hands so that the hands, the repository of power, will be blessed with power and ultimately with dominance.

He transfers it to his right hand to show ascendancy, which indicates that the blessing is to be dominant over his brothers and ascendant over them. The right hand signifies ascendancy as we see in the verse,[73] "The right hand of Hashem is ascendant". Thus the sum of the actions in taking the cup with both hands and transferring it to his right hand creates a blessing of power, dominance and ascendance over his brothers.

[He does not simply pick it up with his right hand in the first place] because using only one hand would reflect deficiency. He uses both hands because that action is more potent; it demonstrates the universality of the power of his hands.[74] When he is dominant he is ubiquitously dominant – and he is unfailingly dominant. Putting it into his right hand after picking it up with both hands thus provides a context that leads to overwhelming ascendancy.

In summary, these two actions together bring about the ultimate level of superiority – lifting with both hands shows that the power extends everywhere (this is the symbolism of both hands)[ii] and putting it into his right hand shows that the power is accompanied by ascendancy. The combination puts [the recipient of the blessing in] the most advantageous possible position. Understand these concepts because they contain deep wisdom. Just as taking [the blessing-cup] in both hands brings out the ubiquity of his power, so does putting it into his right hand show that he will be great and rise to great heights.

There is another implication to taking [the blessing-cup] with both hands and transferring it to his right hand and that is that the power of rulership belongs to the people. The institution of kingship belongs to Yisroel and it is their responsibility to accept the rulership of the king on themselves. [The symbolism of this implication is that] both hands represent the totality of the nation and the lifting of the cup with both hands represents accepting the blessing of the rights of ownership on the institution of kingship.

───────────────────── פירוש בנתיבות לב ─────────────────────

[72] *Beraishis* 16:12. The verse is describing the characteristics of the children of Yishmael and means that Yishmael will be a bandit who overpowers and robs his victims. This corroborates the Maharal's contention that "hand" symbolizes power.

[73] *Tehillim* 118:16. *Rashi* quotes a Medrash that points out the ascendancy of the right hand. It states, "Hashem created the celestial beings with His right hand; therefore, death has no power over them; as it says (*Yeshayahu* 48:13): 'Even my hand laid the foundation of the earth.' This is the **left** hand. 'And My right hand measured the **heavens** with handbreadths.' This is the **right** hand."

[74] The Maharal in *Netzach Yisroel* chapter 8 writes that the right hand represents "initiation" and the left hand, "conclusion". In that context he explains that the misfortunes that befell Yisroel when the Temple was destroyed happened during an inauspicious time in the Jewish calendar – the period between the 17th of the month of *Tamuz* and the 9th of *Av*. The five misfortunes that occurred on the 17th of *Tamuz* were "right hand" misfortunes and thus they were milder, representing the beginning of the tragedy. The five misfortunes that occurred on the 9th of *Av*, the "left hand", conclusion-oriented date, were harsher and more final, representing the culmination of the tragedy. Thus that period represents the full range of tragedy, from initiation through culmination.

Of relevance here is the usage of "right hand" and "left hand" to represent starting and end points, and the implication that when both hands are employed there is a further implication of a complete range – in other words, universality. Picking up the blessing-cup in both hands represents the comprehensiveness of the ascendancy of Yaakov over his brothers.

[In this interpretation of the symbolism] transferring the cup to the right hand represents the designation of a king and the transferring of rulership to him. This is [the way kingship works in Yisroel,] as the verse specifies,[75] "You shall appoint a king over you…" This interpretation is clear.[76]

Section 6 – The Blessings of the Blessing Cup – Part 4

ואמר ומגביה מן הקרקע טפח, זה כנגד וישתחוו לך בני אמך...

The *Gemara* continues, "He holds it a *tefach* off the ground". This corresponds to [the blessing of] "Your mother's sons will bow to you". The reason [bowing is signified by holding the blessing-cup off the ground a *tefach*] is because [The root word used for bowing,] השתחויה, *hishtachavoya*, means [lying completely on the ground[77] with] arms and legs outstretched, per the verse,[78] "For our soul is cast down[79] to the dust". The person bowing is likening himself to the ground in comparison to the object of his bowing.[80] The person being bowed to is therefore distinct from the ground. Being prostrate on the ground is to place oneself on the ground level and [to implicitly state that] the person being bowed to is elevated from ground level.[81] Thus, lifting the blessing-cup a *tefach*[82] signifies [the blessing of] "Your mother's sons will bow to you".[83]

פירוש בנתיבות לב
---

[75] *Devarim* 17:15.

[76] In both interpretations the symbolism of taking the blessing-cup in both hands and transferring it to the right hand is to rulership. In the first interpretation it refers to Yisroel's rulership over the "brothers", the other nations of the world. In the second interpretation it refers to the institution of kingship within the nation Yisroel itself.

It is unclear, however, how, in the second interpretation, the correspondence to the blessing of Yitzchok, "be dominant over your brothers", applies, since Yitzchok's blessing seemingly refers to the dominance of Yisroel over other nations, not to the dominance of the king of Yisroel over his subjects.

Perhaps this can be understood in light of an interpretation of the blessings of Yitzchok presented in *Shem MiShmuel, Toldos* 5678. He explains that Yitzchok was unaware of the wickedness of Esav, the son he intended to bless, and believed that both Yaakov and Esav were destined to be the progenitors of Yisroel, with Esav assuming the political leadership of the nation – kingship – and Yaakov assuming the religious leadership. The blessing that was intended for Esav, but coopted by Yaakov, was therefore the blessing for kingship of Yisroel and in fact it bears a striking resemblance to the blessing that Yaakov himself conferred upon his son Yehudah, who was actually granted kingship over *Yisroel*.

We see, then, according to this interpretation, that Yitzchok's "be dominant over your brothers" blessing is actually a reference to the king of Yisroel ruling over his subjects (rather than a reference to Yisroel ruling over other nations, as in in the straightforward interpretation) and in that light the Maharal's alternate understanding of the lifting-and-transferring of the blessing cup as symbolism for the institution of kingship in Yisroel makes perfect sense.

[77] The *Gemara* in *Brachos* 4b discusses the various kinds of genuflection and defines *hishtachavoya* as lying prostrate on the ground with arms and legs outstretched.

[78] *Tehillim* 44:26.

[79] The word used for "cast down" is שחה, derived from the same root as *hishtachavoya*.

[80] He is in effect declaring that he "like the dust under his feet" in relation to the person to whom he is bowing.

[81] The point of the bowing is to create a distinction between the status of the bower and the status of the person being bowed to.

[82] A *tefach*-height is generally the minimum measure to define separation. For example an enclosure with a height of a *tefach* qualifies to separate pure from ritually impure, or to define the starting height (though not the full required height) of a *sukkah*. See *Sukkah* 15b.

[83] As in the other parallels between the blessings of Yitzchok and the actions involving the blessing-cup, the blessing-cup itself represents the object of the blessings. Thus, for this blessing, the blessing-cup represents the bowed-to brother – Yisroel – so it is elevated to signify its higher status than the ground-level bowers.

The *Gemara* continues, "He gazes at it". Casting one's eyes on a thing creates a concrete and active reality, so gazing at the blessing-cup gives [Yitzchok's] blessing [to Yisroel] a concrete and active reality[84] and thereby bonds Yisroel with blessing.[85] [iii] Such an attachment to blessing makes one impervious to curses, as the verse states,[86] "Do not curse this nation, for they are blessed". Attempting to curse one who is blessed causes the curse to rebound on the one attempting to apply the curse. We have explained this in several contexts. For this reason our Sages advise,[87] "As a rule it is preferable to be the object of a curse rather than one who curses" – better for a person to be cursed by others than for him to curse others because when one who curses a person who is impervious to the curse, the curse boomerangs back on him.[88]

Also, gazing at the blessing-cup shows that the blessing is pervasive and there is no

—————————————————— פירוש בנתיבות לב ——————————————————

[84] In *Nesiv Ayin Tov* the Maharal compares a person with an "*ayin tov*", "a good eye" – a good-hearted person who delights in the good fortune of others – to a blessing-cup. Such a person, the Maharal says, is a full and complete container for blessing, just as a blessing-cup is full and complete. The blessing-cup thus symbolizes the *ayin tov* attribute. Citing the *Gemara* discussed here, the Maharal states that one reason for gazing at the blessing-cup is to associate with the blessing of *ayin tov*.

He also cites a *Gemara* in *Sotah* 38b which says that the honor of holding the blessing-cup should be reserved for those who have an *ayin tov*. In *Chidushei Aggados* on that *Gemara* the Maharal develops the comparison between the blessing cup and the "eye" further, writing that while the *ayin tov* is like a full cup and the evil eye like an empty cup and thus it is inappropriate for someone with an evil eye to be honored with the (full) blessing-cup.

[85] The underlying principle the Maharal is implicitly employing is that thoughts have a power to affect events, both in a constructive and a destructive way. We discuss this principle and its origins and implications at length in end note iii, "The Power of Thought and the Evil Eye".

Moreover, as the Maharal explains in *Derech Chaim* 2:9, vision and intellect are closely related in that they are both metaphysical in nature. They also function closely together; the eye is the primary gateway to the mind as *Rashi* (quoting *Medrash Tanchuma* 15) comments on *Bamidbar* 15:39: the eyes are "spies" for the mind – what the eye sees, the mind focuses on. When the mind focuses it can create positive or negative energy that has a real-world effect.

Thus, focusing on the blessing-cup invokes thoughts of Yitzchok's blessing and this reinforces the blessing, and, as the Maharal says, bonds Yisroel with blessing. This is entirely consonant with the *Gemara's* explanation for gazing at the blessing-cup. The purpose, the *Gemara* says, is to focus attention on it (and as the *Mishna Brurah* cited earlier explains, to focus attention on the blessing). The Maharal is explaining that the reason this focus is so important is that it serves to actually create blessing!

[86] *Bamidbar* 22:12. Hashem is admonishing Bil'am against attempting to curse Yisroel, telling him that they are immune to his curses, since they are already blessed.

[87] *Sanhedrin* 49a.

[88] In *Gur Aryeh, Devarim* 19:19, and in *Beer Hagolah* chapter 2, the Maharal explains how this works in the context of the *aidim zomimim* (false witness) laws. The Torah specifies that false witnesses suffer the sentence that would have been imposed on their scapegoat had their testimony not been disproven. However this applies only if the sentence on the intended scapegoat had not already been carried out. For example, if the false witnesses testified that their scapegoat killed someone – a capital offense – and their testimony was discredited, the false witnesses would themselves be subject to capital punishment, but only if their scapegoat had not yet been executed. If he had been executed the false witnesses would not be executed.

This provision seems counter-intuitive. It would seem that the harsher punishment should apply if the scapegoat had been executed rather than only when he was still alive! The Maharal explains that the will of the false witnesses to harm the scapegoat generates a fatal negative energy that must find release. If the scapegoat is in fact killed that negative energy was expended. If their intent to harm the scapegoat was not actualized, however, the negative energy is active and it bounces back on the false witnesses themselves, causing them to suffer the fate they intended for their scapegoat. The Maharal likens this to throwing a rock with force. If it hits its mark its energy is expended but if it instead hits a wall it bounces back and strikes the thrower.

Similarly if a person curses someone else he releases negative energy that can affect his intended victim. But if that person is impervious to the curse due to his own opposing will, or his merits, the negative energy rebounds against the person who issued the curse and the curse falls on him. See end note iii, "The Power of Thought and the Evil Eye" for additional detail.

leeway for anything but blessing. For these [two] reasons gazing at the blessing-cup corresponds to, "Those who curse you shall be cursed".[89]

The *Gemara* continues, "…and he presents it to his wife, children and household members". This corresponds to, "Those who bless you shall be blessed". Certainly, the wife, children and household members bless the master of the household since they are his beneficiaries, and it is natural to bless someone who favors you. This in turn reflects the master of the household's own blessings onto them, fulfilling, "those who bless you shall be blessed".[90] For this reason [the *Gemara* advises the holder of the blessing-cup to] present from it to his wife, children and household members.

Section 7 – The Blessings of the Blessing Cup – Part 5
הרי לך מבואר ומפורש כי עשרה דברים שנאמרו בכוס...

It is therefore clear and explicit that the ten requirements specified for a blessing-cup correspond to the ten blessings [that Yitzchok gave Yaakov as specified in the *v'yiten l'cha* verses]. Reflect on these correspondences so that they are properly understood. As validation that the correspondences are accurate consider the subsequent *Gemara*.[91] "Rav Yochanan said, 'We observe only four [of the ten,] namely, undiluted, full, exterior washing and interior washing.'" Why did they observe only those four? It was not because they believed that the tradition was for those four alone since there were [roughly contemporaneous] *Amoraim*[92] that also practiced, [for example,] *itur* and *ituf*.[93] Rather, [Rav Yochanan held that] now that we are in exile, we no longer enjoy the blessings of "nations shall serve you", "…bow to you", "…dominant over your brothers", "…mother's sons will bow to you", "those who curse you shall be cursed" or "those who bless you shall be blessed".[94]

Those [six] blessings are inapplicable to Yisroel in their [current] lowly and ignoble state of exile, when the *Shechina* is not with them.[95] However the first four blessings, "from the dew of the skies", "the moisture of the earth", "an abundance of grain" and "…wine", are directed at the land of Israel, not the nation Yisroel, and therefore

────────── פירוש בנתיבות לב ──────────

[89] The two reasons are that gazing at the blessing cup bonds Yisroel with blessing, and that the state of blessing is all-encompassing.

[90] The sequence is as follows: 1) The head of the household, who is holding the blessing-cup, is the primary beneficiary of the blessings of Yitzchok. 2) He share its contents with his household. 3) They, as the beneficiaries of his sharing, bless him. 3) Since the blessings of Yitzchok include, "those who bless you shall be blessed", the household members themselves, having blessed the head of the household, become secondary beneficiaries of the blessings of Yitzchok.

[91] *Brachos* 51a-b.

[92] Sages from the Talmudic era, like Rav Yochanan, including Rabbi Yehudah who, as the *Gemara* cited earlier stated, surrounded his blessing-cup with students., and Rav Chisda who surrounded his blessing-cup with "satellite" cups, to observe *itur*, and Rav Pappa who wrapped himself in his cloak, and Rav Assi who donned his head-covering, to observe *ituf*.

[93] Thus Rav Yochanan had to have been aware that there was a tradition for the other six practices as well.

[94] Since those blessings are dormant in our current state of exile Rav Yochanan held that the blessing-cup practices that correspond to them are also suspended.

[95] The Maharal does not mean that the *Shechina* has literally abandoned us since our Sages teach that the *Shechina* does accompany us into exile (see *Megilla* 29a). However its presence is hidden from us and its protection not as apparent as when we are living in our homeland with the Temple. It is certainly obvious, the Maharal is saying, that those six blessings, which speak of our ascendancy over the other nations, are not in effect in our current circumstances.

they persist. Certainly that are not in force as powerfully as before [the exile] but they did not cease as several sources make clear.[96] Thus Rav Yochanan declared that "we observe only four".[97] [98]

Our editions [of the *Gemara*] have the words, "there are those who add" before, "he must also present it to his wife, children and household". According to this version of the text the implication is that there are ten blessing-cup requirements exclusive of that one.[99] Doubtless, according to this version, "take with both hands" and "place into right hand" are treated as two separate requirements and [if "present to wife…" is also counted] that would yield eleven requirements in total. Since the *Gemara* stated that there were ten requirements for a blessing-cup, they include the text "there are those who add" before the "eleventh" requirement [to show that it is not included in the *Gemara's* ten-count].

I am astonished that this version of the text could be considered authentic since, according to it, the correspondences previously described between the blessings of Yitzchok and the blessing-cup requirements no longer work out, and their validity is unquestionable. Subsequently I studied the view of the *Rosh* [on this matter] and discovered that he does not include the words, "there are those who add" in his version of the text, nor does the *Tur*[100] nor do many other commentators.

Thus the version of the text [that does not include the phrase] can be considered definitive, as we explained, and "take with both hands" and "place into right hand" are counted as a single item.

Section 8 – Structure of the After-Meals Blessing – Part 1

ובפרק שלשה שאכלו ת"ר משה תקן לישראל...

From chapter *Shlosha SheAcholu*:[101]

פירוש בנתיבות לב
---

[96] For example, to this day, the after-blessing for fruits grown in Israel notes that fact by ending with, "For the land and for **its** fruits" rather than with, "For the land and for **the** fruits", and there would be no reason to make this distinction if the land and the fruits of the land were not special in some way. See *Brachos* 44a and *Shulchan Aruch, Orach Chaim* 208:10.

[97] In other words, the "we" in "we observe" is not meant as "we" in contrast to the previously cited opinion in the *Gemara* that listed the ten blessing-cup practices, which would imply that he argued with that opinion. Rather "we" is meant to refer to himself and others in his generation, which lived in exile, in contrast to earlier generations which lived in the time of the Temple.

[98] The Maharal set out to demonstrate that his association between the blessings of Yitzchok and the blessing-cup requirements were valid based on the statement of Rav Yochanan that we observe only four of the requirements nowadays. Given that Rav Yochanan certainly knew of the other six, as the Maharal demonstrates, the only distinction between the four that he kept and the six that he did not keep was that the blessings of Yitzchok that correspond to the four are applicable in exile while the blessings that correspond to the six are not applicable in exile. Thus it is clear that the blessing-cup requirements are based on the blessings of Yitzchok.

[99] Since the *Gemara* started off saying that there were ten requirements for a blessing-cup (and no opinions were presented that claimed eleven requirements, instead of ten) the implication of "there are those who add" is that there is a "bonus" requirement that is not enumerated in the ten, as the Maharal will explain.

[100] *Orach Chaim* 183:4.

[101] *Brachos* 48b.

"We learned in a *Braiso*: Moshe instituted the blessing of "He who sustains"[102] for Yisroel when they first received the *mon*.[103] Yehoshua instituted the blessing of the land[104] for them when they entered the land [of Israel]. Dovid and Shlomo instituted the blessing of "He who builds Yerushalayim"[105] for them [at two junctures]; Dovid[106] instituted [the opening passages] "[Please be merciful, Hashem our G-d,] on Your nation Yisroel, and on Your city Yerushalayim…" and Shlomo[107] instituted, "… and on Your great and sacred house".

"The blessing of "the Good and Bestower of good"[108] was instituted in Yavneh in commemoration of those murdered in Beitar, as Rav Masneh said, 'The day that the murdered of Beitar were permitted to be buried [the Sages of] Yavneh instituted [the blessing of] "the Good and the Bestower of good" – "the Good" in that the bodies did not decompose; "Bestower of good" in that they were permitted to be buried.[109]

"Our Sages taught, 'This is the order of the blessing after meals: The first blessing is *HaZon*, the second blessing is the blessing of the land, the third blessing is "Builder of Yerushalayim"[110] and the fourth blessing is "The Good and Bestower of good". On Shabbos we begin with words of consolation and conclude with words of consolation and we take note of the sanctity of the day in the middle."[111]

The *Gemara's* attribution of the first blessing to Moshe, and the subsequent attributions [of the other blessings], are problematic since the *Gemara* will shortly say that the obligation to recite the blessings after meals is biblical in origin:[112] "How do we know that the after-meals blessing is biblically mandated? From the verse,[113] 'And

───────────── פירוש בנתיבות לב ─────────────

[102] הזן, *HaZon*, the first of the four blessings in the after-meal blessings, in which we thank Hashem for food. The word *HaZon* means, "He who sustains".

[103] See *Shmos* 16.

[104] The second blessing in the after-meal blessings which thanks Hashem for giving us the land of Israel. It begins with the words, נודה לך, "*Nodeh l'cha*", "We thank you".

[105] The third blessing; it thanks Hashem, primarily, for Yerushalayim and the Temple. It begins with the words, רחם נא, "*Rachem na*", "Please be merciful".

[106] Dovid selected the site of the Temple in Yerushalayim.

[107] Shlomo actually built the Temple.

[108] The fourth blessing, הטוב והמטיב, *HaTov v'Hameitiv*.

[109] The events referred to occurred as a result of the Bar Kochba-led revolt against the Romans. The seat of the revolt was in the large metropolis of Beitar. When the Romans, under the leadership of Andrionus Caesar, suppressed the revolt they slaughtered tens of thousands of the Jewish residents of Beitar and did not allow them to be buried. The Jewish leader at the time, *Rabban* Gamliel, and the rest of the Jewish leadership, then based in Yavneh, fasted, prayed and went to great expense to overturn the decree against burial until, finally, the Roman government relented and permitted the burial to take place.

When they entered Beitar to bury the bodies they discovered that the bodies miraculously had not decomposed. The fourth blessing was instituted to thank Hashem for causing the burial to be permitted and for preventing the bodies from decomposing until that happened.

[110] This is the same blessing referred to before as the third blessing; in this citation it is referred to with its ending words rather than its starting words.

[111] The Maharal will discuss the meaning of this portion of the *Gemara* in the next section.

[112] The Torah was completed and sealed before the events that Yehoshua, Dovid and Shlomo commemorated in their respective blessings took place. If the after-meal blessings are biblical in origin how could they have contributed to them?

[113] *Devarim* 8:10.

you will eat and be satisfied, and you shall bless Hashem, your G-d'". The intent [of the *Gemara*], however, is to convey that Moshe [and the others] composed the wording of the blessings [not that they created the obligation to recite them].[114]

We will now discuss why the set of after-meals blessings comprises these three specific blessings[115] and explain why [a blessing dealing with] "Builder of Yerushalayim" is associated with the blessings pertaining to meals.

Hashem bestows three categories of benefit on Yisroel: First, Hashem supplies us with necessities, like [basic] food, since it is impossible for man to survive without food.[116] Second, in addition to necessary food, Hashem gave us the bountiful land [of Israel,] blessed with all manner of things.[117] [As a result of this second category] we enjoy non-essential amenities [in addition to necessities]. [Third,] on top of that, Hashem gave us the ultimate benefit, the pinnacle of perfection, the Temple. The Temple raised all of Yisroel's blessings to the height of excellence, as the *Gemara*[118] states, "The day the Temple was destroyed [full-fledged] blessing ceased". The Temple was the wellspring of perfect blessing in the world.[119] [Now, though,] Since the Temple was, because of our sins, destroyed, we are compelled to beseech Hashem for mercy which we do in the blessing [beginning with] "Please be merciful Hashem, our G-d".[120] This is an entreaty for the Temple to be rebuilt speedily and in our days and thus, for blessing in the world to be restored to its former state of perfection.

We discuss these three categories of benefit in *Nesiv HaChesed*,[121] please refer there.

We understand, then, why these three blessings are associated with the after-meal blessing set – they are all relevant to food.

The fourth blessing, "The Good and Bestower of good" is different in kind from the first three blessings. The first three blessings are [presented from the perspective of their recipients, so they specify] things that people are capable of absorbing. People are certainly capable of taking in food, which is critical for their survival, Yisroel

——————————————— פירוש בנתיבות לב ———————————————

[114] See also the commentary of the *Rashba* on the *Gemara* in *Brachos* 48b.

[115] As the Maharal will explain later only the first three blessings are biblically mandated; the fourth – both the requirement for it as well as its wording – were instituted Rabbinically. However the Maharal will also explain the rationale for the Rabbinic inclusion of the fourth blessing, as well as for its placement in the sequence.

[116] We express our gratitude for this in the first blessing, *HaZon*.

[117] We express our gratitude for this in the second blessing, *Nodeh l'cha*. The emphasis in the second blessing is also on food, albeit food that goes beyond the basic nutrition necessary to sustain life.

[118] *Sotah* 48a. "Rabbi Yehoshua testified that from the day the Temple was destroyed there is no day without a curse, the dew has not descended for a blessing and the flavor has departed from the fruits. Rav Yosi said, the fatness was also removed from the fruits."

[119] In the third blessing the emphasis is still on blessing specific to nourishment.

[120] We beg Hashem to be merciful and to rebuild it so that the blessings can be restored in all their glory. But this text is only appropriate after the Temple's destruction.

The Maharal is alluding to the fact that when Dovid and Shlomo originally composed the text of this blessing it was for a newly consecrated Temple, not one that was destroyed. The text we recite today is therefore not the text originally composed by Dovid and Shlomo. The original text called for the Temple and the Davidic kingdom to be preserved and for the Jews to be able to live peacefully in their land. See the commentary of the *Rashba* on the *Gemara* in *Brachos* 48b.

[121] *Nesiv Gemilus Chassodim*, Chapter 1. The Maharal there utilizes these same three categories of benefit – essential, necessary but non-essential and beyond-necessary – to explain three clauses in the *borei nefoshos* after-blessing for non-grain foods, the three Shabbos meals and the three Levite levies of *challah*, tithes and first-fruit.

is certainly attuned to the blessings of perfection that pertain to the land, since the land of Israel was given to them as their inheritance, and Yisroel even has "receptors" for the ultimate blessings of the Temple.

However the blessing of "The Good and Bestower of good" describes Hashem as inherently good and as an inherently unbounded giver, without reference to any recipient. Hashem, independent of a relationship with any receiving entity, is good and giving. This is why the blessing is couched in terms of "Good and Bestower of good"[122] – to convey that Hashem, detached from any potential beneficiary, is intrinsically good and giving. When we ascribe to Hashem [the ability to bestow] an abundance of good we are speaking about an abstract property that is not associated with any recipient waiting to receive it.[123]

Moreover this property of Hashem to bestow an abundance of good is actualized only at intervals, not continually.[124] For this reason the "Good and Bestower of good" blessing is not recited at all times [as are the first three blessings] but only when others have benefited along with him, which symbolizes an abundance of blessing.[125] The blessing was instituted with this condition in mind. And since it deals with an abundance of good it only mandated Rabbinically, not biblically.[126]

Section 9 – Structure of the After-Meals Blessing – Part 2

ועוד יש לך לדעת ולהבין כי הברכה הזאת שהיא ברכת המזון...

Know and understand as well[127] that the after-meals blessing was established to acknowledge that Hashem completed Yisroel in every possible way. This certainly merits blessing, as the verse indicates,[128] "And you will eat and be

————————— פירוש בנתיבות לב —————————

[122] "Good and Bestower of good" is a phrase that describes properties, not actions that have an object. In contrast the first three blessings describe Hashem as "Sustainer **to the entire world**", or as one who has "bequeathed **to our forefathers** a land…" or as being merciful **to Yisroel, Yerushalayim and Israel**.

[123] Moreover, since we are speaking of an abstract property that is unlimited, it would in any event be impossible for a finite and limited creation of Hashem to be a receptacle for an unlimited property.

[124] Nonetheless, Hashem's property of "Good and Bestower of good" is continual, only its actualization is not.

[125] This law originates in *Brachos* 49b and is cited in *Shulchan Aruch Orach Chaim* 212:2, however those sources deal with a different version of the "Good and Bestower of good" blessing – a standalone blessing that is recited when hearing good news that affects others as well as oneself.

The *Mishna Brurah* 189:1 writes that the original version of this blessing was much shorter, closely resembling the aforementioned standalone blessing. The Maharal seems to view the two blessings as variants stemming from a single root, which is why he equates them here. (See also section 31 where the Maharal similarly equates the two blessings.)

Apparently the Maharal is saying that in both instances of the "Good and Bestower of good" blessing there is a status diminution in the blessing brought about by the occasional nature of this property of Hashem. In the case of the standalone blessing the diminution takes the form of a limitation in when the blessing is recited (only when others have benefited). In the case of the version of the blessing that appears in the after-meals blessings the diminution takes the form of a mandate that it is only Rabbinic, not biblical.

[126] *Shulchan Aruch Orach Chaim* 191:1 per *Brachos* 46a. The relationship between an abundance of good and the Rabbinic nature of this blessing in the after-meals context is fully discussed in section 31.

[127] The Maharal presents a second approach to understanding the structure of the three blessings included in the after-meals blessing. In the previous section the Maharal explained the three blessings as a progression from essential to non-essential to perfect – a hierarchy based on how vital the particular blessing is. In this section the focus is on a hierarchy based on exclusivity – from blessings that apply to everyone to blessings that apply only to Yisroel.

[128] *Devarim* 8:10.

satisfied, and you shall **bless** Hashem, your G-d". To be satisfied is to be complete and thus this verse, [which deals with physical sustenance,] is instructing us to bless Hashem [for completing us in terms of our physical sustenance]. And, having entered into the matter of blessing Hashem for completeness [in one respect,] we proceed to bless Him as well for completing Yisroel in all other respects.

We begin with the blessing for food itself. This is a need that Yisroel has in common with all creatures that require sustenance. We proceed to the next blessing, which is for a level of completeness that is above and beyond that provided to anyone else – the completeness inherent in Yisroel's having been granted the unique and holy land [of Israel] which is distinguished from all other lands – and in this Yisroel is distinguished from all other nations. [Since this blessing deals with a level of completeness that is unique to Yisroel] we mention in it the Torah and the covenant of circumcision[129] as we will discuss later.

The third blessing was instituted in commemoration of the level of completeness that was granted to Yisroel with the construction of the Temple. This is the final and ultimate completeness – Hashem's presence [in the Temple]; the *Shechina* among them in the Temple and in Yerushalayim. This goes beyond the [prior] blessing of the land. True, in bequeathing to Yisroel the exceptional land of Israel Hashem granted them an unparalleled level of completeness [130] but it was not yet apparent that there would be no holding back in terms of the extent of completeness to be granted to Yisroel. This changed when they were granted Yerushalayim and the Temple – the supreme completeness.[131] For this reason in the portion of the Pesach *Hagaddah* that enumerates "the many benefits that Hashem bestowed upon us"[132] the final benefit is, "and he built the Temple for us".[133]

These three things, taken together, represent different aspects of completeness that are appropriate for Yisroel and which brings them to a state of full completeness.

However, the blessing of "Good and Bestower of good" deals with bestowal of good in a quantitative sense – Hashem is good and bestows good in great measure [in the context of the categories of blessing mentioned in the first three blessings].[134] This blessing is therefore only Rabbinically mandated.

פירוש בנתיבות לב

[129] The Torah and *bris milah* are unique to Yisroel and contribute to Yisroel's unique status *vis a vis* Hashem.

[130] More than was granted to any other nation.

[131] Thus the uniqueness of Yisroel was brought into sharper relief as the gap between the blessings they enjoy versus blessings that are granted indiscriminately to all mankind, widened into a chasm.

[132] כמה מעלות טובות למקום עלינו, *kamah maalos tovos lamokom aleinu.* This portion of the Hagaddah is presented as a progression from lesser to greater benefits so the final benefit enumerated is the ultimate benefit.

[133] The Maharal discusses the progression of fifteen benefits that culminate in the building of the Temple in *Gevuros Hashem*, chapter 59.

[134] That is, while the first three blessings describe three qualitatively different categories of blessing, the fourth blessing does not present a new category. It merely quantifies the previous three categories.

Section 10 – Structure of the After-Meals Blessing – Part 3
ועוד אלו ג' ברכות ברכת הזן הוא השלמת הטבע...

There is yet another way to understand the progression of these three blessings.[135] The *HaZon* blessing signifies completeness from the standpoint of the [physical] laws of nature; people by nature need food. Completeness in terms of the land, however, while possessing a physical component, is also completeness from a spiritual and G-dly standpoint. It is known, for example that the atmosphere of Israel sharpens the mind;[136] this in addition to other characteristics [that are of a spiritual nature].[137] This needs no further elaboration.

Nonetheless, even though the completeness inherent in giving us the land of Israel has a spiritual component, it is not entirely spiritual as are Yerushalayim and the Temple. The holy city of Yerushalayim and the Temple, the holy and G-dly abode, are unadulterated spiritual completeness. That is why, as our Sages taught, ten miracles occurred in the Temple.[138] The essence of the Temple is pure holiness and Yisroel's [possession of the Temple] positions them at the height of holiness as well. This explanation is similar to the preceding one.[139]

All three of these forms of completeness are appropriate for the after-meals blessings because these blessings were established to acknowledge fulfillment – Hashem completes us by supplying our lacks – and [with the elements that are described in] these three blessings we are sated and rendered complete in all respects.[140]

───────────── פירוש בנתיבות לב ─────────────

[135] In this approach the blessings are distinguished from one another by level of sanctity.

[136] *Baba Basra* 158b. The Maharal also discusses this concept in *Nesiv HaTorah*, chapter 10 where he uses it to explain a *Gemara* in *Pesachim* 113a that states that one who lives in Israel inherits the world-to-come. The reason, writes the Maharal, is that the world-to-come is entirely spiritual in nature and one who lives in Israel is already living in a spiritual environment; in a holy and non-materially-oriented place – as we see from the fact that the atmosphere of Israel sharpens the mind.

[137] For example, prophecy was extant exclusively in the land of Israel; see *Mechilta Bo, Parsha Aleph.*

See also *Kesubos* 110b: "Whoever lives in Israel is likened to one who has a G-d, whoever lives outside of Israel is likened to one who does not have a G-d". The *Ramban* on *Vayikra* 18:25 explains that while other lands are "administered" by Hashem through angelic intermediaries, Israel is under His direction supervision and thus immoral behavior is intolerable there – it results in miscreants being ejected from the land.

Similarly the verse in *Devarim* 11:12 declares that Israel is "the land that Hashem your G-d looks after continually" and the *Sifri* writes, "*Rebbi* said, is this the only land that Hashem looks after? He looks after every land, as the verse says… Rather, His focus, as it were, is only on Israel and as a "by-product" he looks after other lands along with it."

[138] *Avos* 5:6. The Temple was an "island" of holiness where the physical laws of nature were suspended and miracles were commonplace.

[139] The second (previous) explanation of the progression of the three after-meals blessings is that it is based on exclusivity, with the third, most sacred level reserved for Yisroel. This third explanation bases the progression on level of sanctity, with the third, most sacred level being Yerushalayim and the Temple. The Maharal is saying that the two explanations converge with respect to the third blessing since in both, the most sacred level is Yerushalayim and the Temple and in both, this level is reserved for Yisroel.

[140] The Maharal is reiterating the point he made in his introduction to this topic at the beginning of Section 9: "…The after-meals blessing was established to acknowledge that Hashem completed Yisroel in every possible way… And, having entered into the matter of blessing Hashem for completeness [in one respect,] we proceed to bless Him as well for completing Yisroel in all other respects.".

The reiteration is presented to draw a contrast with the fourth approach toward understanding the three blessings, presented in the next section, which associates all three blessings with food, rather than generalizing the after-meals blessings to all manner of completeness, as is the case with the first three approaches.

Section 11 – Structure of the After-Meals Blessing – Part 4

ועוד יש לפרש כי כל אלו ג' ברכות הכל הם השלמה אחת לגמרי...

O ne may take a different approach [to understanding the progression of the three blessings in the after-meals blessings] and that is, that they are all referring to a single aspect of completeness – that all three blessings were established to acknowledge that Hashem made Yisroel complete with respect to sustenance.

The first blessing, *HaZon*, acknowledges that Hashem bestows food upon them from Above. [For this blessing to be effective] it requires a receptacle ready and suited for it, and capable of capturing the abundant blessing flow. For this Hashem gave them the land [of Israel] – the ideal receptacle for this form of blessing.

Now, since the blessing flows from the heavenly to the earthly realm, which are fundamentally different from one another, an intermediary is required that spans both realms to serve as a conduit to transmit the blessing to the earthly realm. This is the Temple, which bridges the heavenly and earthly realms and transports blessings from the heavenly to the earthly realm. This concept is elucidated in the Medrash[141] on the verse,[142] "...And behold, a ladder set up on the ground and its top reached to heaven...". The Medrash states that this is a reference to the Temple which resembles a ladder in that it transports [blessing] from above to below and [prayer and sacrificial service] from below to above – in other words, the Temple bridges the heavenly and earthly realms.[143]

According to this approach the [fourth] blessing of "Good and Bestower of good" does not signify completeness.[144] Rather it refers to an extra measure of good; an abundance of good. These are not completeness-related, thus this blessing only has a Rabbinic standing.

There is another reason this blessing is Rabbinic and that is that the first three blessings are continual – even though the Temple was destroyed[145] it was intended at the time it was built to be a permanent structure and was only destroyed because of sin.[146] However the fourth blessing of "Good and Bestower of good" is only in

───────── פירוש בנתיבות לב ─────────

[141] *Sifri, Bamidbar, piska* 119.

[142] *Beraishis* 28:12. The context is Yaakov's overnight stay on the consecrated grounds of Mount Moriah, the site of the *Akeida* and future site of the Temple. During that stay he had a vision of a ladder reaching from earth to the heavens with angels going in both directions.

[143] *Rashi* on that verse explains that the center of the ladder was directly over the Temple site. The Maharal explains that this was so because the Temple strikes a balance between the heavenly and the earthly. On the one hand, it is the abode of the *Shechina*. On the other hand it is a place where man comes to serve Hashem. And the balance is precise – neither side can lay claim to the Temple; each side has an equal share in it.

Similarly the Maharal explains that the heavenly realm was created with what is referred to as Hashem's "right hand", the earthly realm with His "left hand" – two disparate entities represented by the two "hands" at opposite sides. But the Temple was created with both "hands" because it is the nexus of the heavenly and the earthly.

[144] Since, according to this approach the only aspect of completeness the first three blessings deal with is completeness with respect to food and the "Good and Bestower of good" blessing has nothing specific to do with food.

[145] Apparently disrupting its continuity.

[146] Similarly the land of Israel (subject of the second blessing) may not always be in Jewish hands but it is the permanent birthright of the Jewish nation. The Maharal elaborates on this point in chapter 13 of

effect at certain times. It is not continual, as is derived from the verse,[147] "… And I will favor **whom** I wish to favor", which is interpreted to mean, "… **when** I wish to favor".

For these reasons[148] the four blessings [we have been discussing] were incorporated into the after-meals blessings. Understand these reasons for they are all valid.

We now consider the statement[149] that, "The blessing of 'the Good and Bestower of good' was instituted in Yavneh in commemoration of those murdered in Beitar… 'the Good' in that the bodies did not decompose; 'Bestower of good' in that they were permitted to be buried". [The *Gemara's* point is that the juncture in history represented by] Yavneh was precisely the time for this blessing to be instituted. When Beitar was destroyed it was apparent that Hashem's attribute of strict justice was dominant with respect to Yisroel because of their sins. It was a time of reckoning.[150] Nonetheless Hashem displayed benevolence toward them.

This behavior is more remarkable than Hashem's other acts of benevolence since, even in the midst of imposition of strict justice, the benevolence of Hashem, evidenced by not allowing the bodies to decompose and by allowing them to be buried, persisted. This demonstrates the absolute nature of Hashem's attribute of benevolence. [151]

─────────── פירוש בנתיבות לב ───────────

Netzach Yisroel.

[147] *Shmos* 33:19, as explained in *Medrash Tanchuma* 23. The Hebrew text of the verse is written וְחַנֹּתִי אֶת אֲשֶׁר אָחֹן. The first letter of the highlighted word "*es*" is *aleph* and with that spelling the word means "whom". However the letters *aleph* and *ayin* are often interchangeable in order to glean additional meaning from a verse. If that replacement is made the verse reads וְחַנֹּתִי עַת אֲשֶׁר אָחֹן and with that spelling the word is pronounced "*ais*" and means "when". The message is that Hashem does not bestow favor continually but only at selected points in time.

It is noteworthy that *Rashi* on the verse, based on a *Gemara* in *Rosh Hashanah* 17b, comments that although the assurance offered by Hashem here was only for favor at certain times, when the covenant to seal Hashem's assurances was consummated, as documented in verse 34:10, it contained a guarantee that the favor of Hashem would not be limited to select points in time and the prayers of Yisroel would never be ignored. This seems to call into question the Maharal's explanation that the fourth blessing is Rabbinic because it is not always in effect. According to this *Rashi*, the final promise was that the blessing of "Good and Bestower of good" would in fact always be in effect. צריך עיון. Further study is required to resolve this question.

[148] That is, the four sets of explanations the Maharal has provided for the construction of the after-meals blessings. The following table provides a summary of the four explanations.

	Explanation Basis	1. Food - הזן	2. Land - ארץ	3. Temple - מקדש	4. Good –טוב ומטיב
1	*Progression of necessity*	Essential	Non-essential	Perfection	Attribute of Hashem [(1)]
2	*Progression of exclusivity*	Universal	Yisroel only	Yisroel only – higher level	Quantifier of other blessings [(1)]
3	*Progression of spirituality*	Physical	Physical/spiritual blend	Spiritual	(Not specified)
4	*Aspects of food receptivity*	The food blessing	Food blessing receptacle	Conduit for food blessing	Food blessing is abundant

[(1)] *The fourth blessing is not part of the sequence in this explanation of the after-meals blessings set.*

[149] From the *Gemara* in *Brachos* cited earlier.

[150] See footnote 109 for a full description. The event represented the final failure of the Bar Kochba revolution and crushed the hopes of Yisroel for an impending redemption. It involved the slaughter of tens of thousands of Jews. It was patently obvious that Yisroel was still under the harsh decree of divine retribution that led to the destruction of the Temple.

[151] The *Meshech Chochma* on *Devarim* 8:10 provides a similar explanation of the fourth, "Good and Bestower of good" blessing. He writes that the first three blessings deal with the obvious hand of G-d in the progressive building up of the nation Yisroel, from the *manna* (with which he associates the absorption of the Torah), to their taking possession of the land of Israel, to the construction of the

Thus, just as the first three blessings were instituted by personalities [in commemoration of events that took place in their time,] – Moshe, the blessing for food when Yisroel was sent the *Mon*, Yehoshua, the blessing for the land when they arrived at the land [of Israel], Dovid, the blessing of "Builder of Yerushalayim" [when the preparations for the Temple started] – so also did the Sages of Yavneh institute the blessing of "the Good and Bestower of good" when, in the darkness of suffering the consequences of [national] sin, Hashem treated them benevolently because of his innate attribute of benevolence. This is the genesis of the "Good and Bestower of good" blessing.

[The double language conveys the double nature of the miracle.] As the *Gemara* explains, "'the Good' in that the bodies did not decompose; 'Bestower of good' in that they were permitted to be buried". The confluence of good on top of good such as occurred here when the bodies did not decompose and, on top of that, they were permitted to be buried, is called "Good and Bestower of good" – a simultaneous double portion of good.[152]

Section 12 – The After-Meals Blessing Introduction – Part 1

ובפרק שלשה שאכלו ר' אומר ובטובו הרי זה תלמיד חכם...

ברוך שאכלנו משלו **ובטובו חיינו**

From chapter *Shlosha SheAcholu*:[153] "Rebbi said, one who recites,[154] '... and

───────────── פירוש בנתיבות לב ─────────────

Temple. But the fourth blessing deals with the nation in decline; the epoch beginning with the destruction of the Temple and the exile, the last hopes of the nation for imminent salvation dashed with the terrible Bar Kochba defeat – Yisroel at its apparent nadir, seemingly destined for destruction with no hope of redemption.

Yet we survived and continue to survive. Our endurance in the hostile exile environment is indeed an ongoing miracle and the first sign of that miracle was the twin miraculous events at Beitar. It demonstrated that although we were "a sheep among seventy wolves", Hashem controls events, belligerent monarchs mysteriously rescind their decrees, nefarious plots against us suffer unlikely failures and against all odds, we retain our glory.

The fourth blessing commemorates our recognition of this state of affairs and authenticates the prophecies that predicted them, along with the prophecies that foretell our ultimate redemption.

[152] Perhaps the Maharal means to say that when there is double benevolence, as there was in Beitar, the first instance of benevolence is a result of Hashem's innate benevolent nature and is irrespective of a particular recipient. When it evinces itself, it is applied indiscriminately. This corresponds to the fact that the bodies did not decompose – there was no distinction between one body and the next; they all were all uniformly protected against decomposition. This is referred to as טוב, *tov*, or "Good" with no reference to a particular target of "Good".

When, on the other hand, Hashem's benevolence is directed at a particular recipient, Hashem is described with the word מטיב, or "Bestower of Good", where the reference to "bestower" implies the existence of a "bestowee". In this situation each of the Beitar martyrs was an individual "bestowee" and had his own grave, in its own particular place that was not shared with anyone else. The benevolence was specifically aimed at each particular recipient.

Thus, the miracles of Beitar demonstrated both sides of Hashem's benevolence – that which emanates from His natural goodness and is indiscriminate and that which is relationship-based and is aimed at a particular individual. הטוב והמטיב, *hatov v'hamaitiv*, "the Good and Bestower of Good".

(Note that this explanation interprets the meaning of "the Good and Bestower of Good" differently from the explanation presented by the Maharal in Section 8, where he interprets both "Good" and "Bestower…" as descriptors of Hashem's nature and independent of any recipient.)

[153] *Brachos* 50a.

[154] This is the nucleus of the responsive *birchas hazimun* introduction to the after-meals blessings, recited when three or more individuals have eaten together. It's full text is, "Blessed is our G-d of whose food we have partaken and through His benevolence we live". The words, "our G-d" are recited when there

through His benevolence,[155] [He has given us life]' is a scholar. But one who recites, '… and **from [part of]** His benevolence,[156] [He has given us life]' is a boor… Rebbi said, one who recites, '… and through His benevolence, He has given **us** life'[157] is a scholar. But one who recites, '… and through His benevolence, [He has given life]'[158] is a boor. The *Naharblai*[159] reverse the preference.[160] But we do not rule like the *Naharblai*."

Halacha הלכה

The permitted and prohibited text variants for the after-meals blessing introduction are presented here.

Shulchan Aruch Orach Chaim 192:1.

The reason "through His benevolence" is preferable to "from [part of] of His benevolence" is because the latter choice of words implies that Hashem only bestows part of his benevolence upon us.[161] Thus one must say "through His benevolence" and not "from [part of] His benevolence".

Similarly one who says, "… and through His benevolence, [He has given life]" acknowledges that Hashem is the source of life [in the abstract] but his praise is incomplete in that he does not acknowledge that he, personally, receives life from Hashem. Thus one must say, "… and through His benevolence, He has given **us** life". The minority view [162] which prefers, "… and through His benevolence, [He has given life]" over the version which has, "… given **us** life" holds that the "us" is actually more limiting because it implies that only "we" are recipients of life from Hashem, to the exclusion of all other creatures. Thus the version without "us" is preferred since it is inclusive of all things and that is why the *Naharblai* take issue with Rebbi and opt for the no-"us" version, which implies that all creatures obtain life from Hashem.

However in practice we do not follow the ruling of the *Naharblai* since their version [without the "us"] does not sufficiently emphasize that we, ourselves, are recipients of life from Hashem. Thus we say, "… and through His benevolence, He has given **us** life", and we discount the objection of the *Naharblai* that this language is not inclusive enough because the person making the blessing must, first and foremost, emphasize that he is thanking Hashem for the life that **he** is receiving from Hashem.

פירוש בנתיבות לב

are ten or more meal participants present; otherwise "He" is substituted.

The Gemara is discussing the proper wording of this introduction.

[155] וּבְטוּבוֹ, *u'ṯetuvo*. This is the "scholar" version that is actually used because the implication is that Hashem allows us to benefit from the full extent of his benevolence.

[156] וּמִטּוּבוֹ, *u'metuvo*. This is the "boor" version that should not be used because the false implication is that Hashem allows us to benefit only from a limited portion of his benevolence. This diminishes the extent of Hashem's benevolence.

[157] חִיֵּינוּ, *chayinu*. This is the "scholar" version that is actually used because the implication is that we are declaring that we have personally benefited from Hashem's life-giving.

[158] חיים, *chayim*, omitting the "us". This is the "boor" version that should not be used because it does not acknowledge the we personally benefited from Hashem's life-giving.

[159] This is a reference either to the custom of a place called *Naharbel* or (according to the *Gemara* in *Sanhedrin* 17b) a pseudonym for the *Amora Rami bar Bruchi*.

[160] That is, they disagree with Rebbi and favor *chayim* over *chayinu*, for reasons the Maharal will explain. (They do not, however, disagree with Rebbi on the first issue and agree that "… through His benevolence" is preferred over "from part of His benevolence".)

[161] That is, it would imply that Hashem is stingy in sharing His benevolence with us.

[162] The *Naharblai*.

Section 13 – The After-Meals Blessing Introduction – Part 2
ברכת הזימון המברך אומר נברך שאכלנו משלו...

שאכלנו משלו נברך

ברוך שאכלנו משלו ובטובו חיינו

ברוך שאכלנו משלו ובטובו חיינו
ברוך הוא וברוך שמו

Halacha הלכה

The leader initiates the after-meals blessing with רבותי נברך, to which the others respond, "Blessed be the name of Hashem from this time and forever".

Mishna Brurah 192:1.

I n the *birchas hazimum* introduction to the after-meals blessings the leader says, "Let us bless He[163] of whose food we have partaken". The other participants respond with, "Blessed is He of whose food we have partaken and through His benevolence we live". The leader repeats, "Blessed is our G-d of whose food we have partaken and through His benevolence we live" and he adds, "Blessed be He and blessed be His name".

This is correct way [to conduct the responsive *birchas hazimum* dialogue] since at each step additional praises are added. [This is similar to the way the *Borchu* prayer[164] is conducted.] The prayer leader says, "Let us bless Hashem, the blessed One" and the congregants respond, "Blessed is Hashem the blessed One for all eternity".[165]

Similarly, in the *birchas hazimum* introduction to the after-meals blessings, the leader says, "Let us bless He of whose food we have partaken", the other participants respond with, "Blessed is He of whose food we have partaken and through His benevolence we live" and the leader responds, "Blessed is our G-d of whose food we have partaken and through His benevolence we live, blessed be He and blessed be His name".

Section 14 – The First Blessing – Part 1
הזן את העולם כלו בטובו, ר"ל הש"י מצד טובו...

הזן את העולם כלו בטובו בחן
בחסד וברחמים

" He nourishes the entire world with his goodness": This means, in a general sense, that Hashem, with His innate trait of goodness, provides nutrition to all beings. The blessing continues by dividing His approaches to providing nutrition into three specific categories [based on type of recipient]. There are those who justly earn their nutrition – these are the world's righteous people. The blessing refers to them when it says that Hashem nourishes the world with חן, *chen*, favor. Such people obtain their nutrition because they find favor in the eyes of Hashem, as was the case with Noach, about whom the verse says,[166] "… and Noach found favor [in the eyes of Hashem]".

There are those who obtain their nutrition from Hashem through His חסד, *chesed*, benevolence. These are people who, from the standpoint of intelligence, are on the level of animals.[167] Their nutrition can only be provided through the benevolence of Hashem.[168]

<hr>
פירוש בנתיבות לב

[163] The name of Hashem is substituted if there are ten or more participants.

[164] Recited before the *Shma* blessings during the *Shachris* and *Maariv* services; see chapter 7.

[165] Here, too, the response echoes the leader's opening and adds a clause to it.

[166] *Beraishis* 6:8.

[167] The Maharal is referring to people whose lives revolve around the physical, who do not give much thought to their purpose for being in the world or to obligations higher than those necessary to sustain their day to day existence. In this respect they are very much like animals.

[168] They have done nothing to earn their keep, so to speak, so they are not entitled to *chen*, as are the righteous. They are also not eligible for the next sustenance method, *rachamim*, or mercy, since, per the *Gemara* in *Brachos* 33a, it is prohibited to be merciful to the unintelligent. Benevolence has less stringent eligibility requirements than mercy so, since Hashem sustains "the entire world", those without intelligence are limited to receiving their sustenance through the benevolence door.

Then there are those who obtain their nutrition from Hashem through his רחמים, *rachamim*, mercy. These are children, who, because of their innocence, require mercy, thus they are nourished via the *rachamim* approach.[169]

הוא נתן לחם לכל בשר

The blessing continues, "He provides *lechem*[170] to all living beings". This refers to the sustaining life-flow that Hashem provides to all beings equally.[171] The reason the word *lechem*, [specifically,] is used to describe sustenance, "…to all living beings" is because *lechem* satisfies and strengthens the heart.[172] The sustenance that Hashem provides universally is termed *lechem* since it [too] supports and sustains the heart, the repository of man's life-force.

כי לעולם חסדו

This [sustaining life-flow] emanates from Hashem's benevolence and all creatures

─────────── פירוש בנתיבות לב ───────────

Benevolence is one of the thirteen attributes of Hashem enumerated in *Shmos* 34:6-7. *Rashi* on that verse, citing a *Gemara* in *Rosh Hashanah* 17a, similarly writes that benevolence is the attribute available to those without much merit.

[169] They have not earned *chen* since they are as yet incapable of earning on the basis of merit at all. They do not deserve to be labeled unthinking "animals" since they are too young to be capable of thinking. Thus they subsist on the basis of mercy alone.

[170] Although the word לחם, *lechem*, is often used as a generic term for food, per, for example *Rashi* on *Beraishis* 31:54, it specifically means "bread" and, as we will explain, the Maharal is using it in that context but generalizing it metaphorically to refer to sustenance, including non-food sustenance.

[171] The Maharal will explain that while nourishment is stratified according to the recipient's spiritual level, Hashem sustains the life of all living beings with an undifferentiated flow. The phrase, נֹתֵן לֶחֶם לְכָל בָּשָׂר, "…provides *lechem* to all living beings, itself is a verse in *Tehillim* 136:25.

Although we utilize the literal translation, "…all living beings" it is clear from the end of section 15 that the Maharal views this phrase as referring only to human beings.

[172] *Rashi* on *Beraishis* 18:5, "And I will take a morsel of bread, and sustain your hearts…", quotes *Medrash Rabbah* 48:11 to the effect that *lechem* is referred to as a "heart sustainer" in the Torah, Prophets and Scriptures (*kesuvim*). This verse is the Torah reference, *Shoftim* 19:5, "Refresh your heart with a morsel of bread…", is the reference in the Prophets and *Tehillim* 104:15, "…and bread, which sustains man's heart", is the reference in Scripture.

The *Be'er B'sadeh* on the verse in *Beraishis* explains that the heart is the seat of the spirit and intellect and that bread made from one of the five halachically recognized grains (wheat, spelt, barley, oats, and rye) has a unique ability to nourish the spirit and the intellect – the capabilities of his heart. He cites the opinion of Rav Yehudah in *Brachos* 40a that the forbidden fruit that Adam consumed and which enhanced his intellect was actually wheat; we see that wheat affects intellectual capabilities from the fact that a child cannot learn to call his parents – a harbinger of intellect – until he has begun to consume grain.

He goes on to explain that the three verses mentioned by *Rashi* refer to three levels of bread that Hashem granted us – mundane bread, the *matzo* of the Egyptian exodus and the *manna* we consumed in the desert after the exodus – and that these levels form a progression from physical sustenance to a high and then a still-higher level of spiritual sustenance. Each level nourishes and opens up for us successively higher gradations of spiritual attainment.

It is possible that the Maharal is alluding to something similar in that *lechem*, including the full range of bread-types enumerated by the *Be'er B'sadeh*, is an all-encompassing sustainer to the full gamut of capabilities encapsulated in man's spirit and intellect – that is, in the parlance of our Sages, encapsulated in man's heart, the crux of his existence since man is essentially spirit and intellect. To say that Hashem provides *lechem* to all living beings, then, is to say that Hashem provides an encompassing sustaining life-flow to all living beings.

Whether or not the Maharal is fully following the reasoning of the *Be'er B'sadeh*, with respect to the three levels of *lechem*, though, he **is** saying that because of the central importance of *lechem* as a staple of life it is used to describe life-giving in a generic sense, independent of providing nutrition, and this life flow is distributed to all living beings on an equal basis, without the stratification that characterizes Hashem's provision of nutrition.

The Maharal also discusses *lechem* at the beginning of Chapter 17 in the context of the pre-blessing on bread and in that context he makes clear that on a simple and literal level *lechem* means "food" and since bread is the primary food for man, it also means "bread".

benefit from it in an undifferentiated manner.[173] Distinctions come into play with respect to nourishment. Nourishment provided through favor is different from that provided through benevolence; nourishment provided through benevolence is different from that provided through mercy. Each creature draws nourishment through the channel appropriate to him. But the [basic] sustaining life-flow is benevolence-based and is the same for all creatures. Hashem's benevolence extends to all and all are entitled to it.

The fact that Hashem indiscriminately sustains everything signals that this sustenance comes from His attribute of benevolence, since it is His benevolence that extends to everything and is shared equally by everything. This is the import of כי לעולם חסדו, "His benevolence is universal" – meaning that it is boundless and not quantifiable. When Hashem's benevolence is active do not imagine that it is finite or limited, for, "His benevolence is universal". Hashem's benevolence is without end and without restriction.[174]

Why, it may be asked, is this [quality of boundlessness] true specifically about Hashem's attribute of benevolence [and not of his other attributes]? It may further be asked, why does the phrase, "For His benevolence is universal" repeatedly recur in the *Tehillim*-song, "*Hodu*"?[175] Similarly in the *Hallel* prayer[176] we say, "Give thanks to Hashem, because He is good, for His benevolence is universal".

The reason is as follows. Most transmissions [from Hashem to man] are recipient-driven. For example, when judgement is imposed it is because the recipient is deserving of [that particular imposition of] judgement. This is true of mercy as well; mercy flows to a recipient who is entitled to mercy. Benevolence is the sole exception to this rule. Benevolence is an intrinsic property [that does not require a recipient for it to manifest itself]. Hashem emanates kindness and benevolence because it is his nature, so to speak, to do so, and He does so without regard to any particular beneficiary. He does so because He, Himself, is good.

Attributes of Hashem that are intrinsic [and independent of external elements, such as recipients] share Hashem's property of limitlessness. Thus His attribute of benevolence is infinite; without end or limitation. It is universal. Attributes like judgement or mercy, on the other hand, require objects; recipients for whom judgement is fitting by virtue of their actions or for whom mercy is fitting [by virtue of their status]. Recipients, [being non-divine,] are by definition finite and thus extensions of judgement or mercy to them must be finite.[177]

──────────────── פירוש בנתיבות לב ────────────────

[173] The corresponding Hebrew phrase in the blessing is כי לעולם חסדו, which is generally translated, "…for His benevolence is **eternal**". However as the Maharal understands it the translation is, "…for His benevolence **universal**". The word לעולם, *l'olom*, can connote either "eternal" or "universal".

[174] "Universal" in this context means not bound either by target (recipient type) or by time.

[175] *Tehillim* 136. This chapter of *Tehillim* expresses thanks to Hashem for his many acts of benevolence. There are twenty-six verses, each expressing gratitude for a different act of benevolence and each ending in "…For His benevolence is universal". The Maharal is reinforcing his question – apparently all aspects of Hashem's benevolence possess this attribute of universality but only benevolence-related acts are included in the list. Why? And why is universality associated only with "good"?

[176] *Tehillim* 118:1. Here too we reiterate the verse, "Give thanks to Hashem, because He is good, for His benevolence is universal" leading to the same questions.

[177] Since it is impossible to extend judgement or mercy or any object-dependent behavior to a non-existent being. And by extension, since mankind itself is finite, and our needs for judgement and mercy are finite (as the Maharal will shortly explain), these behaviors will not always manifest themselves in

This is the import of "Give thanks to Hashem, because He is good, for His benevolence is universal". We praise Hashem because He is good – and his goodness is manifest since "His benevolence is universal". Just as Hashem is infinite, so, [in lockstep,] is his intrinsic attribute of benevolence infinite – in contrast to attributes that are bound to recipients, which are not infinite.

We can add another dimension to this explanation by noting that when we describe Hashem's benevolence as infinite and without end, we mean to include the world-to-come in our description. In that epoch, when imposing judgement on sinners will no longer be necessary,[178] and there will be no need for mercy,[179] Hashem's goodness and benevolence will persist. "His benevolence is universal" even in the world-to-come.[180]

This is an extension of our basic concept, which is that Hashem's benevolence is an intrinsic trait; thus, just as He is infinite so is His benevolence infinite and without end or limitation. Understand this.[181]

Section 15 – The First Blessing – Part 2

ובטובו הגדול לא חסר לנו...

ובטובו הגדול תמיד לא חסר לנו ואל
יחסר לנו מזון לעולם ועד

" And in His great goodness, nourishment **is** never withheld from us [and will never **be** withheld from us, for all eternity]".[182] The word [used for what is

──────────── פירוש בנתיבות לב ────────────

Hashem as will benevolence, which is not object-dependent.

[178] In the world-to-come man's inclination for evil will disappear so judgement will be irrelevant.

[179] Mercy is reserved for the undeserving but with no evil inclination everyone will be deserving.

[180] Hashem created the world because He is intrinsically benevolent and without the world there would be no beneficiary of His benevolence. Indeed, the ongoing emanation of the world on the part of Hashem is itself an act of benevolence. Thus although Hashem would retain the attribute of benevolence regardless of whether or not there would be a world, since benevolence is an intrinsic trait, the world is a Hashem-desired manifestation of His benevolence, and this desire is unchanged even in the radically different world-order of the world-to-come.

[181] In a similar vein the Maharal in *Gevuros Hashem* chapter 7 explains why a positive prophecy has a guaranteed outcome while a negative prophecy can be rescinded based on a change in circumstance (e.g. repentance on the part of the intended victims of the prophecy). He explains that Hashem is intrinsically good so when He issues a positive prophecy it is not based on the behaviors of the intended recipients. It is a function of His inherent goodness, which is immutable. On the other hand a negative prophecy is a withholding to his inherent goodness based on the negative behavior of the object of the negative prophecy. Thus the negative prophecy is not immutable and if the behavior changes the negative prophecy is cancelled.

[182] This section requires some understanding of Hebrew grammar. We will attempt to provide enough background to understand the Maharal's points without going into unnecessary detail. However a basic knowledge of Hebrew and the Hebrew alphabet and vowels is presumed.

Every Hebrew verb may have of up to seven grammatical paradigms, most of which can be conjugated in various tenses (past, present, future). The differences between the paradigms in meaning are generally those of perspective (who is doing the action described by the verb) and intensity of the action. The different paradigms are distinguishable one from another primarily on the basis of their vowelization.

The two grammatical paradigms that are relevant for this discussion are *kal*, or simple aspect and *pi'el*, or emphatic aspect. (The Maharal refers to *pi'el* as "*dagesh*", which means "emphasis".) The root שבר, for example, which means "break", in the *kal* first-person present tense would be conjugated שָׁבַרְתִּי, *shovarti* (note the vowelization, a *komotz* under the *shin* and a *patach* under the *vais*) which means, "I **broke** [some object]". The same root in the *pi'el* first-person present tense would be conjugated שָׁבָּרְתִּי, *shivairti* (vowelized with a *chirik* under the *shin* and a *tzairai* under the *vais*), which means, "I **smashed** [some object]". The difference between *kal* and *pi'el* is the intensity of the action described. The verb root is the same שבר but the meaning is modified based on the grammatical paradigm used.

translated here as] "never withheld" is חָסַר, *chosar*,[183] which is in the *kal* grammatical paradigm. Similarly, the word [used for what is translated here as] "will never be withheld" is יֶחְסַר, *yechsar*, with a *segol* under the *yud*, and which is [therefore also] in the *kal* grammatical paradigm. The object of the verb [חסר, in both cases,] is "nourishment" – that is, we have never lacked nourishment because Hashem supplies it to us continuously. So we are not now nourishment-deprived. And, for eternity, we never will lack nourishment because Hashem will continue to supply us with nourishment forever. So we will not be nourishment-deprived in the future, either.

There is another view that holds that we should say חִסַּר, *chisair*, with a *chirik* under the *ches*, which is in the *pi'el* grammatical paradigm. The meaning would then be, "And in His great Goodness **He** has never withheld nourishment from us…" but rather supplies it to us continuously. Similarly [this view holds that we should continue with] יְחַסַּר, *yechasor*, with a *shva* under the *yud* and a *patach* under the *ches*, to be consistent with the *pi'el* grammatical paradigm. The meaning would then be, "… and **He** will never withhold nourishment from us, for all eternity".[184]

[The second variant is also valid. However,] there is no [apparent] rhyme or reason to ["mixing and matching" by] starting with חִסַּר, *chisair*, in the *pi'el* grammatical paradigm and continuing with יֶחְסַר, *yechsar*, in the *kal* grammatical paradigm.

There are those who counter, however, that this [switch from *pi'el* to *kal*] is grounded in wisdom, because once we establish, [with the use of *pi'el*,] Hashem's more intense role in providing our nourishment in the past, a precedent is created that will carry forward into the future.[185] Thus the use of *kal* to describe the future is sufficient, since the language is merely building on the status quo [of the past, as described by the previous *piel* language]. Therefore it is valid to describe past [sustenance] using the more intense *pi'el* and revert to the more relaxed *kal* when discussing future [sustenance].[186]

We may add [in justifying a mixed grammatical paradigm model beginning with *pi'el* and ending with *kal*] that we must begin with *chisair*, in *pi'el*, to shine the spotlight on Hashem as the party responsible for not withholding nourishment from us. When we speak of nourishment Hashem must be the focus. Once we have accomplished that, however, there is no need to dwell on the point and we may revert to *kal* and say *yechsar*, with a *segol* under the *yud*, and shift our focus to the nourishment, which "will never be withheld from us", since Hashem will continually supply it to us.

––––––––––––––––––––––––––––––– פירוש בנתיבות לב –––––––––––––––––––––––––––––––

[183] With a *komotz* under the *ches* and a *patach* under the *samech*.

[184] The difference in the two variants of this phrase of the blessing is in how strongly we express the immediacy of Hashem's involvement in our non-deprivation of nourishment. In the first variant the emphasis is on the nourishment and we declare that we have not been and will not be deprived of it. Obviously the agent behind our non-deprivation is Hashem but in this variant he is not as explicitly acknowledged as the impetus behind our satiety as he is in the second variant. In the second *pi'el* – "*dagesh*" variant Hashem's role in maintaining our past and future non-deprivation is very much front-and-center.

[185] We now know that Hashem's involvement is intense and there is no reason to assume that in the future it would be anything less.

[186] However, to be inconsistent in the use of the grammatical paradigms by reversing them, starting with *kal* and ending with *pi'el*, would make no sense.

Section 16 – The First Blessing – Part 3

בעבור שמו הגדול, ר"ל כי הש"י מפרנס לכל...

בעבור שמו הגדול...

❝ For the sake of His great name…". That is to say that Hashem sustains all of creation so that it will persist and therefore will perpetuate His great name – for if the world ceased to exist, how and to whom would the greatness of His name be perpetuated? Similarly Yehoshua, speaking [to Hashem] about Yisroel, said that if, G-d forbid, Yisroel were to be destroyed, "…and what will You do for Your great Name?"[187] Are stones and rocks capable of bringing out the greatness of Hashem? Therefore the blessing states that it is for the sake of His great name that He nourishes and sustains everyone.[188]

Moreover[189] sustenance is what allows people to continue to exist and Hashem's ineffable name is the name associated with maintaining the continued existence of the universe.[190] Indeed, it is for this reason that immediately after the [original] creation, when the [newly-created] universe first required continuity maintenance, the verse [alludes to its inception by] stating, "…on the day that the **Hashem**,[191] G-d

———————————— פירוש בנתיבות לב ————————————

[187] See *Yehoshua* 7:9. The context is the unexpected defeat of Yisroel in the city of Ai subsequent to their previous victories against the Canaanite inhabitants of Israel after their forty years in the desert following their exodus from Egypt. Unbeknownst to Yehoshua, one of the soldiers had violated a ban on taking spoils, and that precipitated the defeat. But at the time of Yehoshua's prayer he feared the imminent destruction of Yisroel and cried out, "For the Canaanites and all the inhabitants of the land shall hear and shall encircle us and cut off our name from the earth; and what will You do for Your great Name?"

It is Yisroel's role to perpetuate the greatness of Hashem's name in the world and if they were to disappear there would be no one to perform that function. Hashem's name is embedded in the name "Yisroel", as *Rashi* on that verse points out. Moreover, as the Maharal mentions in *Ohr Chodosh*, Haman's attack on Yisroel was considered an attack on Hashem because Yisroel is Hashem's primary creation and if they cease to exist Hashem loses His identity as Creator, as it were.

The *Ramban* (*Devarim* 32:26) explains this concept in detail. He writes that the purpose of creation is to enable man to recognize his Creator and acknowledge Him, but man was given free choice and the nations of the world elected to ignore mankind's mission, spurning recognition of Hashem. The only nation to live up to their mission is Yisroel; through them Hashem "reminds" the other nations of the purpose of Creation by making Himself known through miracles that are performed on behalf of Yisroel. Were Yisroel to disappear from the scene the world would be bereft of these reminders and Hashem would be forgotten and creation would no longer have a purpose.

Although the Maharal here is talking in general terms it seems clear from the context that "all of creation" is a specific reference to sustaining Yisroel.

[188] In this interpretation of, בעבור שמו הגדול, *ba'avor shmo ha'gadol*, the meaning is as we translated it, "for the sake of His great name". The word כי, *ki*, which can have multiple meanings, here means, "it is the case that". In other words, for the sake of His great name it is the case that Hashem sustains…

[189] This is a second, independent explanation of the phrase beginning with *ba'avor shmo ha'gadol*, but in this explanation the translation is not "for the sake of His great name", as described in footnote 188, but rather, "through the use of His great name". In other words, through the use of His great name it is the case that Hashem sustains…

[190] Hashem is essentially unknowable but the attributes that He shares with us, as it were, are represented by his "names". Hashem's ineffable name is spelled with the letter *yud* followed by *hai* following by *vov* followed by *hai* but it has no vowelization and is therefore unpronounceable in our current world. It is often referred to as the "*Havaya* name" – a rearrangement of its letters that means "existence" – since, as the Maharal is explaining, it describes Hashem's attribute of maintaining the continuity of existence.

The Maharal is telling us that this is the name referred to in the first after-meals blessing as "His great name".

[191] "Hashem" simply means "the Name" and is the generic reference to G-d we use in this text. In this verse, however, where we write "Hashem", the "*Havaya* name", which refers to continuity of existence, actually appears. See footnote 190. The point is that, from the moment of original creation and continually thereafter, Hashem is refreshing creation to maintain the existence of the world and if that process were to stop, there would be no coasting along on the basis of status quo – the world would just

made earth and heaven…"

It is for this reason as well that King Dovid, in the Psalm, "Praise Hashem for He is Good",[192] has twenty-six verses,[193] all ending in כי לעולם חסדו, *ki l'olom chasdo*, "His benevolence is for the sake of [maintaining] the world"[194] and the ultimate, twenty-sixth verse – which corresponds to the Hashem's ineffable name – highlights, "He gives bread to all living things; His benevolence is for the sake of [maintaining] the world". [In the realm of all the forms of Hashem's benevolence mentioned in this Psalm,] giving bread to all living things is the highest form of benevolence.[195] This is why it is mentioned last, why it completes the sequence of twenty-six praises and why it is the final entry in the count that equals the value of the ineffable name.

Another explanation[196] is that nourishment is provided directly by Hashem,[197] with no heavenly intermediary and thus it is associated specifically with the ineffable name. Further elaboration is inappropriate.[198]

כי הוא קל זן ומפרנס לכל ומטיב
לכל ומכין מזון לכל בריותיו…

The blessing [next] enumerates four forms of sustenance that Hashem provides. The first is זן, *zan*, food nourishment, what one eats in order to stay alive. The second is פרנסה, *parnasa*, livelihood. All the other things a person needs to live[199] fall under that category of livelihood. ומטיב לכל, *u'maitiv la'kol*, "and He is benevolent to all", is the third form of sustenance. This category includes the "bonus" benevolence of [non-

──────────── פירוש בנתיבות לב ────────────

cease to exist. The property of Hashem that manages the process of continuity of existence, as it were, is referred to with the "*Havaya* name".

[192] *Tehillim* 136. For additional discussion of this Psalm, known as *Hallel HaGadol*, see footnotes 6, 171 and 175.

[193] Twenty-six is the numerical *Gematria* value of the *Havaya* name.

[194] The phrase *ki l'olam chasdo* is generally translated, "for his benevolence is forever" but the word *l'olam* can mean both "forever" and "for the sake of (*l'*) the world (*olam*)". Since the Maharal is now discussing the continual perpetuation of the world by Hashem, through His benevolence, via the attribute of his ineffable name, and is saying that Psalm 136 is is a song of praise to Hashem for this perpetuation, he is clearly reading the phrase as meaning, "His benevolence is for the sake of the world" – that is, His benevolence motivates, as it were, His perpetuation of the world through the *Havaya* name.

(Interestingly, although the Psalm begins with praises that are universal, lauding Hashem for maintaining natural phenomena like the oceans, sun, moon, etc., fifteen of the praises are specific to Yisroel and detail the acts of benevolence and the miracles that Hashem performed during the exodus from Egypt and entry into the land of Israel. According to the way the Maharal understands the theme of this Psalm, "His benevolence is for the sake of the world", one can perhaps conclude that these actions on behalf of Yisroel are as integral to the survival of the world as maintaining the laws of nature.)

[195] And therefore praising Hashem for it is the ultimate praise. In *Gevuros Hashem* chapter 65 the Maharal explains the sequence of praises to Hashem found in "*Hallel HaGadol*". He says that the fact that Hashem provides sustenance to all is the most significant of His kindnesses and miracles, superseding even redemption, and therefore appears last in the list. See section 1 and footnote 6.

[196] This explanation is an extension of the previous one. *Ba'avor shmo ha'gadol* again means "through the use of His great name"; the complete phrase, though is read slightly differently: "Through the use of His great name it is the case that Hashem [**himself**] sustains…"

[197] The *Gemara* in *Taanis* 2a,b quotes Rabbi Yehuda as saying that the "key" to rain is one three "keys" that is never entrusted to a heavenly agent but is kept exclusively in the hands of Hashem. The *Gemara* then cites a point of view that adds the key of sustenance to the list and wonders why Rabbi Yehuda omitted it. The *Gemara* answers that conceptually he did not omit it; he merely did not list it separately because it is included in the "rain" key – since sustenance is inextricably bound with rain.

[198] The Maharal means that this concept is based on Kabbalistic principles that are beyond the scope of the current work. To get an idea of what the Maharal is alluding to, though, consider that in Chapter 25 of *Gevuros Hashem* he writes that the *Havaya* name refers to Hashem in isolation from his creations. There are no intermediaries in that context.

[199] Items such as shelter, clothing, furnishings, work implements, etc.

essential items] as we discussed earlier.[200] [Finally we have] ‫ומכין מזון לכל בריותיו‬, *u'machin mazon l'chol briyosav*, "He prepares nourishment for all His creations". This refers to non-human creations. For these creations "He prepares…" is the appropriate phrase rather than "He provides…" [which was said earlier regarding man][201] because "provides" implies a recipient capable of [actively] accepting that which was provided, such as man, whereas for non-reasoning beings [like animals], it is only possible to use [the weaker] "prepares" [since there is no process of active acceptance, only the consumption of that which the animal happens to find].

Section 17 – The First Blessing – Part 4

‫ברכה זאת פותחת הזן את העולם ומסיים הזן את הכל...‬

‫הזן את העולם... הזן אה הכל‬

This blessing opens with, "He nourishes **the entire world**" and concludes with "…Who nourishes **everything**". The conclusion seems more encompassing than the opening since "everything" [by definition omits nothing. The reality, however, is that the conclusion is not expanding the scope of Hashem's catalog of intended beneficiaries. Rather, the language of the conclusion is designed to communicate a change in perspective, not a change in scope.]

The opening is written from the standpoint of the recipient – the world – which requires sustenance and therefore Hashem provides it and enables the world to persist. However the conclusion, "Who nourishes everything", is written from the standpoint of Hashem, who intrinsically yearns and desires to sustain everything, [independent of any potential recipient].[202]

Our Sages have already taught us[203] that the Holy One, blessed is He, yearns for the prayers of the righteous. What is the basis of this yearning? It is a consequence of Hashem's intrinsic desire to impart good. Hashem yearns for the prayers of the righteous to enable this desire to come to fruition. Prayers are required to enable Hashem to fulfill His desire to impart good because [good is only good if it is appreciated and] praying for something is an indicator of appreciation. Thus Hashem yearns for the prayers of the righteous[204] so that he can [satisfy His natural inclination to] impart good.

Thus this blessing concludes with, "Who nourishes everything" – that is, with a

──────────────── ‫פירוש בנתיבות לב‬ ────────────────

[200] At the end of section 8 of this chapter. In that context the Maharal associates the blessing of an abundance of good with the fourth after-meals blessing. The Maharal is evidently saying here that although there is a separate blessing for this level of benevolence in the fourth Rabbinically mandated blessing, it is alluded to as well in the first, Torah-mandated blessing.

[201] "He provides *lechem* to all living beings", which appears at the beginning of the first after-meals blessing and is discussed at the beginning of section 14.

[202] In other words the opening describes Hashem's actions while the conclusion describes His nature, as it were.

[203] *Yevamos* 64a.

[204] Why is it that the *Gemara* in *Yevamos* specifies that Hashem yearns specifically for the prayers of the righteous – why cannot anyone's sincere prayers serve the same purpose? The Maharal answers this question in *Chidushei Aggados* on that *Gemara*. He answers that Hashem's desire to impart good is a function of His role at the Cause of creation and therefore it's protector. The "Cause" role exists only when there are "Effects", or created beings. To the extent that these created beings recognize their absolute dependence on Hashem and their complete inability to function independently of Him, they are effective demonstrators of Hashem's role as Cause. Only the righteous achieve that level of recognition. The average person is incapable of it. Thus the average person is not effective evidence of Hashem's role as Cause and his prayers are not declarations of his total dependence on Him. They are therefore too weak to elicit a flow of good from Hashem.

paean to Hashem's intrinsic property of yearning to nourish everything.[205] Understand this well.[206]

Section 18 – The Second Blessing – Part 1

ברכה שניה נודה לך...

נודה לך... אנו מודים לך

The second blessing is נודה לך, *nodeh l'cha*, "We thank You". This blessing begins with "We thank you" and the concluding paragraph [of the blessing] similarly begins with "For all… we thank You".[207] This structure [is unique to the *nodeh l'cha* blessing; it] is not shared by the first or the third blessings. The reason for this distinction is that the gift of the land [of Israel was a perpetual gift of life] since man's livelihood derives from the land. The first blessing focuses on nourishment and the moment-to-moment sustenance that Hashem provides but this cannot be called "livelihood" since the emphasis is not on the long term. However the land is a perpetual gift and it is therefore a continual life-giving source for its owners.[208]

Expressing gratitude with "thank you" is a uniquely suitable response to life-providing forms of assistance[209] so we employ it as a response to Hashem's bequeathing us the land and we bracket this blessing with expressions of thanks beginning and end.[210]

פירוש בנתיבות לב

[205] At the end of section 8 of this chapter the Maharal associates the intrinsic desire of Hashem to bestow good with the fourth, Rabbinic blessing of the after-meals blessing and he links it with the blessing of an overabundance of good. In this Torah-mandated blessing these two properties – overabundance of good and intrinsic good – are alluded to separately. See footnote 200.

[206] The conclusion or *chasima* of a *brocho* encapsulates the content of the *brocho* and represents its crescendo. Thus it is appropriate to present the *raison d'etre* for Hashem's benevolence at the end of the blessing that has been describing it.

[207] This structure is dictate by the *Gemara* in *Brachos* 49a which states that the *Nodeh l'cha* blessing must begin and end with thanks to Hashem. In this and subsequent sections the Maharal will explain why this is so.

[208] The distinction is rooted in the fact that by definition nourishment is a moment-to-moment concept whereas livelihood is a concept that extends in time. However no value judgment is implied here – the Maharal is not stating that livelihood is somehow more important or necessary than nourishment, or that the gift of the land somehow supersedes or moots the provision of nourishment. Both are necessary; they are separate channels through which Hashem benefits us. The point, as the Maharal will detail, is that the "thank you" mode of gratitude-expression is specifically appropriate to the livelihood gift that is the subject of the second blessing.

[209] The word we are translating as "thank you" is הודאה, *ho'daah* in Hebrew. Why is it that this word is particularly appropriate as a response to life-providing forms of assistance, as the Maharal states? After all it is customary to say "thank you" even for mundane things that are far from life-providing. Perhaps we can answer this question with a profound concept articulated by Rav Yitzchok Hutner in *Pachad Yitzchok, Chanukah, Maamar* 2:5. He writes that the word *ho'daah* has two meanings: it means "thank you" but it also means "admission", as in, "I admit that I owe you this money". Admission is a statement of dependence; when a person makes an admission he is effectively stating that he is not an independent and standalone being but has to come onto others for some aspect of his existence.

The word, *ho'daah*, carries both these meanings because they are related. Thanking someone is more than just an expression of gratitude, is a tacit admission of dependence on him for the item or service he is being thanked for. Now, our most fundamental possession is our life and we are totally dependent on Hashem for our lives – for our creation, our continued existence and our subsistence. If *ho'daah* is an expression of dependence, there is nothing that more deeply calls for *ho'daah* than the life-providing forms of assistance that Hashem provides us. This is why, as the Maharal says, expressing gratitude with *ho'daah* ("thank you", as we translate it) is a uniquely suitable response to life-providing forms of assistance.

[210] Perhaps the begin/end bracketing symbolizes the perpetual nature of this gift.

The building of the Temple[211] is not life-giving in the same sense as the granting of the land, which provides [actual] livelihood.[212] The giving of the land, [uniquely,] evokes an emphatic expression of thanks.

"Thank you" is always used in the context of,[213] "for our lives which are deposited into Your hand and for our souls which are entrusted with You". [We similarly use an expression of thanks here in the second after-meals blessing] since Hashem gave us life when he gave us the land just as he did when he first gave us our actual lives. Therefore our Sages instituted expressions of "thank You" at the beginning and end of this blessing.

נודה לך... על שהנחלת לאבותינו
ארץ חמדה טובה ורחבה

They further instituted the language, "We thank you... because you have bequeathed to our forefathers an appealing, good and spacious land...". Why is the land described as "appealing"?[214] Because it contains appealing things, as the verse[215] describes: "...a land with brooks of water, fountains and depths, that emerge in valleys and mountains" – and because it has beautiful gardens and orchards, because people find its fruits appealing.

[Now, it is not true that is everything that is appealing is also beneficial;] there are things that people want that are not necessarily healthy or strength-giving. For this reason we declare that the land is "good" – it is intrinsically good; it's produce is good, health-giving and strengthening. This is what is meant by "good".

We continue with "a spacious land" which means as the words imply – [capacious]. This too is a result of divine blessing,[216] as our Sages taught in chapter *HaNizakin:"*[217] [The land of Israel] is called[218] "the land of the deer" because it [miraculously] accommodates, comfortably and without cramming, all [Jews] who settle in it.[219] This is why "a spacious land" is also enumerated [as an item for which we thank Hashem].

פירוש בנתיבות לב

[211] Subject of the third after-meals blessing.

[212] Thus the "thank you" mode of expression is not suited to the third blessing just as it is not suited to the first, nourishment-oriented blessing.

The Temple's primary benefit was spiritual, not physical. Although the Temple certainly also brought physical blessing to the land and in fact to the entire world, livelihood is possible, albeit in a weakened state, even in the absence of the Temple, as indeed we see in our present time, when we unfortunately lack the Temple but still possess some measure of livelihood.

[213] This expression appears in the *Modim*, "Thank You" blessing of the *Shmoneh Esrai* prayer. "Our lives" is a concept that extends over time, thus justifying the "thank You" expression, says the Maharal.

[214] The origin of this expression which associates "desirable" with the land of Israel is a verse in *Yirmiyahu* 3:19, "I will give you a desirable land...".

[215] *Devarim* 8:7.

[216] The implicit question is that "desirable" and "good" are absolute values which are therefore achievable through Hashem's blessing, whereas "capacious" seems to be relative to the number of inhabitants that are destined to occupy the land. It will either be big enough or it will not. What effect can blessing have?

[217] *Gittin* 57a.

[218] *Daniel* 11:16, "...and he will stand in the land of the deer". The expression figuratively means, "land of beauty" but the literal meaning is "land of the deer" and the *Gemara* in *Gittin* explains why this expression is used.

[219] That is, just as the hide of a deer is remarkably stretchable, so too the land of Israel miraculously expands to accommodate all Jews who settle in it. Obviously this unnatural phenomenon can only be achieved via a blessing from Hashem.

Section 19 – The Second Blessing – Part 2

ויש לך להבין כי אלו ג' דברים חמדה טובה ורחבה...

It is important to understand that these three attributes [of the land of Israel] – appealing, good and spacious – came about in the merit of our forefathers, to whom the land was [originally] given. Here is how each attribute is associated with its corresponding forefather.[220]

Avrohom was beloved by all because he was kind to all; his signature trait was to act benevolently and pleasantly to his fellows beings. Certainly such a person will be appealing to everyone, and accepted by everyone, as a result of his conduct. This is why [the people of Chevron] told Avrohom,[221] "You are a prince of Hashem in our midst".[222] It is why the valley of *Shaveh* is known as the valley of the king.[223] Avrohom did not impose himself upon his subjects with force. Rather, everyone acknowledged his likable and appealing behavior [and they therefore accepted his kingship on themselves willingly]. Thus the land's appealing nature is in the merit of Avrohom [to whom the land was first bequeathed].

The land was "good" in the merit of Yaakov. Good implies freedom from dross and the trait of "good" is associated with Yaakov because his offspring were without dross.[224] In his merit, therefore, the land was good in every respect and without dross.

The land was spacious in the merit of our forefather Yitzchok for whom spaciousness is particularly apropos – as Yitzchok himself said,[225] "For now Hashem has made room for us, and we will be fruitful in the land". There is deep meaning attached to the association between Yitzchok and spaciousness.[226] [In fact] all three associations of the forefathers with the attributes of the land of Israel have deep meaning associated with them, which is why these attributes [in particular] are singled

–––––––––––––––––––––– פירוש בנתיבות לב ––––––––––––––––––––––

[220] In this and the following two sections the Maharal will present three sets of three items each that appear in this blessing and that are in the merit of the forefathers and he will then explain the significance of three sets of three.

[221] *Beraishis* 23:6. The context is the start of Avrohom's negotiation with the residents of Chevron over the purchase of the *Machpela* cave as a burial place for his wife.

[222] They recognized his innate benevolence and goodness.

[223] See *Beraishis* 14:17. This is where the epic "battle between the four kings and the five kings" took place. The Torah relates that during that battle, Lot, Avrohom's nephew, was captured, compelling Avrohom himself to enter the fray in order to rescue him. *Rashi* on this verse, based on *Beraishis Rabbah* 42:5 explains that "the valley of the king" got its moniker because that was where all the nations concurred and crowned Avrohom over them as a prince of Hashem.

[224] All of Yaakov's children were righteous and all were destined to become branches of the nation of Yisroel. Our Sages call this concept מיטתו שלימה, *mitaso shlaimo*. Yaakov was the only one of the forefathers with that distinction since Avrohom had Yishmael and other children that were not destined to become part of the Jewish nation and Yitzchok had Esav who similarly did not become part of the Jewish nation.

[225] *Beraishis* 26:22. The context is Avimelech's banishment of Yitzchok from the land of the Philistines because of his wealth. The Philistines continued to harass him until he distanced himself from them considerably, at which point he exclaimed, "For now Hashem has made room for us, and we will be fruitful in the land".

[226] Perhaps we can associate this concept with an idea the Maharal presents in *Gur Aryeh, Beraishis* 26:34. He writes that the signature trait of Yitzchok is *din*, justice, which implies perfection with no room for error. Yitzchok had children at age sixty because the number six (and power-of-ten multiples of it) represents expansion in all directions (north, south, east, west, up and down). Therefore when Yitzchok reached that age it was the precise time for his own family to expand and to achieve perfection. We see, in any event, that Yitzchok, with his attribute of *din*, is associated with expansion in all directions, which is tantamount to spaciousness.

out in this blessing.

Section 20 – The Second Blessing – Part 3

ואומר ועל בריתך שחתמת בבשרנו...

ועל בריתך ... ועל תורתך ... ועל
חקיך ...

The blessing continues, "… and for the *bris* covenant that you inscribed on our flesh, for Your Torah which You have taught us and for Your statutes which You made known to us…". These three things [correspond to the three aspects of our beings]. The *bris* is on our bodies. "Your Torah" refers to the Torah which pertains to our intellects. "Statutes"[227] are laws [whose reasons] are not susceptible to human understanding; they are decrees [which we must follow whether we understand them or not]. These are the province of our animating spirit;[228] they bypass our intellect and are actualized [directly] by our spirit, which can perform actions even when they are not susceptible to understanding.

[With these three gifts] Hashem made man complete in every respect – for our bodies he gave us the *bris* covenant which is fulfilled on our physical persons [and brings our bodies to a state of perfection], for our intellects he gave us the Torah [which brings our minds to a state of perfection] and for our animated spirit he gave us the statutes which the spirit fulfills even though they are beyond comprehension [and thereby brings our spirit to a state of perfection].

[The wording of the blessing is carefully chosen to reflect the basic difference between the gift that our intellect processes and the gift that is relegated to our spirit.] Actions that man performs are channeled through his spirit, as is known, since the spirit is man's animating force. Therefore the statutes, for which the focus in on **fulfilling** their requirements[229] [rather than on **understanding** them,] since they are impervious to understanding, are the province of the spirit. This is why the blessing uses the phrase, "that you **taught** us" with respect to the Torah whereas the phrase, "that you **made known** to us" is used with respect to the statutes. The statutes are not suited to being taught since the goal of teaching is to impart intellectual understanding.[230]

If we reflect, we will understand that, [as was the case with respect to the properties of the land of Israel][231] these three things – the bris covenant inscribed on our flesh, the Torah that Hashem taught us and the statutes that he made known to us – were also granted to us in the merit of the forefathers. The *bris* covenant is associated with Avraham.[232] "Your Torah" is in the merit of Yaakov as the verse says,[233] "And He

––––––––––––––– פירוש בנתיבות לב –––––––––––––––

[227] חוקים, *chukim*, in Hebrew.

[228] נפש, *nefesh*. This is the animating force that we share with animals; it controls activity but does not require understanding as a prerequisite to action. Of course while animals act on instinct and are incapable of rational thought, human beings are supposed to use their intellects to dominate and control the actions of their spirits. With respect to the statutes, which have no known reason, our intellects "command" the spirit to carry them out regardless, since they are incumbent on us as Hashem's will, but they are nonetheless considered primarily the province of the spirit since the intellect is accustomed to acting on the basis of a reason that pertains to the action itself, not to a reason based on the need to fulfill an unexplained command.

[229] Which requires action.

[230] And the statutes cannot be understood intellectually.

[231] Discussed in the previous section.

[232] Since it was originally commanded to him. See *Beraishis* 17.

[233] *Tehillim* 78:5.

established testimony in Jacob, [and He set down a Torah in Israel]". We explained this at length in our commentary on the first chapter of tractate *Avos*;[234] refer there. "Your statutes…" are decrees from Hashem that emanate from His attribute of strict justice and we obtained those in the merit of Yitzchok [whose signature trait was strict justice].[235] Thus, these three things were also in the merit of the forefathers.

Section 21 – The Second Blessing – Part 4

ועל חיים חן וחסד גם אלו שלשה...

ועל חיים חן וחסד...

" … and for the life, favor and benevolence [which you granted us]". A proper understanding of these three benefits makes it clear that they, too, are in the merit of the forefathers.[236] [iv] We thus have three sets of benefit triads [that

—————————— פירוש בנתיבות לב ——————————

[234] *Derech Chaim* 1:2. The association begins in *Beraishis* 25:27 where the Torah reports that "Yaakov was a straightforward man, dwelling in tents". "Tents", *Rashi* explains (based on the *Beraishis Rabbah* 63:10) is a reference to the Torah study halls of Shem and Ever. Similarly, Yaakov informs his apparently malevolent brother Esav, "I have dwelled with Lavan…" (*Beraishis* 32:5) and *Rashi* explains that the *Gematria* of the word for "dwelled", גרתי, *garti*, is 613, signifying the number of commandments in the Torah. Yaakov was declaring that he lacked not one iota of Torah observance. The Maharal points out that although Avraham also observed all the Torah's commandments, Yaakov excelled in Torah **study** and therefore it was in his merit that Yisroel received the Torah. See the *Derech Chaim* in context for additional associations between Yaakov and Torah.

[235] Strict justice is justice untempered by mercy. Yitzchok willingly allowed himself to be offered as a sacrifice to Hashem at the *Akeida* (see *Beraishis* 22), which, had it been actually implemented, would have been the ultimate example of strict justice. Yitzchok was thus willing to submit to strict justice and he lived under its aura and comported himself accordingly, as the Maharal writes in *Netzach Yisroel* chapter 52.. Indeed, Hashem would have preferred to govern the world only on the basis of strict justice but he tempered the justice with mercy because the world would not otherwise have been able to endure. In *Netzach Yisroel* chapter 13 the Maharal writes that Yitzchok was particularly "close" to Hashem because Yitzchok's signature trait was strict justice.

The Gemara in *Brachos* 26b states that Yitzchok instituted the afternoon prayer service, deriving this from the verse in *Beraishis* 24:63, "And Yitzchok went out to meditate in **the field** towards evening". "The field" is a reference to the Temple mount, the optimum location for prayer. Avrohom and Yaakov also instituted prayers there but it is referred to as "the field" only with respect to Yitzchok. The reason, the Maharal explains in *Netzach Yisroel* chapter 52, is that typically a field is undeviatingly flat, in the same way that strict justice is undeviating. Yitzchok prayed from the standpoint of strict justice, his signature trait, so "the field" reference is applicable only to him. The Maharal discusses the role of our forefathers with respect to prayer at length in Chapter 3, Section 2.

[236] The Maharal does not specify the correspondences in this case. They are as follows: *chesed*, benevolence, is the attribute of Avrohom as discussed in Section 19. That Hashem bestows benevolence upon us is measure for measure payback for Avrohom's benevolence.

As noted in Section 20, the attribute of Yitzchok is *din*, strict justice, also known as *gevurah*, the power of discipline. The Maharal explains in *Gevuros Hashem* Chapter 64 that from the standpoint of strict justice there are no "entitlements" since no one can measure up to the standard of strict justice. The best we can hope for is that we find favor in Hashem's eyes, as it were, and to be gifted with sustenance that is not conditioned on merit. See also *Chidushei Aggados* on *Sanhedrin* 98b for more on the association of favor with Yitzchok. In any event our acknowledgement of sustenance from the perspective of Yitzchok is an acknowledgment that we find favor in Hashem's eyes. See endnote iv for an extended discussion of Yitzchok and the attribute of *din*.

Yaakov represents a balance between unremitting benevolence and unremitting justice – the attributes of Avrohom and Yitzchok. His middle ground is referred to as *tiferes*, which literally means beauty – the beauty of a harmonious blend of contrasts. It is also known as *emes*, truth, since it creates the reality that allows the world to exist – the reality of benevolence and strict justice in proper balance. A benevolence-only world, where merit plays no role, would not allow us the opportunity to earn the reward that Hashem wants to give us; we would be living on "handouts" and that would rob us of our dignity. A world of strict justice would be unsurvivable since it would have no tolerance for error and human beings are prone to error. Life thus depends on Yaakov's middle ground and the "life" in this blessing is in the merit of Yaakov. See Chapter 9 of *Gevuros Hashem* for additional discussion of the attributes of Yaakov.

Another association of Yaakov with life: The Maharal writes in *Netzach Yisroel* chapter 4 that life is associated with Yaakov because the *Gemara* in *Taanis* 5b says that "Our forefather Yaakov did not die".

Hashem bestowed upon us in the merit of the forefathers. The first triad is] "an appealing, good and spacious land", the next triad is "the *bris* covenant that you inscribed on our flesh, for Your Torah which You have taught us and for Your statutes which You made known to us" and the final triad is "the life, favor and benevolence". In this, the blessing of acknowledgment, it is appropriate to acknowledge to Hashem that none of the benefits He provides us are in our own merit; they are all in the merit of our forefathers.

ועל אכילת מזון...

The three sets of triads constitute nine benefits for which we thank Hashem. The tenth benefit [in this blessing] is "for the provision of food…". This benefit is the tenth[237] because provision of food is the [single most] overarching benefit, for, as we detailed earlier, "Providing man's sustenance is more difficult than anything else.[238] Thus it is appropriate to make food the tenth benefit for which we give thanks.[239]

Section 22 – The Second Blessing – Part 5

ואמר שאתה זן ומפרנס כו' בכל יום ובכל עת ובכל שעה...

שאתה זן ומפרנס... בכל יום ובכל
עת ובכל שעה

The blessing continues, "[and for the provision of food] with which you nourish [and sustain us constantly] in every day, at every time-interval and in every hour". The reason [for the apparently redundant time references] is that a person's sustenance requirements vary according to his circumstances, which are changeable. Today he may need this, tomorrow he may need that; as his situation changes over time, so do his sustenance needs. [But it is not only a change in day that may change his sustenance needs;] on a separate track his needs may also change from one moment to the next.

──────────── פירוש בנתיבות לב ────────────

This is obviously not to be taken in a literal sense (since the Torah describes his embalming and burial). Rather, says the Maharal, this is a reference to the fact, cited in *Yevamos* 76a, that Yaakov never experienced a wasted seminal emission. Wasting seed in this manner partakes of the nature of murder since the wasted seed would otherwise have had the potential to become a living human being. Yaakov's avoidance of this behavior bespeaks (among other things) the high value he placed on life. This is why the *Gemara* says that Yaakov did not die and why he, in particular, is associated with life.

[237] In *Gevuros Hashem*, end of chapter 46, the Maharal explains that the number 10 signifies an elevation into a higher stratum, as in fact happens numerically when we progress from singles units (1-9) to units of 10. When the Torah, or our Sages, specify that a particular item is the tenth item in a list of ten, it is not just happenstance, but a statement that there is a status change taking place when that item is encountered. Because of its vital nature, provision of food is not just another benefit or even just a more important benefit, it is a fundamentally different kind of benefit; one that is on a different level than the others. Thus is appears as the tenth and final benefit enumerated in this blessing. The Maharal will have more to say on the meaning of the number ten in this context in the next section. See, in particular, footnote 244.

[238] This statement is based on a *Gemara* in *Pesachim* 118a which compares provision of sustenance to various difficult things, such as splitting of the Red Sea and bringing on the redemption, and declares it to be either equal to or greater in difficulty than those things. In section 1 of this chapter we discuss this *Gemara* and address the question of how the concept of "difficulty" applies to Hashem, the omnipotent power.

[239] The following table encapsulates the ten benefits we thank Hashem for in this blessing.

Second-Blessing Benefits Table

	ארץ - The Land		תורה ומצות - Torah and Mitzvos		טובות - Benefits	
Avrohom	חמדה	appealing	ברית	Bris	חסד	Benevolence
Yitzchok	רחבה	spacious	חוקים	Statutes	חן	Favor
Yaakov	טובה	good	תורה	Torah	חיים	Life
# 10	מזון		Food			

Days are comprised of disparate moments where we can distinguish between this or that different moment [where the sustenance requirements will vary]. Thus the blessing includes "at every moment" [to express that Hashem's food blessing is granular to the moment level].

Moments are not associated with fixed time intervals, hours are. Hours take up non-varying slices of time but moments are slices of time of indeterminate [juncture or] interval and no two are [necessarily] alike, such that we can pinpoint when we will have our moment-oriented needs.[240]

"In every hour" refers to [fixed-length] subdivisions of the day. The day is divided into hours and a person's needs differ from hour to hour.

The underlying idea is that people are in a continual state of flux and their sustenance needs change as their circumstances change. Hashem adjusts the flow of sustenance every day to the particular needs of that day and the same is true with respect to [the particular needs of] each indeterminate moment of the day and of each fixed-length hour of the day. This is clear.

Why is moment mentioned [in the blessing] before hour? [Since the word "moment" is not associated with fixed time intervals] it can refer to intervals as long as a full day or a half or quarter of a day.[241] Thus it follows the mention in the blessing of "day" [and precedes the mention of "hour".[242]

ועל הכל... אנחנו מודים לך... [The second blessing continues with] "For everything... we thank You...". [What is the significance of the word "everything" in this context? The reference is to the ten benefits previously enumerated and the point being made is that] we are giving thanks to Hashem for a full set of ten benefits. For, just as the formal thanking blessing [HaGomel] takes place in an assemblage of ten,[243] so also should the size of the grouping [of benefits] for which we give thanks be ten. [When both conditions are present] the thanks is complete. For this reason the Todah offering[244] includes

—————————————— פירוש בנתיבות לב ——————————————

[240] In other words, while the hour defines **the** need, the moment is defined **by the** need. Consider, for example, the need to eat lunch. If lunchtime is noon, then when it is noon, we know that it is time for lunch. The hour defines the need. But consider the need to scratch an itch. That need is spontaneous; we can speak of the moment we scratch only after the itch. The moment is defined by the need, not vice-versa.

[241] Although the Maharal initially speaks of the word עת, eis, which we translate "moment", as a single point on the timeline, from the subsequent context it is apparent that this is the lower limit of a moment's duration but a "moment" can actually also extend over an indeterminate amount of time.

[242] The sequence is from larger to smaller intervals and although moment intervals can also be very small, nonetheless, since they can also be quite large they follow immediately after the longest of the intervals, the day, and precede the hour interval which is generally the smallest of the three.

[243] The reference is to the Birchas HaGomel, recited when spared from one of four specific categories of misfortune. A quorum of ten men is required when reciting this blessing per the Gemara in Brachos 54b, which derives this requirement from the verse, "And they shall exalt Him in an assembly of people" (Tehillim 107:32). The Gemara in Megillah 23b demonstrates that than a קהל, khal, "assembly" is a group of ten; the Shechina is present when a group of ten are engaged in prayer or Torah study. The straightforward reason a quorum of ten is required for HaGomel is, as the verse alludes, is to cause a greater sanctification of Hashem's name by publicizing the personal salvation of the one reciting the HaGomel blessing in front of a significant group of people.

Although there is no quorum requirement for the second after-meals blessing, it, like HaGomel, is a blessing of thanks and the Maharal is pointing out the affinity between issues having to do with thanks and the number ten.

[244] The Todah thanksgiving offering was required when the Temple was standing, in the same set of four circumstances that today engenders the HaGomel blessing.

four kinds [of bread], ten loaves of each kind. Those versed [in hidden wisdom] will understand this allusion.

ועל הכל... אנחנו מודים לך
ומברכים אותך

"For everything… we thank You and bless You". [What is the difference between thanking Hashem and blessing Him?] We have already explained[245] that הודאה-*ho'daah* level thanks is applicable to benefits that, but for Hashem supplying them to us, we would not be able to exist. This level of thanks pertains to being saved from imminent danger. Blessing [on the other hand] is applicable [also] to good. Hashem provides us sustenance; if He failed to do so we could not survive. For this we owe Hashem הודאה -*ho'daah* level thanks. But Hashem does not stop there [as it were]; in addition He benefits us until we are sated with goodness. For this, blessing is appropriate.[246]

Section 23 – The Gemara on the Second and Third Blessing – Part 1
ובגמרא פרק שלשה שאכלו תניא ר' אליעזר אומר...

From chapter *Shlosha SheAcholu*:[247]

────────────────── פירוש בנתיבות לב ──────────────────

The number ten carries several related implications as explained in various contexts by the Maharal. It conveys a promotion in status, as from single units to units of ten, as detailed in footnote 237. At the beginning of *Nesiv HaTorah* chapter 1 the Maharal writes that ten signifies "coherent multiplicity" – quantity that is organized and united. In *Gur Aryeh, Beraishis* 17:5 (as added in the Hartman edition from a manuscript) the Maharal writes that ten straddles the fence between the single unit numbers and the aggregate numbers and is able to fill both roles with equal facility. Possibly this is why ten signifies, as the Maharal says in *Nesiv HaTorah*, "coherent multiplicity" – since it partakes of the nature of both single units and aggregate numbers, it can unify them.

Now, the Maharal writes in his *Drasho L'Shabbos HaGadol* that the letter *yud* (numerical value ten) represents Yisroel – the nation of many members, united in their fealty to Hashem. The *yud's* shape is theoretically a single point and a single point is indivisible, just as Yisroel is indivisible with respect to its devotion to Hashem. This is presumably the underlying reason why a quorum is ten and the *Shechina* rests of a group of ten – it is the smallest congregation of Jews that actually possesses this ten-related quality of unity. A Jew reciting the *HaGomel* blessing in front of a quorum of ten is effectively reciting it to a microcosm of all of Yisroel.

The ten loaves of different varieties that accompany the *Todah* offering presumably symbolize the full-faceted completeness of Hashem's blessing in different areas.

As applied to the second after-meals blessing, the tenth benefit enumerated is that of food, which, as explained in footnote 237, is a different category of benefit due to its critical importance. But it is also the tenth in a set of ten, signifying that all ten blessings together comprise the complete set of blessings for which thanks are appropriate in the after-meals blessing context.

[245] Section 18.

[246] As the Maharal explains in Chapter 8 (and discussed in this chapter as well) the word *bracha*, which is commonly translated as "blessing", actually means "wellspring" and denotes a gushing flow of abundance. Our "blessing" to Hashem is an acknowledgement that he is the source of that abundant flow. In fact "blessing" is appropriate not only to "extras" but also to "basics", such as food, which are included in that flow, and the Maharal is not attempting to imply otherwise here. The Maharal speaks of the universality of blessing in section 8 – indeed, the first blessing in the after-meals blessings is for an essential: food.

Ho'daah on the other hand, as the Maharal explains in section 18, is targeted specifically at essentials, since it is an admission of indebtedness and dependence as well as thanks. When a person makes an admission he is effectively stating that he is not an independent and standalone being but has to come onto others for some aspect of his existence. If *ho'daah* is an expression of dependence, there is nothing that more deeply calls for *ho'daah* than the life-providing forms of assistance that Hashem provides us. This is why expressing gratitude with *ho'daah* is a uniquely suitable response to the essentials of life. See footnote 209 for additional detail on this concept.

[247] *Brachos* 48b. The Maharal will analyze this *Gemara* in this and the following three sections, revisiting some of the concepts regarding the second and third blessings that are also covered in their respective

Halacha הלכה

One who omits any of the phrases mentioned in this paragraph must repeat the after-meals blessings.

Shulchan Aruch Orach Chaim 187:3

"We learned in a *Braiso*: Rabbi Eliezer said, whoever omits, "an appealing, good and spacious land" from the [second] land-blessing[248] and [mention of] the kingdom of Dovid from the [third] "Builder of Yerushalayim"[249] blessing has not satisfied his obligation. Nachum the Elder said, one must mention *Bris* [in the land blessing].[250] Rabbi Yosi said, one must mention Torah [in the land blessing].[251] Plimo said, one must mention *Bris* before Torah[252] because the Torah was given with [only] three covenants[253] and *Bris* was given with thirteen covenants.[254]

"[Rabbi Abba said] one must express thanks at the beginning and end [of the second blessing][255] and at the very least must express thanks at least once. One who fails to express thanks even once is repulsive.[256]

"One who ends the land blessing with, "He who bequeaths lands" [instead of with "for the land and for sustenance"][257] and [ends the "Builder of Yerushalayim" blessing with] "Savior of Yisroel" [instead of with[258] "He who builds Yerushalayim with mercy"] is a boor.[259]

"Whoever omits *Bris* and Torah from the land blessing and [mention of] the kingdom of Dovid from the "Builder of Yerushalayim" blessing has not satisfied his obligation.

"This *Braiso* supports the position of Rabbi Ilai, for Rabbi Ilai said in the name of Rabbi Yaakov bar Abba, who quoted our Rabbi as saying

───────────────── פירוש בנתיבות לב ─────────────────

sections.

[248] These positive adjectives appear in various verses as praises of the land of Israel so it is appropriate to mention these attributes when speaking of the land.

[249] King Dovid and his dynasty were responsible for the sanctification of Yerushalayim, and the Messianic restoration of Yerushalayim is only achievable in conjunction with the restoration of the Dovidic dynasty.

[250] The reference is to *bris milah*, circumcision. Avrohom was promised the land of Israel in the context of his being given the commandment of circumcision (*Beraishis* 17:8).

[251] Torah observance is a condition to Yisroel's inheritance of the land of Israel per *Devarim* 8:1).

[252] As we say in our rendition of this blessing, "…for Your covenant which You sealed in our flesh; for Your Torah which You taught us…".

[253] The Torah was given and/or reviewed with Yisroel at three junctures, each time with a covenant between Hashem and Yisroel: at Sinai, shortly after their exodus from Egypt, at the plains of Moav and at Mount Gerizim.

[254] The word "*bris*" is mentioned thirteen times in the Torah chapter that describes the presentation of this commandment (*Beraishis* 17). The *Tosfos Yom Tov* on *Nedarim* 3:11 comments that these thirteen mentions of the one *Bris* covenant outweigh the three actual covenants of the Torah in terms of precedence in the after-meals blessings. The Maharal in Section 24, in explaining this passage of the *Gemara*, discusses the thirteen *Bris Milah* covenants as on a level with actual covenants.

[255] "We thank You, Hashem" at the beginning and "For all Hashem… we thank You" at the end (at the beginning of the second and last paragraph of this blessing, which is considered the end).

[256] We translate the *Gemara* according to the common understanding of its meaning, however the Maharal in Section 24 apparently understands this *Gemara* differently.

[257] All nations were bequeathed their lands by Hashem; this blessing is supposed to be describing the unique relationship between Yisroel and Hashem.

[258] Translated according to the understanding of most commentators on the *Gemara*. As will be evident in section 26, however, the Maharal understands that the Gemara is objecting to one who says, "He who bequeaths lands" **in addition to** "for the land and for sustenance".

[259] He ignores the fact that the salvation of Yisroel will take place through the rebuilding of Yerushalayim. However the *Gemara* subsequently cites an opinion that "Savior of Yisroel" is an acceptable variant.

that whoever omits *Bris* and Torah from the land blessing and [mention of] the kingdom of Dovid from the "Builder of Yerushalayim" blessing has not satisfied his obligation.

We have already explained[260] the meaning of "an appealing, good and spacious land" and detailed how these are the primary attributes of the land [of Israel] and constitute its primary praises.

What, however, is the relationship between *Bris* and Torah to the land [of Israel], such that they are, as the *Gemara* says, vital to the second blessing,? The answer centers around the fact that the land is sanctified, and apart from other lands. For this reason the nation that possesses the land similarly has to be apart from other nations. This is why Hashem commanded us to be circumcised. The land demands that its inhabitants be apart from other nations just as it is apart from other lands, and *Milah*, and the sanctity that it brings, are the only characteristics that definitively set Yisroel apart from the other nations. *Milah* is the excision of the foreskin, which represents lowliness, degradation, corporeality, physicality.[261] Its removal thus brings sanctity.[v] This is why we say [in the *Milah* blessing] "...Who sanctified the beloved one from the womb".[262]

We are further required to mention the Torah in the land blessing. The Torah catapults us to a higher level of sanctity [than does *Milah*]. *Milah's* level of sanctity results from a removal of that which is lowly, degraded and corporeal, as represent by the foreskin but the Torah creates a level of sanctity that is entirely divorced from the physical.[263] Both levels of sanctity – *Milah's* removal of the lowly and the Torah's

——————————— פירוש בנתיבות לב ———————————

[260] In sections 18 and 19.

[261] All of which are the antithesis of sanctity.

Although our entire bodies are physical the foreskin represents the depths of physicality, to the extent that it prevents our having a close relationship to Hashem. In *Tiferes Yisroel* chapter 19 the Maharal writes that the difference between our physical nature and Hashem's purely spiritual nature made a relationship between man and Hashem impossible until the advent of Avrohom, who "discovered" Hashem and made a degree of closeness with Him possible. The totally physical nature of the foreskin precluded implementing that closeness so Hashem commanded Avrohom to remove his foreskin, thus doing away with the final impediment to achieving closeness with Hashem. Avrohom's progeny, Yisroel, were commanded to maintain this practice so that they, too, could achieve closeness with Hashem. As the *Zohar* says (3:14a, 93b and 73b), "In what way does Yisroel form a bond with Hashem? Through the holy seal that is impressed on their flesh [- their *Bris Milah*]".

Milah, which enables a closeness with Hashem, thus became the *Bris*, the covenant, that formalizes and finalizes our close relationship with Hashem. The Maharal elaborates on this concept further in *Chidushei Aggados* on *Nedarim* 31b, where he writes that *Milah* represents man's "finishing touch"; an act by man, on his person, that completes Hashem's creation of him. This "partnership" in man's person is the basis for the covenant.

Now, the source for the Maharal's statement that the land mandates *Milah* is a *Medrash* in *Beraishis Rabbah* 46:9 which says, "If Avrohom's children uphold *Bris Milah*, they will enter the land and if not they will not enter the land". Israel is the land where the *Shechina* resides, the land that is under Hashem's direct supervision, as it were, as the Maharal explains in *Gur Aryeh* on *Beraishis* 17:8. Since Hashem "lives" in Israel and since He cannot interact with people who retain their foreskins, it follows that the nation that is destined to inherit the land and "coexist" there with Hashem must practice *Milah*. For more on *Milah* see end note v.

[262] The text of the *Milah* blessing appears in *Shabbos* 137b. *Rashi* there explains these words to mean that from the time Avrohom was originally commanded to perform *Milah* all Jewish males are sanctified in potential form even while still in the womb, in anticipation of their forthcoming *Milah*.

[263] In *Gur Aryeh* on *Devarim* 11:18 the Maharal quotes and endorses the view of the *Ramban* (*Beraishis* 26:5) that the commandments of the Torah were "designed" to be performed exclusively in Israel. Of course we know that most of the commandments, except for the ones that are specifically tied to the land, do apply everywhere. The reason, the *Ramban* explains, is that Divine Wisdom understood that the Jews

rarefied level of physicality negation – are apropos to the land blessing since it was the land and its sanctity-separation from other lands that enabled Yisroel to achieve the states of holiness that separate Yisroel from the other nations. *Milah* creates a separation between Yisroel and the other nations by freeing us from the lowliness of the foreskin, which represents a degrading physical state. The Torah breaks the bond with physicality entirely since it is wisdom that is pure intellect-based,[264] unlike other forms of wisdom.

One might think that the land that Hashem gave Yisroel exists, after all, in the physical realm and therefore does not have a G-dly nature. This is why the *Gemara* insists that we mention *Bris* and Torah in the land blessing. [It does so to reinforce the fact that] it was because of the [spiritual nature of the] land that we merited *Bris* and Torah and were thereby transformed into a totally differentiated and G-dly people. *Milah* transformed us by separating us from the physical lowliness of the foreskin; Torah transformed our very nature into one of separation from the physical.

Again, these achievements came about solely through the land [of Israel] which stands apart, in its holiness, from all other lands. [Our connection to] the land elevated us through *Milah* and elevated us even more through the Torah. The Torah elevation has a particular connection to the merit of the land because Israel is the natural home of the Torah, as the *Gemara* says, "the atmosphere of Israel brings wisdom".[265] It is therefore clear why mentioning *Bris* and Torah in the land blessing is obligatory. Understand these concepts well.

Section 24 – *The Gemara on the Second and Third Blessing – Part 2*

צריך להקדים ברית לתורה שזה נתן...

" One must mention *Bris [Milah]* before Torah because the Torah was given with [only] three covenants and *Bris [Milah]* was given with thirteen covenants". This

---

פירוש בנתיבות לב

would be spending many years in exile from their land before ultimately returning to it, and if the commandments would not be in effect during the exile they would be forgotten and would have to be re-learned from scratch – a difficult process fraught with the risk of key details being forgotten. Thus the commandments remain in force even outside the land of Israel – despite the fact that they are out of their native element.

The Torah's commandments are native to the land and, as the Torah makes clear in several contexts, the land demands their observance – it cannot tolerate the presence of those who flout the Torah's laws. In *Devarim* 11:21, we are adjured to keep the Torah's commandments "…in order that your days may increase and the days of your children, on the land which Hashem swore to your forefathers to give them". In *Vayikra* 18:28 we are admonished to adhere to the Torah's commandments in order that, "…the land not vomit you out for having defiled it, as it vomited out the nation that preceded you". In *Devarim* 4:26 we are warned of the consequences of violating the Torah: "…you will speedily and utterly perish from the land to which you cross the Jordan".

We see that just as the commandments belong to the land, so does the land protect the commandments. We appreciate, therefore, why it is that the *Gemara* says in *Baba Basra* 158b that, "the atmosphere of Israel brings wisdom". Wisdom is required to understand the Torah and if we are unable to understand the Torah we are unable to properly observe it – and that leads to ejection from the land. Thus, to enable Yisroel, the rightful owners of the land, to remain in it, the land itself supports our efforts by facilitating our knowledge of, and therefore our observance of, the Torah.

For more on the bond between the nation Yisroel and the land of Israel see *Kuzari, Maamar* 2:22-24.

[264] The word שכלי, *sichli*, which literally means intellect-based, is used by the Maharal to refer to wisdom that is completely detached from any physical component whatever.

[265] *Baba Basra* 158b.

requires explanation; it seems odd that *Bris [Milah]* was given with thirteen covenants while the Torah was given with only three.[266] The explanation is that a *Bris*-covenant creates a bond between two things. So [while *Bris [Milah]* and Torah are both covenants between Yisroel and Hashem] *Bris [Milah]* is on a person's body; it is part of his being and thus it forms a more potent bond with Hashem than does the Torah. Thus thirteen covenants sealed the *Milah* bond, which is an absolute bond since it is impressed upon our flesh. *Bris [Milah]* then enabled Yisroel to become worthy also of the covenant of the Torah, elevating them to a transcendent spiritual plane.[267]

[Even though the Torah covenant is more exalted] *Bris [Milah]* precedes it since it is an absolute bond and is impressed on our bodies. This is why *Bris [Milah]* was given with thirteen covenants and why it comes first. As to why there were specifically three covenants associated with the Torah and thirteen with *Milah*, that is out of scope of our present discussion.[268]

─────────── פירוש בנתיבות לב ───────────

[266] The Maharal pointed out in the previous section that the Torah elevates a person to a higher degree of spirituality than does *Bris Milah*, so one might expect Torah to surpass *Bris Milah* in number of covenants as well.

[267] In the previous section the Maharal explained that the sanctity of the land brought about Yisroel's entitlement to both *Bris Milah* and Torah. The Maharal is now adding a crucial detail: *Bris Milah*, too, is a prerequisite for the Torah. In order for Yisroel to merit the Torah it needs the holy environment of the land of Israel as well as the *Bris Milah* impressed on their bodies. The Torah, after all, is Hashem's most precious possession (see *Shir HaShirim Rabbah* and other *Medrashim*). How can He give it to an uncircumcised people who are distant from Him, as explained in detail in footnote 261.

[268] Regarding the association of the number three with the Torah, we begin with a *Gemara* in *Shabbos* 88a: "Blessed be Hashem who gave a three-fold Torah (*Torah, Neviim, Kesuvim*) to a three-fold people (*Kohanim, Leviim, Yisraelim*) through a third-born (Moshe, who followed Aharon and Miriam) on the third day of the third month (*Sivan*)". The Maharal in *Gur Aryeh* on *Bamidbar* 21:34 explains that the number three signifies pure intellect, completely separated from the physical. The number two implies extension in two direction, signifying the space-occupying physical. Three implies the central point from which the extensions emanate. As a point, it occupies no space; thus is signifies pure intellect and is therefore associated with the Torah.

As a central point it also signifies ישרות, *yashrus* absolute fairness, a hallmark of the Torah (and of Moshe, Hashem's messenger to convey the Torah to Yisroel). In fact the Maharal in *Derech Chaim* 1:2 adds that the Torah was given in the merit of Yaakov, the third of the forefathers, who is referred to as *Yeshurun* (*Yeshayahu* 44:2), to the nation of Yisroel, the third nation to emerge from Avrohom (after Yishmael and Esav), who is also referred to as *Yeshurun* (*Devarim* 33:5). This explains why there were specifically three covenants associated with the Torah.

The author of this commentary is unable to find an explicit source in the extant works of the Maharal for an association between *Bris Milah* and the number thirteen. Perhaps, however, the association can be understood on the basis of a concept discussed by the Maharal at the end of *Derech Chaim* 3:6. The Maharal is explaining a *Gemara* in *Brachos* 6a which states that the *Shechina* is present in a group of ten Jews and also in a group of three Jews. The *Gemara* asks, if the *Shechina* will descend for a group of three why mention that it is present in a group of ten – it will have already joined when that group comprised only three members! The *Gemara* answers that for a group of ten Jews the *Shechina* will precede their arrival whereas for a group of three, the group must assemble first; the *Shechina* will join them only after they assemble.

The Maharal explains that there is a relationship of "mutual dependency", as it were, between Hashem and Yisroel. Hashem is the עלה, *ahlo*, Cause – the creator of all that exists – but that appellation applies only if there are actually created beings. In that sense Hashem's identity as Cause depends on Yisroel, his primary creation. When there are created beings a desire is engendered in Hashem, as it were, to associate with the creations that enabled His Cause title. On the other hand, we, as Hashem's created beings, עלל, *ahlul*, are of course dependent on Hashem for our very existence and we crave a relationship with our Cause.

A group of ten represents wholeness and completion and thus is substantive enough to constitute an *ahlul* relative to Hashem. Hashem precedes a group of ten since in the relationship of Cause to Created the Cause always comes first. A group of ten, then, enables an expression of Hashem's desire to associate with his creations.

The *Gemara* continues,[269] "If one chooses to omit [either Torah or *Milah* from the blessing] he should be sure to retain at least one", because even one of them indicates the specialness of the land of Israel – and [demonstrates that] Yisroel merits a distinctive status relative to all other nations in that they are the possessors of the land that is distinctive from all other lands.

Section 25 – The Gemara on the Second and Third Blessing – Part 3

וצריך שיאמר בברכת הארץ נודה לך תחלה וסוף...

" One must express thanks at the beginning and end of the second blessing". At the beginning he says, "We thank You, Hashem…" and afterwards he says, "For all, Hashem, our G-d, we thank You…"; this is considered "at the end".[270]

A possible reason for the double thanks is that the first thanks corresponds to the first time Yisroel was given the land[271] and the second thanks corresponds to the second time [they were given the land].[272] [Two thanks are necessary because] the first sanctification of the land, which took place when they first entered it, was effective only as long as they dwelled in the land and not for the future [after they were exiled from it], whereas the second sanctification of the land, [which took place when they re-entered it after the Babylonian exile] was effective not only as long as they dwelled in the land but also perpetually.[273] We therefore express our thanks twice.[274]

The primary reason thanks are needed at the beginning and end, however, is because

———————————————————————— פירוש בנתיבות לב ————————————————————————

A group of three, however, represents the other side of the coin – the craving of the Created to have a relationship with their Cause. Even though three is insubstantive relative to a group of ten it nonetheless merits a relationship on the basis of the Created yearning for its Cause. Since they are the initiators of this "call" to the *Shechina*, they are first and the *Shechina* joins them only after they convene.

The number ten is significant with respect to Hashem's desire to have a relationship with us. The number three is significant relative to our desire to have a relationship with Hashem. Now, remember that *Bris Milah* is the first covenant that allowed for a relationship between Hashem and man as discussed in footnote 261. A covenant is a mutual relationship with benefits for both parties. *Bris Milah* cleared the way for Hashem to associate with His creations, as represented by the number ten, and for Yisroel, His creations, to have a relationship with Him, as represented by the number three. Thus it is very fitting for *Bris Milah* to be associated with thirteen, the sum of those two numbers and we understand why there were specifically thirteen covenants associated with *Milah*. (See also end note i where we cite the Maharal which explains that there are thirteen attributes that "describe" Hashem, as it were, because thirteen is the epitome of perfection. Since Milah "perfects" man it is apropos that thirteen covenants be associated with it.)

[269] This is the *Gemara* referenced in footnote 256. We translate it differently here because the Maharal apparently understands it differently from the common understanding.

[270] The second blessing appears in most editions of the after-meals blessings as two paragraphs that begin, נודה לך, *nodeh l'cha*, "we thank You", and ועל הכל... אנחנו מודים לך, *v'al ha'kol... anachnum modem lach*, "for all, Hashem… we thank You". Thus the double expression of thanks is not, strictly speaking, at the beginning and end of the second blessing but rather at the beginning and middle of the second blessing. However, the Maharal says, the appearance of the second thanks at the beginning of the last paragraph counts as thanks at the end.

[271] After the exodus from Egypt.

[272] When they returned to the land after the destruction of the first Temple, at the conclusion of the seventy year Babylonian exile.

[273] Whether or not the sanctification of the land that took place at the first entry was enduring, or expired when the first exile took place, is the subject of a disagreement in the *Gemara, Zevachim* 107b. The *Rambam* rules like the opinion which holds that it expired. See *Mishna Torah, Terumos* 1:5 and *Bais HaBechira* 6:16. This view is accepted by the Maharal.

[274] The first thanks is for the first entry but the sanctification of the first entry expired, rendering that thanks moot as far as the present is concerned. The second thanks is for the second entry which, along with our thanks for it, endures.

of the special association between thanks and the land blessing, as we discussed earlier.[275] Now, there is a principle that any blessing that does not directly follow another blessing requires the formula, "Blessed are You, Hashem…" at its beginning and at its end.[276] Since the land blessing is thanks-focused it has [instead] an expression of thanks at the beginning and end. [Bracketing the blessing with thanks beginning and end] indicates a complete thanks, just as the "blessed are You…" formula at the beginning and end of a [typical] blessing indicates complete blessing.[277]

There is, however, another reason,[278] a reason laden with deep meaning, to explain why thanks is associated with the land blessing. To give thanks [to Hashem] in the הודאה, ho'daah sense of the word is to put oneself completely in the hands of Hashem in acknowledgment of the favor Hashem bestowed upon him. This is what ho'daah means, as we explain elsewhere;[279] that ho'daah is giving oneself over to Hashem. We might think, since Hashem did after all gift us with the land, that "the heavens belong to Hashem but the land was given to [flesh and blood] people"[280] and that, G-d forbid, mankind, [being denizens of the land that Hashem gave away to them,] is outside of Hashem's sphere of influence. This is why, [specifically in the land blessing,] we bracket the blessing with thanks beginning and end. In so doing we put ourselves and our souls under the control of Hashem, who favored us [by giving us

———————————————— פירוש בנתיבות לב ————————————————

[275] At the beginning of Section 18, where the Maharal wrote, "However the land is a perpetual gift and it is therefore a continual life-giving source for its owners. Expressing gratitude with "thank you" is a uniquely suitable response to life-providing forms of assistance so we employ it as a response to Hashem's bequeathing us the land and we bracket this blessing with expressions of thanks beginning and end". See footnote 209 for additional detail on the relationship between הודאה, ho'daah and the land.

The Maharal will shortly present another reason for the special association with thanks to the land blessing.

[276] When a blessing directly follows another blessing the "Blessed are You Hashem" at the beginning is generally omitted from the text of the blessing. See Gemara, Pesachim 104b and Rambam, Mishna Torah, Hilchos Brachos 11:1.

[277] The Maharal is saying that הודאה, ho'daah, thanks (or "admission", as we explained in footnote 209), in the land blessing, plays the same role that ברוך, baruch, blessed, plays in other blessings. In other blessings the primary theme is blessing. In the land blessing, though it is technically still classified as a blessing, the primary theme is thanks. The Maharal interprets the "formula" in the rule of "any blessing… requires the formula… at its beginning and at its end" as being dependent on the primary theme of the blessing. For a standard blessing the formula is "Blessed are You Hashem.." but for the land blessing, whose theme is thanks, the formula is "thanks" at the beginning and end.

[278] In addition to the reason cited in footnote 275.

[279] See Nesiv HaTeshuva 5 and elsewhere. In fact the concept that ho'daah is giving oneself over to Hashem, and the idea of giving oneself over to Hashem in general, מוסר עצמו אל השם יתברך, recurs frequently in the works of the Maharal; it is a nuanced concept that has numerous facets. As noted earlier (see footnote 209) the word ho'daah implies not only thanks but also "admission", as in owning up to an action and at the same time acknowledging a debt as a result of that action. To acknowledge a debt is one sense of giving oneself over. One who sins and owns up to his sin (ho'daah) is giving himself over to Hashem, as the Maharal points out in Nesiv HaTeshuva.

In Nesiv Ahavas Hashem, Chapter 1 the Maharal writes that ho'daah is an expression of inadequacy in the face of a flow of beneficence from Hashem. In so doing a person is giving himself over to Hashem in that he is acknowledging that without that flow he would have and would be nothing. In Gevuros Hashem, Chapter 64 the Maharal writes that ho'daah is "payment of self"; it is acknowledgment of a debt so great that the only possible payment is one's person. Since all of mankind benefits from Hashem in this manner ho'daah implies that there is in fact no one that is not under Hashem's dominion. In Chidushei Aggados to Baba Kama 16a the Maharal writes that the reason we bow by the Modim blessing in Shmoneh Esrai is to express that we are giving ourselves over to Hashem, that the Created is returning to its Creator. For additional detail on this concept so Rabbi Yehoshua Dovid Hartman's note 29 in the Nesiv HaTeshuva reference cited at the beginning of this footnote.

[280] This is a quote from Tehillim 115:16 but the Maharal is using it sardonically and counter to its actual meaning in the verse, as an expression of rejection of Hashem's supervision of the world.

the land]. As a result [it is clear that] both man himself as well as his land and everything else are Hashem's and that nothing is outside His domain.

This is the deeper reason why thanks are appropriate in the land blessing. And in order for our thanks to be complete we express it twice, once at the beginning and once at the end of the blessing [as explained earlier]. Our blessing is then complete and perfect.

Therefore in the land blessing we must [still] use the thanks-formula both at the beginning and end of the blessing, even though it is the second of two consecutive blessings, since the prior blessing did not end with the thanks-formula.[281]

Section 26 – The Gemara on the Second and Third Blessing – Part 4

החותם מנחיל ארצות הרי זה מגונה...

❝ One who ends the land blessing with, "He who bequeaths lands" [instead of with "for the land and for sustenance"]... is repulsive".[282] This is because the land blessing is specifically for the land of Israel and to change the text to "He who bequeaths lands" is to generalize it to other lands as well. In fact, though, Israel is in a different category from other lands.[283] Therefore [one who lumps other lands together with Israel] is a boor.[284]

Similarly, one who ends [the "Builder of Yerushalayim" blessing] with "Savior of Yisroel" [in addition to[285] "He who builds Yerushalayim with mercy"] is a boor, because he concludes the blessing with two [praises of Hashem] and this is inappropriate.[286]

"Whoever omits Bris and Torah from the land blessing and [mention of] the kingdom

---

פירוש בנתיבות לב

[281] The Maharal is addressing a "technicality": We said earlier that "any blessing that does not directly follow another blessing requires the formula … at its beginning and end". But it is also true that a blessing that does directly follow another blessing does not require the formula at its beginning. The land blessing, though, does follow another blessing, since it is the second of the after-meal blessings, so why does it require the formula – in this case containing a reference to thanks – at its beginning? The answer is that this exemption from the beginning formula applies only if the formulas are the same – either blessing or thanks – in both of the two consecutive blessings. In this case they are not the same since the formula in the first, food blessing is blessing-based while the formula in the second, land blessing is thanks-based.

[282] The Gemara's actual wording, and as the Maharal quoted it earlier, and uses it later in this section, ends in "… is a boor" so this is an apparent typographical error.

[283] See sections 18, 19 and 23.

[284] The word בור in Hebrew, pronounced similarly to the English pronunciation of boor, means "uncultivated". Its primary usage is with regard to a plot of land but it has a similar meaning when applied to a person. It conveys that he is unlearned and unaware of distinctions and differentiations that better educated people take for granted – such as the distinctions between Israel and other lands.

[285] The Maharal is understanding this Gemara passage differently from most commentators; see footnote 258.

[286] The source for this is a Gemara in Brachos 49a which states, "Rebbi ruled that it is inappropriate to conclude a blessing with two". The reason as explained by Rashi is the principle of "one may not perform commandments in 'bundles'", אין עושים מצוות חבילות חבילות, which is laid down in Sotah 8a. The rationale for this ruling is that "bundling" commandments makes them appear burdensome; like something one wants to get out of the way as expeditiously as possible. Moreover, as Tosfos explains in Moed Katan 8b, "bundling" does not allow one to properly focus on and savor the full implications of each commandment.

of Dovid from the "Builder of Yerushalayim" blessing has not satisfied his obligation." We already explained[287] the connection between *Bris* and Torah to the land blessing] and detailed how they pertain to praise of the land.

...על הארץ ועל המזון

The blessing concludes with, "[Blessed are you Hashem,] for the land and for the nourishment". This is not considered "concluding the blessing with two praises"[288] because we are really saying, as the *Gemara* explains,[289] "for the land, which produces nourishment".[290]

This that [the *Gemara* we are discussing mentions that] me must mention the kingdom of Dovid in the "Builder of Yerushalayim" blessing will be explained in the next section.

[Returning to the "Blessed are you Hashem, for the land and for the nourishment" conclusion of the blessing,] one may ask, why do we not conclude with a simple mention of the land [without referring to its nourishment aspect]?[291] The answer is that the conclusion should always be more encompassing [than the body of the blessing which preceded it], as we explained in our discussion of the conclusion of the food blessing.[292] By referring, [as explained above,] to "the land, which produces nourishment" we allude to the fact that the nourishment is actually being produced by Hashem, and this is one of the distinctions of the land – that its nourishment is special because Hashem directly supervises its production, as it were, and does not delegate the task to any angel or other intermediary. [By the addition of "for the nourishment" to the blessing conclusion] we are declaring, therefore, Hashem's [direct] rulership over the land, as the verse indicates,[293] "for the entire world is Mine".[294]

Section 27 – The Third Blessing

ברכה ג' רחם ה' וכו', כבר אמרנו...

רחם (נא) השם...

The third blessing is, "Have mercy [please] Hashem…". We already explained[295] why this blessing is appropriate for the after-meals blessings; it is [an expression of] the ultimate level of completion. The building of Yerushalayim and the Temple represent wholeness and completion to the highest possible degree. That is why this blessing is the last of the biblically mandated blessings.[296]

It also explains why this blessing includes the subsection beginning with, "Our father,

──────────────── פירוש בנתיבות לב ────────────────

[287] Sections 23 and 24.

[288] Which we declared to be inappropriate two paragraphs prior to this one.

[289] *Brachos* 49a.

[290] Thus the praise is single, and for the land exclusively, and mention of the nourishment qualifies the praise of the land but is not a praise in and of itself.

[291] Granted that we are no longer bothered by the question of dual praise, as the Maharal previously explained, but what is to be gained by adding the nourishment qualifier?

[292] Section 17.

[293] *Shmos* 19:5.

[294] The context is a guarantee that Hashem is offering Moshe prior to the giving of the Torah that if Yisroel observes the Torah they will remain Hashem's chosen nation. The entire world is Hashem's but, as *Rashi* says on that verse, "the other nations [and their lands] mean nothing to Me". Hashem's entire focus is on Yisroel and the land of Israel.

[295] See section 11.

[296] Last equates with ultimate.

(ונא) אל תצריכנו ... לא לידי מתנת
בשר ודם ולא לידי הלואתם

our King"[297] even though the things [we beseech Hashem for] in it have nothing to do with a blessing dealing with the building of Yerushalayim. They are included because the blessing dealing with the building of Yerushalayim represents the ultimate degree of wholeness and completion with no imperfection whatever, as we said, and therefore we graft these other requests onto the blessing so that [by association] they too may be free of imperfection, [as is illustrated by the request,] "[please][298] make us not needful... of the gifts of human hands nor of their loans". This is tantamount to a request that we not lack anything whatever.

רענו זוננו פרנסנו וכלכלנו והרויחנו
והרוח לנו... ו(נא) על תצריכנו...

There are, [significantly,] seven specific requests including this one [in this subsection of the blessing]. They are: "tend us" (1), "nourish us" (2), "sustain us" (3), "support us" (4), "relieve us... and grant us speedy relief from our troubles" (5), "...make us not needful..." (6) and "rebuild Yerushalayim..." (7). The number seven signifies completion and wholeness as we have explained elsewhere.[299] That is why the word for seven is שבעה, *shiv'ah*, from the same root as שביעה, *svia*, satisfaction.

The reason this subsection begins with "Our father, our King" [is that these are our grounds for beseeching on behalf of our needs]. Since You are our Father, who brought us into the world, as a [flesh-and-blood] father brings a child into the world, and since, after you brought us into the world, You are our King, and the job of a King is to sustain his subjects,[300] for these two reasons it is inappropriate for us to be left lacking in any respect. For if we are left lacking people will murmur that Your creations are deprived, since you are our Father.[301] Since you are also our King, from this standpoint as well, if we are lacking people will murmur that a King's role is to support His subjects [and You are not doing so]. Therefore, [the subsection continues,] "tend us, nourish us", etc.[302]

פירוש בנתיבות לב

---

[297] Our version of the blessing begins, "Our G-d, our Father".

[298] Not in the Maharal's version of the prayer.

[299] In *Derech Chaim* 6:10 the Maharal explains that seven represents seven layers of creation including the full range of diversity – that is, the multitude of different things – possible in this world. In *Chidushei Aggados* on *Nedarim* 31a the Maharal writes that the physical world is represented by seven – a central point (1) with arcs extending towards each of the four points of the compass (4), up and down (2). See also Chapter 1, Section 2 and end note v of this chapter.

There are seven requests in this subsection to signify the full gamut of full blessing, covering all possible areas of our lives and all our needs.

[300] In *Netzach Yisroel* chapter 54 the Maharal explains that a nation has only one King and that attribute of oneness funnels down to the nation, who are united under the King's banner. Unity implies wholeness and indeed the King's job is to assure that his nation's needs are filled and that no lacks remain unfilled. He is referred to as *Parnas*, "sustainer" because just as sustenance completes by satisfying a lack of food, so does the King complete his nation and make them whole by satisfying all their deficits and assuring that the diverse elements of his kingdom are functioning together harmoniously.

Hashem is our ultimate King so we turn to Him in this blessing, in that role, and implore Him to sustain us.

[301] Based on a *Gemara* in *Kesubos* 49a-b the *Shulchan Aruch* rules in *Even HaEzer* 71:1 that a father is obligated to support his children until they reach adulthood. At that point they can presumably function without their father's assistance and the father's obligation ceases. Hashem's "children", however, are never capable of functioning without His assistance and thus we can and do turn to Him perpetually for sustenance since his "paternal" obligations never cease.

[302] We provide a "shopping list" of areas where we need help from Hashem in the hope that for His sake, as our Father and King, he will not want his children/subjects to appear deprived in any way, to the world-at-large, since this would be a desecration of His name.

It is required to mention the kingdom of Dovid in the "Build Yerushalayim" blessing, as the *Gemara* specified.[303] This is because, as we said, this blessing represents the ultimate completion of Yisroel and the kingdom of Dovid, in particular, completes Yisroel. This is well-known because every kingdom completes its nation and [with respect to Yisroel in particular,] the kingdom of Dovid provides an additional layer of completion in that it enables the *Shechina*, Yisroel's ultimate King, to reside among them. This is why the kingdom of Dovid must be mentioned in the "Build Yerushalayim" blessing.[304]

[305]The Ibn Ezra strenuously objected to the pronunciation רְעֵנוּ זַנֵנוּ, with the [first letter of the second word,] *zayin*, vowelized with a *chataf*, [and pronounced *zaneinu*] and he elaborated on his reasons in his commentary on *Koheles*.[306] His argument is that that vowelization implies that the root of the word is זנה, [and behaves, when conjugated in causative present tense, plural] much like the leading *ayin* in the root ענה, which is vowelized with a *chataf*[307] [when similarly conjugated] in the word עֲנֵנוּ, *aneinu*. He maintains, however, that the root [of זננו] is, rather ז"ון, *manchi ayin*;[308] similar to the [*manchi ayin*] verb שוב, [which derives from the three-letter verb שבה] and which

פירוש בנתיבות לב

303 *Brachos* 48b.

304 The connection between completion and the Kingdom of Dovid can be understood as follows. The Maharal in *Nesiv HaSholom* chapter 3 writes that there is a special association between the Kingdom of Dovid and *sholom*, or peace. Dovid and his descendants were divinely destined for Kingship over Yisroel. When others, such as Shaul, Dovid's predecessor, held the title there was dissension and disunity. But Dovid's grasp on the rulership was fitting, and dissension over his rule was out-of-place.

Now, completeness and peace are two sides of the same coin and in fact they share a common root. Completeness is שלמות, *shlaimus* and peace is שלום, *sholom*. Completeness in Yisroel is achieved when individual Jews, in all their diversity, are functioning together cooperatively – that is, peacefully – with each individual focusing on his role and its relationship to the role of others in building a cohesive whole in the nation Yisroel's service of Hashem; where people do not encroach on others and do not work in a vacuum, without regard for the communal mission.

All monarchs unify, as discussed in footnote 300, but the monarchy of the house of Dovid has a special predisposition for unification.

There are various names used to refer to Hashem and various "bynames" that do not have the same level of sanctity as the names themselves. One of the bynames is *sholom* – and this byname has a level of sanctity beyond that of the others. The *Sifsei Chaim* in his volume on *Shmoneh Esrai*, explains why, in the context of the *sim sholom* blessing. He writes that Hashem craves the ultimate *sholom* of Yisroel functioning as a united and smoothly running organism, focused on its divine mission, as described above. This craving for *sholom* is so deep that Hashem coopted the word as one of his "names", as it were. When we achieve that goal we will have enabled Hashem – the *Shechina* – to dwell with us as in days of yore. And the Kingdom of Dovid, with its unique unifying power, will play a central role in enabling us to achieve that goal.

305 The rest of this section requires some understanding of Hebrew grammar. We will attempt to provide enough background to understand the Maharal's points without going into unnecessary detail. However a basic knowledge of Hebrew grammar is presumed.

306 *Koheles* 5:1.

307 Which has an "ah" sound.

308 In Hebrew, מנחי עי"ן. Hebrew verbs generally have three letters. The first letter is referred to as the פ, *pay* letter, the second as the ע, *ayin* letter and the third as the ל, *lamed* letter, from the word פעל, which means "verb". A verb with only two letters is referred to as *manchi ayin*, "rests on the *ayin*"; i.e. the *ayin* letter is the last one in the verb; there is no *lamed* letter. Some verbs have two variants; a three-letter variant and a *manchi ayin* variant.

The Ibn Ezra maintains that the root of the word זננו in this after-meals blessing is not the three-letter זנה, which would justify the זַנֵנוּ vowelization but rather the two-letter ז"ון root (the internal ו *vov* is a vowelization, not a root letter).

is vowelized as in the [first word of the] verse,[309] שׁוּבֵנוּ אֱלֹקֵי יִשְׁעֵנוּ, *shooveinu elokai yishainu* since [the *manchi ayin* variant] שׁוּב [is pronounced with a *meloopam*[310] instead of a *chataf*]. Therefore [the Ibn Ezra concludes that] the proper vowelization in this blessing is זוּנֵנוּ, *zooneinu*, using what the *Ashkenazim*[311] call the *meloopam* vowel.

Truthfully, after a careful grammatical analysis, I accustomed myself to pronouncing the word *zooneinu* [as the Ibn Ezra recommends].[312] If, however, early editions of this blessing are found to have the [*zaneinu* pronunciation with] a *chataf* under the *zayin* then I recommend against changing away from it,[313] [notwithstanding the Ibn Ezra's objections]. The Ibn Ezra also, after all, also objected strenuously to the custom of reciting *piyutim*[314] during prayer [yet we continue that tradition notwithstanding]. See our earlier discussion on this topic.[315]

Section 28 – The Shabbos Addition

ובשבת פותח בנחמה ומסיים בנחמה...

רחם (נא) השם... ❝ On Shabbos one begins [the third blessing] with words of solace and ends with words of solace and mentions the sanctity of the day in the middle."[316] Why is

───────────── פירוש בנתיבות לב ─────────────

[309] *Tehillim* 85:5.

[310] Which has an "oo" sound.

[311] The Ibn Ezra, who was born in Spain, followed the *Sephardic* customs.

[312] The Maharal is apparently acknowledging a switch from his prior pronunciation to that recommended by the Ibn Ezra.

[313] Evidently the prevailing custom in the Maharal's milieu was *zaneinu* but in acknowledgment of the strength of the Ibn Ezra's argument he was willing to switch to *zooneinu* – but not in the face of concrete evidence that there was an established tradition for *zaneinu*.

The prevailing custom today is to pronounce the word *zooneinu*.

[314] Poetic prayers and praises to Hashem that were generally composed later than the main order of prayers, and added to the services on holidays and special occasions. The Ibn Ezra objected to them on several grounds, and was particularly upset at their occasional departures from the strict rules of grammar under the guise of poetic license.

Notwithstanding the Ibn Ezra's objections, there are venerable traditions going back centuries earlier than the time of the Maharal – and of the Ibn Ezra – that embraced the *piyutim*. Therefore the Maharal, with some qualifications, does not object to their use. Here too, the Maharal declares that although the Ibn Ezra may seem to be technically correct, we do not reverse long-standing traditions on the basis of our own reasoning. The presumption is that the Sages of earlier generations were aware of our logic and discounted it for valid reasons unknown to us and we are safe in following their lead whether we know their reasons or not.

[315] At the end of Chapter 12.

[316] *Brachos* 48b. Some background is necessary in order to understand this section. There are two variants of the third after-meals blessing: the first, which we will call variant A, opens with רחם (נא) השם, *rachem (nah) Hashem*, "Have mercy [please] Hashem", and closes with בונה (ברחמיו) ירושלים, *boneh (b'rachamav) Yerushalayim*, "Who rebuilds Yerushalayim (in his mercy)". (The Maharal omits the words in parenthesis, while the prevailing custom today is to include them, but that is not germane to our current discussion.) The second variant, which we will call variant B, opens with נחמנו השם אלוקינו בירושלים עירך, *nachameinu Hashem Elokeinu b'Yerushalayim irecha*, "console us, Hashem, our G-d, in Yerushalayim Your city", and ends with מנחם עמו ישראל בבנין ירושלים, *menachem amo Yisroel b'binyan Yerushalayim*, "Consoler of His nation Yisroel with the rebuilding of Yerushalayim".

There are differing views regarding when these variants apply. One point of view holds that either variant can be used on weekdays or Shabbos (*Rambam Hilchos Brachos* 2:4, *Shulchan Aruch Orach Chaim* 188:4). Another view holds that variant A is used on weekdays and variant B is used on Shabbos (*Gra, Shulchan Aruch, ibid*). A third view, that of *Rashi* on the *Gemara* in *Brachos*, holds that variant A is used all the time. Each view interprets the *Gemara* in its own way by explaining how the beginning and end of the variant(s) they prescribe for Shabbos fit the definition of נחמה, *nechama*, "solace" – necessary because the *Gemara*

Shabbos mentioned specifically in the "have mercy" blessing? The reason is that Shabbos and Yerushalayim/the Temple have in common that they are holy so it is appropriate to mention Shabbos particularly in this blessing.

When the Gemara says that, "one begins with words of solace and ends with words of solace" it means that [on Shabbos] one opens the [third] blessing with "console us… in Yerushalayim Your city" and closes it with "Consoler of His nation… with the rebuilding of Yerushalayim". [317] It is not appropriate to open with "Have mercy [please] Hashem" [318] because the word רחם, *rachem*, mercy, pertains to someone who is in distress, and it is as if he were saying, "have mercy on me in my misfortune!" – and it is inappropriate to declare oneself in distress on Shabbos, the day of respite [from the travails of the week].

True, we do say [in the main body of the third blessing] "grant us… [speedy] relief from all our troubles" [319] but that phrasing is hypothetical – [we are saying that] in the event we have trouble, grant us relief from it. [320]

[The real problem with declaring distress on Shabbos is not so much in beginning the blessing in that manner but in closing it that way.] To close with a declaration of distress, in light of the fact that the closing is the sum and substance of the blessing, is out of place, and since it is inappropriate to end the blessing that way, we do not begin it that way either. [321]

The נחם, *nachem*, "console us" variant [of the opening,] on the other hand, does not refer to someone [currently] in distress, rather it refers back to an ancient sorrow, the sorrow over [the destruction of] Yerushalayim, and one may have a feeling of sorrow of this nature on Shabbos. [322] Not so "have mercy" which implies that someone is [currently] in distress. This is totally inappropriate for Shabbos.

There are those who justify the *rachem* "have mercy" variant on Shabbos, relying on the point of view that holds that there is no fundamental difference between the meanings of the words רחם, *rachem*, and נחם, *nachem* [323] but this is erroneous because there is a significant difference between *rachem* and *nachem* to those with a proper understanding.

────────────── פירוש בנתיבות לב ──────────────

specifies that the begin/end of the third blessing on Shabbos references "solace". All opinions hold that the insert for Shabbos that is "sandwiched" between the begin/end "solace" is רצה והחליצנו, *retzai v'hachlitzeinu*, and that it is recited immediately before the ending "solace" blessing.

The prevailing custom today is like *Rashi*. The Maharal, however, holds, like the *Gra*, that only variant B may be used on Shabbos, and in this section he justifies that position.

[317] That is, as explained in footnote 316, the Maharal specifies variant B, exclusively, for Shabbos.

[318] That is, as explained in footnote 316, the prevailing custom, following the view of *Rashi*.

[319] Which, seemingly, is also a declaration of distress on Shabbos.

[320] Since the statement is hypothetical there is no declaration of a current trouble and no Shabbos impropriety.

[321] There is a rule, cited in the *Gemara* in *Brachos* 49a in connection with the third after-meals blessing but generally applicable, that the conclusion of a blessing has to be topically in line with the blessing's opening, חתימה מעין הפתיחה, *chasima mai'ain ha'pesicha*. Since we cannot close this blessing on a note of distress we therefore cannot open it that way either so the Maharal rules out "have mercy" as the opening of the blessing.

[322] And thus one may beseech Hashem for consolation for this sorrow on Shabbos.

[323] They hold that both words can mean "console", even though, following the Maharal's position, we have translated רחם, *rachem*, as "have mercy" in this section.

Section 29 – The Omain of the Third Blessing

וחותם בונה ירושלים ואומר המברך אמן על ברכת עצמו...

...בונה (ברחמיו) ירושלים, אמן

He then concludes the blessing with "[Blessed are you Hashem] Who rebuilds Yerushalayim" and he answers *Omain* to his own blessing. Even though it is inappropriate to respond *Omain* to one's own blessing, we discussed earlier[324] that at the end of [a sequence] of one's own blessings one does respond *Omain*.

[Let us delve further into this issue.] The *Gemara* states[325] that a person who responds *Omain* after his own blessings is repulsive. The *Gemara* asks, was it not said that a person who responds *Omain* after his own blessings is praiseworthy? The *Gemara* answers that it is not a contradiction; the latter statement [which describes the action as praiseworthy] is referring to the "rebuilds Yerushalayim" blessing, the former statement is referring to other blessings.

Rashi comments [on this *Gemara*] that included in the "praiseworthy" case is [not just the "rebuilds Yerushalayim" blessing but also] any blessing that culminates a string of consecutive blessings; in all such cases one should say *Omain* on his own blessing [at the end]. When the Gemara answers that that "one who answers *Omain* on his own blessing is praiseworthy" refers to "rebuilds Yerushalayim", it does not mean [to limit this rule] only to that blessing. Rather, it is using "rebuilds Yerushalayim" as a paradigm for all grouped blessings and teaching that one must self-answer *Omain* on the last blessing in the group.[326]

The reason "rebuilds Yerushalayim" is selected as the example is to convey an additional facet of this rule, and that is that it qualifies for a self-answered *Omain* even though it is actually followed by the blessing "Good and Bestower of good" [and thus is not the last blessing in the sequence that comprises the after-meals blessings]. This is because "Good and Bestower of good" is only of Rabbinic origin[327] and does not cancel the self-answered *Omain* obligation of "rebuilds Yerushalayim".

In our discussion of *Omain* earlier[328] we explained why *Omain* in general may only be recited by someone other than the person making the blessing. The reason is based on the *Gemara*[329] that states that, "One who responds with *Omain* has done something greater than the person who recited the blessing itself".[330] That is why only an

─────────── פירוש בנתיבות לב ───────────

[324] Chapter 11, section 5.

[325] *Brachos* 45b.

[326] The Maharal at the end of this section will take issue with *Rashi* and favor the commentators who hold that the Gemara specifically means that one should say *Omain* only after the "rebuilds Yerushalayim" blessing and not at the end of other multi-blessing sequences. However he begins by providing a rationale for *Rashi's* point of view based on principles he articulated earlier in this chapter.

[327] And thus it does not deprive the "rebuilds Yerushalayim" blessing of its status as last in a series, since it in fact ends the series of three Biblically mandated blessings.

[328] Chapter 11, section 5.

[329] *Brachos* 53b.

[330] The Maharal *op. cit.* explains that the root of the word *Omain*, אמן, derives from the word אמונה, *emunah*, or faith. A person responding with *Omain* is affirming his faith in the content of the blessing he just heard. Faith is a heart-based undertaking and as such it is more rarefied and less material than the blessing itself, where articulation of the words is the critical factor in determining the efficacy of the blessing. A blessing is valid even if the person making it was not focused on the meaning of the words, as long as they were uttered correctly. But an *Omain* is only valid if the focus was there since that is the essence of what *Omain* is all about. That is why "One who responds with *Omain* has done something greater than the person who recited the blessing itself".

outside party can respond with *Omain* – *Omains* are "additive"; they build on the blessing itself, as we explained earlier. The one who recited the blessing is incapable of doing this.[331]

[The *Gemara* declares that] a person who responds *Omain* after his own blessings is repulsive[332] [for reasons we described]. But this does not apply to the last blessing in a sequence; in such a case the status of "last" creates an independent existence [that is separate from the blessing itself] and the *Omain* latches onto that independent existence and is thus able to eclipse the blessing [even if uttered by the same person who made the blessing]. One must understand the *Gemara* in this way [according to *Rashi*].[333]

However, according to the explanation we provided above[334] the three [Biblical] blessings in the after-meals blessing [represent stages of perfection that Hashem bestowed on Yisroel] culminating in the ultimate perfection of "rebuilds Yerushalayim". This stage converges with the rarefied heights of *Omain* about which the *Gemara* states that "One who responds with *Omain* has done something greater than the person who recited the blessing itself". Therefore [on the "rebuilds Yerushalayim" blessing and only on that blessing] the person making the blessing may himself respond with *Omain*.[335] When this concept is properly understood it is evident that this is the correct way of understanding the *Gemara*, and therefore the *Gemara* can be understood straightforwardly – that is, that the only time one who responds *Omain* on his own blessing is praiseworthy is when he is doing so on the "rebuilds Yerushalayim" blessing, since it represents the ultimate level of completion.[336]

───────────────── פירוש בנתיבות לב ─────────────────

Moreover the Maharal explains that while a blessing is directed at a specific commandment or benefit, *Omain* is a general expression of faith in Hashem as omnipotent and unlimited in every way. Thus *Omain* is superior not only because it is an expression of rarefied faith but also because that expression of faith encompasses the full gamut of Hashem's capabilities, as it were, not just the capability that pertains to the current blessing that was uttered.

[331] The idea of *Omain*, as discussed in the previous footnote, is to build on the edifice of the blessing itself. That requires an intelligence apart from the one that uttered the blessing. For A to be greater than B, A has to be distinct from B; a thing cannot be greater than itself.

[332] The text of the Maharal here is actually "boor" but this is evidently a transcriber's error since the Maharal earlier quoted the *Gemara* with the word "repulsive", as we have it in current editions of the *Gemara*.

[333] As mentioned in footnote 326 the Maharal will now take issue with *Rashi* and adopt the position that the *Gemara* means that one may say *Omain* only after the "rebuilds Yerushalayim" blessing.

[334] Section 9.

[335] As discussed in footnote 330 the distinction of *Omain* over the blessing itself is that it is that is a declaration of Hashem's omnipotence and complete and utter mastery over every aspect of creation. This declaration emanates from man's intellectual/spiritual side. So *Omain* is generally a step up from the blessing itself, which is at it should be; it is why the *Omain* must be said by someone other than the person making the blessing, as explained earlier.

The pinnacle of faith represented by *Omain* is, however, identical to that achieved in the spiritual atmosphere of the holy Temple where the laws of nature were routinely suspended and Hashem's supreme mastery of the universe was palpable. Thus the third, "rebuilds Yerushalayim" blessing itself achieves the pinnacle of faith normally achievable only by *Omain*. There is nowhere higher to go. Therefore it would be superfluous to have someone else respond with *Omain*; on the contrary, in order to indicate that the blessing itself has achieved the level of *Omain* and the maximum height has already been achieved it is appropriate for the person making the blessing himself to answer with *Omain*.

[336] This follows the view of *Tosfos* on the *Gemara*, who holds that "rebuilds Yerushalayim" is the only blessing after which one may self-answer *Omain*. This in fact is the prevailing custom in Ashkenazic communities.

Section 30 – The Fourth Blessing – Part 1

ברכה רביעית הטוב והמטיב...

הטוב והמטיב

T he fourth blessing is "the Good and Bestower of good". We explained this blessing's place in the after-meals blessings earlier.[337]

From the *Gemara* in chapter *Shlosha She'achlu*:[338]

"Rabbi Yochanan said, the "Good and Bestower of good" blessing requires mention of Hashem's Kingship.[339] The *Gemara* asks, what is Rabbi Yochanan coming to teach? Is his point that a blessing with mention of Hashem's Kingship is not a valid blessing? But he already taught us this ruling![340]

"Rabbi Zeira explained that Rabbi Yochanan was teaching that [the "Good and Bestower of good"] blessing requires two mentions of Hashem's Kingship: one in its own right and another [to compensate for the lack of mention of Hashem's Kingship] in the [third] "rebuilds Yerushalayim" blessing. The *Gemara* asks, if so, let [the "Good and Bestower of good"] blessing have three mentions of Hashem's Kingship: one in its own right, another to compensate for the lack in the "rebuilds Yerushalayim" blessing and a third to compensate [for the lack of mention of Hashem's Kingship] in the [second] land blessing?

["We must say, then, answers the *Gemara*, that the reason the land blessing does not mention Kingship is because it is a blessing that directly follows another blessing.[341] But if this is so then "rebuilds Yerushalayim" should also not require Kingship mention![342]]

"The *Gemara* answers, it is true that by rights "rebuilds Yerushalayim" should not require Kingship-mention.[343] However that blessing does mention the Kingship of the house of Dovid so it is unseemly for it to

פירוש בנתיבות לב

---

[337] Sections 8, 9 and 11 each present a different perspective on the order of the after-meals blessings and each examines the fourth blessing from its own particular perspective. See the table in footnote 148.

[338] *Brachos* 49a.

[339] That is, the words מלך העולם, *melech ha'olam*, "King of the universe" must appear in the blessing, as in fact is the case in our version of the blessing, which begins, "Blessed are you, Hashem, our G-d, King of the universe…".

[340] On *Brachos* 40b Rabbi Yochanan laid down a blanket rule that all blessings require mention of Hashem's Kingship. Why, then, repeat the ruling with respect to this specific blessing?

[341] As discussed in Section 25 there are differences in the blessing "templates" between blessings that are adjacent to other blessings and blessings that are standalone. One of these differences is that a blessing that directly follows other blessings, ברכה הסמוכה לחברתה, *bracha hasemucha lachaverta*, does not require mention of Hashem's Kingship. The land blessing, which directly follows the first food blessing, is therefore exempt from the Kingship-mention requirement.

[342] Since it directly follows the second, land blessing. And if this is so then there is no need for "Good and Bestower of good" to have an extra mention of Kingship to compensate for the one missing in "rebuilds Yerushalayim", since that blessing, being adjacent to another blessing, did not require Kingship mention in the first place! This would seem to negate Rabbi Zeira's explanation of Rabbi Yochanan's statement that "Good and Bestower of good" needs a Kingship mention.

Thus we are left with our original question – why did Rabbi Yochanan repeat his requirement of Kingship-mention in "Good and Bestower of good" when he already taught us that it is a general requirement?

[343] Since it directly follows another blessing.

omit mention of Hashem's Kingship.[344]

"Rav Pappa [provided an alternative answer and] said, Rabbi Yochanan actually did mean to add two Kingship-mentions to the "Good and Bestower of good" blessing [in addition to its intrinsic Kingship-mention]."[345]

Let us analyze this *Gemara*. [In the end there are two approaches to understanding the ruling of Rabbi Yochanan. The first is that] since we mention the Kingship of Dovid in "rebuilds Yerushalayim", it is unseemly to omit mention of Hashem's Kingship, and since it is inappropriate to insert it side-by-side with that of Dovid's Kingship our Sages decreed that it should be mentioned instead in "Good and Bestower of good". [The second approach is that of] Rav Pappa who adds that we should incorporate a compensatory mention of Kingship for the land-blessing] into "Good and Bestower of good"] as well.

The blessing of "Good and Bestower of good" [is a general blessing that] incorporates all manner of good things that emanate from Hashem,[346] so the Kingship mention that should have been, but could not be, included in "rebuilds Yerushalayim" (since it is inappropriate to insert it side-by-side with human Kingship) was added to "Good and Bestower of good" – the blessing that is inclusive of every kind of good.[347] What is omitted from "rebuilds Yerushalayim" and the land

––––––––––––––––––––––––––– פירוש בנתיבות לב –––––––––––––––––––––––––––

[344] Despite the fact that Kingship is not required in "rebuilds Yerushalayim" following the ordinary rules governing the text of blessings, we require it out of respect to Hashem, once mortal Kingship is mentioned. Thus Rabbi Zeira's explanation of Rabbi Yochanan's statement is justified – Rabbi Yochanan is instructing us to insert a second mention of Hashem's Kingship into "Good and Bestower of good" to compensate for the lack of mention of Hashem's Kingship in "rebuilder of Yerushalayim".

The commentators provide various explanation for why we do not simply insert the Kingship-mention directly into the third blessing, where it belongs. The explanation supplied by *Rabbeinu Yonah*, which the Maharal will also adopt, is that it is disrespectful to mention mortal Kingship and Hashem's Kingship side-by-side, as if they were equivalent. Thus the additional mention of Hashem's Kingship is deferred to the next blessing – "Good and Bestower of good".

[345] Rav Pappa is of the opinion that as long as we add one Kingship-mention to "Good and Bestower of good" to compensate for the one missing in "rebuild Yerushalayim", for reasons as stated above, we add another one to compensate for the missing one in the land blessing. The commentators provide various reasons to explain why Rav Pappa felt the need to do this, in light of the fact that the land blessing is exempt from Kingship mention since it immediately follows another blessing. *Tosfos* explains that since the first three blessings were instituted at different times (see Section 8) they do not have the full status of blessings that are adjacent to other blessings and thus it is appropriate to create compensatory Kingship-mentions for them.

Our practice is to follow the ruling of Rav Pappa and we therefore have three Kingship-mentions in the fourth, "Good and Bestower of good" blessing, as the Maharal will explain.

[346] From the text of the "Good and Bestower of good" blessing: "… the King who is good and does good for all… He did good, He does good and He will do good for us… He bestows upon us… with grace and with kindness and with mercy, with relief, salvation, success, blessing, help, consolation, sustenance, support, mercy, life, peace and all good and of all good things may He never deprive us". See also Section 8 for a more detailed discussion of the role of this blessing.

[347] "Every kind of good" in a general sense includes the specific subject matter of third blessing, Yerushalayim and the Temple, so a Kingship reference that really belongs in the third blessing "fits" in the "Good and Bestower of good" blessing as well. The Maharal's point is that placing it there is not an arbitrary "transplant"; it is actually appropriate there.

The same is true according to Rav Pappa with respect to the Kingship mention in the land blessing. "Every kind of good" also includes the specific subject matter of the land blessing so the Kingship reference that should have gone there, but could not, for reasons as explained, "fits" in the "Good and Bestower of good" blessing as well.

blessing is included in the all-encompassing "Good and Bestower of good" blessing.

Thus this blessing has two ["foreign"] Kingship mentions in addition to its own native mention for a total of three Kingship mentions. They are, "Blessed are You, Hashem, our G-d, **King** of the universe" (1), "our Father, our **King**" (2) and "the **King** Who is good" (3).

There are those who ask that the text that we use for the "rebuilds Yerushalayim" blessing has the words, "our Father, **our King**, tend us…"[348] as well so why does that not qualify as a Kingship mention, and why is it necessary to add the extra Kingship mention, "our Father, our **King**", to the "Good and Bestower of good" blessing? This does not present a difficulty, however, because the Kingship mention that is mandated in blessings is one of praise to Hashem; a declaration that He is King. That sort of reference to Kingship qualifies as "Kingship mention" [and satisfies the requirement to have Kingship mention in a blessing]. That is not, however, the nature of the Kingship mention in "rebuilds Yerushalayim". Rather we mention Kingship there to justify our request that he "tend us, nourish us, sustain us…" on the basis that it is a King's responsibility to do those things on behalf of his subjects. That does not qualify as a [praise-driven] "Kingship mention".

On the other hand the Kingship mention ["stand-in" for "rebuilds Yerushalayim"] in the "Good and Bestower of good" blessing is, "our Father, our **King**, our Sovereign, our Creator, our Redeemer, our Holy One, Holy one of Yaakov, our Shepherd, the Shepherd of Yisroel…". This contains no requests, it is a declaration that Hashem is King [with no ulterior motives]. This is what the [mandated] Kingship mention is supposed to be: [unadulterated] praise to Hashem in that He is our King.

Halacha הלכה

See the cited reference for laws and text versions pertaining to the "Good and Bestower of good" blessing.

Shulchan Aruch Orach Chaim 189

It is true that the text continues, "G-d,[349] Who every single day He did good…".[350] However, these [requests] are directed at the word "G-d" that directly precedes them; [they are not directed back at the earlier Kingship mention]. Thus [these requests] do not present a difficulty; [they do not call into question our motives for the Kingship mention].[351]

––––––––––––––––––– פירוש בנתיבות לב –––––––––––––––––––

[348] As indicated in footnote 297, our version of the blessing begins, "**Our G-d**, our Father", so the question is specific to the Maharal's version of the text.

[349] Our version of the text omits the word, א-ל, "G-d".

[350] See footnote 346 for the full subsequent text. It is clear that we are in fact seguing into a list of benefits that we anticipate that Hashem will grant us, which calls into question, the Maharal's asks, our assumption that the preceding Kingship mention is "pure" praise.

[351] It is interesting how the two key textual differences between the Maharal's version of the third and fourth blessings and our version work in tandem to form two different understandings of the workings of the compensatory Kingship mentions in the "Good and Bestower of good" blessing.

The Maharal is forced to distinguish between altruistic Kingship mentions and non-altruistic Kingship mentions because his version of the text of the "rebuilds Yerushalayim" blessing, unlike ours, also has a Kindship mention. To explain why this does not suffice, and why we need a compensatory Kingship mention, the Maharal needs to invalidate the internal Kingship mention on the basis of its non-altruistic nature. Thus another Kingship mention for this blessing is required in the "Good and Bestower of good" blessing and that Kingship mention is completely altruistic. Having made the distinction between altruistic and non-altruistic Kingship mentions, the Maharal must confront his final question in this section, namely, that the compensatory Kingship mention for "rebuilds Yerushalayim" in the "Good and Bestower of good" blessing is also apparently non-altruistic because it is followed by a list of requests. The Maharal disposes of this question by attributing the requests to the reference to "G-d" that intervenes between the Kingship mention and the requests, and not to the earlier Kingship mention.

However according to our version of the texts there is no Kingship mention in "rebuilds Yerushalayim"

Section 31 – The Fourth Blessing – Part 2

ובברכה זאת הזכיר עשרה שבחים...

הטוב והמטיב

The fourth blessing contains ten praises [to Hashem]. They are, "Our G-d" (1), "our Father" (2), "our King" (3), "our Sovereign" (4), "our Creator" (5), "our Redeemer" (6), "our Maker" (7), "our Holy One" (8), "Our Shepherd, the Shepherd of Yisroel (9) and "the King Who is good" (10).

We have already explained[352] that the blessing of "Good and Bestower of good" is most exalted as it depicts Hashem as intrinsically good and as the universal conferrer of good. That is why this blessing progresses through ten levels [of praise] culminating in the tenth, completely holy praise,[353] for ten represents holiness and Hashem's attribute of "Good and Bestower of good" emanates from the tenth level.[354] Understand this well.

הוא הטיב הוא מטיב הוא ייטיב לנ

This blessing was instituted [as a paean] to Hashem's abundance of goodness – as we say [in the blessing, that] Hashem is "Good and Bestower of good". Conferring good with an abundance of goodness implies that Hashem's goodness is unrestricted [and applies to everyone]. This is why, [in describing the flow,] we say that Hashem "did good" [starting in the past tense], to show that the flow of good is continual and traverses the past, the present and the future.[355]

We continue with three "bestowals".[356] These refer to acts of benevolence that Hashem confers on the world; [they too qualify as "good" since] every act of benevolence is an act of providing good.[357] When a person is delivered from hardship, that [too] is a bestowal of benevolence – for example [the *Gemara*[358] teaches that]

────────────── פירוש בנתיבות לב ──────────────

at all. Thus there is no need to distinguish between altruistic and non-altruistic Kingship mentions and non-altruistic Kingship mentions presumably also satisfy the requirement to have Kingship mentions in blessings. Therefore, according to our version of the texts it is perfectly acceptable for the compensatory "rebuilds Yerushalayim" Kingship mention that appears in "Good and Bestower of good" (necessary, according to us, because in our text versions there is no Kingship request in "rebuilds Yerushalayim" at all) to have requests associated with it, as in fact it does. We cannot explain that these requests are not associated with the Kingship mention because there is an invocation of "G-d" intervening, since our version of the text does not have that invocation. Fortuitously, however, we are fine with our Kingship mentions being non-altruistic, so the omission of the word "G-d" does not create Kingship mentions problems for our version of the texts as it does for the Maharal's version of the texts.

[352] Sections 8 and 11.

[353] That is, the praise that incorporates all the others: "the King Who is good".

[354] In *Gevuros Hashem* chapter 46 the Maharal writes that the tenth always has a predisposition toward holiness since before ten there are only single digits but ten breaks through into a new dimension of groups of ten (just as holiness transcends the mundane world and inhabits a different dimension of reality). This is why the supremely holy day of Yom Kippur falls on the tenth of the month of *Tishrei*. Similarly in chapter 36 of *Gevuros Hashem* the Maharal writes that this was also the reason that Yisroel was commanded to take the lamb for the Pascal offering on the tenth of the month of *Nissan*. It is also the reason, as the Maharal writes in his *Drasha l'Shabbos HaGadol*, that the sanctified *Maaser* tithe was specified to be one part out of ten.

See more on the significance of the number ten in footnote 244.

[355] The text is, "He did good, He does good, He will do good for us". To be truly unrestricted Hashem's goodness has to apply to all of us, including those are not alive now but lived in the past or will live in the future.

[356] "He bestowed upon us, He will bestow upon us, He will forever bestow upon us".

[357] Which is why they feature in this blessing.

[358] *Brachos* 54a. The four situations that require thanks to Hashem in the form of a special blessing called *Gomel*, or "bestows", are returnees from an ocean or desert voyage, inmates released from prison and illness recoverees. The text of the blessing is, "Blessed are You, Hashem our G-d, King of the universe,

people who escape from four kinds of situations are obligated to thank Hashem.

The blessing[359] of "Good and Bestower of good" does not have a concluding invocation.[360] This is because, the *Gemara* explains, it is [only] Rabbinically mandated. The primary reason that this blessing does not have a concluding invocation, though, is that concluding invocations are used only when the blessing [that Hashem is granting, and which is the subject of the verbal blessing that is being recited] is complete and well-defined.[361] For example the [first of the after-meals] blessings, "He nourishes", is well-defined in that food [is an item that] makes a person whole; when a person lacks food, food fills the lack.[362] Since this blessing [from Hashem] reflects an absolute state of completion, the blessing [that is being recited] itself can be complete and it thus has a concluding invocation.[363]

The same thing can be said of the [second] land blessing; the land [fills a specific void and thereby] makes a person whole.[364] The Temple [which is the subject of the third blessing] renders the entire universe complete so this blessing, too, has the property of completeness and is eligible for a concluding invocation. This concept is similar to what we articulated with respect to the land blessing;[365] that bracketing the blessing with thanks beginning and end indicates a complete thanks. [Similarly we end a blessing with a concluding invocation when the blessing that Hashem supplied completely satisfies a lack.]

The "Good and Bestower of good" blessing, however, was instituted on all manner of good that Hashem bestows [regardless of whether or not it completely fills a void and creates a state of wholeness]. As evidence, note that if a person [is already drinking wine and] and is brought a new variety of wine he is obligated to recite the

───────────────── פירוש בנתיבות לב ─────────────────

Who bestows benevolence upon the culpable, for He has **bestowed benevolence** upon me". This demonstrates the Maharal's point, which is that avoiding bad things, such as being saved from danger, is considered a benevolence as much as being provided with good things, like food.

[359] The word "blessing", like the word ברכה, *bracha* that we are translating as "blessing", can refer either to a specific flow of beneficence from Hashem, or to the formula that we recite to acknowledge and thank Hashem for that flow. Usually the context makes clear which of the meanings is intended but in this section both senses of the word are used in close proximity so to avoid confusion we will write "blessing [from Hashem]" or similar turn of phrase when referring to the flow from Hashem and "blessing [that is being recited]" when referring to the formula that we recite.

We use "invocation" to refer to the classic opening and closing of most blessings, "Blessed are you Hashem, King of the universe…"; see footnote 360.

[360] Standalone blessings generally begin with "Blessed are You Hashem…", continue with the specific subject of the blessing and end with another invocation of "Blessed are You Hashem…".

[361] The Maharal does not mean to supersede the *Gemara's* answer but rather to elaborate upon it. The reason this blessing is Rabbinic is precisely because it is not "complete and well-defined".

[362] The Maharal is defining several interrelated criteria necessary to trigger an ending invocation. 1) There has to be a specific lack – such as (in the case of the first blessing) a lack of food. 2) There has to be something specific that Hashem will supply to fill the lack – such as food. 3) The status once Hashem has addressed the lack is that of wholeness – the lack is completely gone and the recipient of the food is complete and no longer suffers from that lack.

[363] Users of the London Hebrew edition of *Nesivos Olam* should be aware of a confusing typographical error in this paragraph. A complete line was erroneously inserted on page 144 (קמ"ד), second column, third line from the top. This line, which reads הקרקע. ולפיכך הוא מגביה כוס של ברכה מן, should be omitted in its entirety. Corrected in the *Yad Mordechai* edition which was based on original manuscripts.

[364] In section 18 the Maharal explains that the land is a perpetual source of livelihood and is fundamentally different than *ad hoc* provision of food, which is the subject of the first blessing. Until we were granted the land this was an unfilled void. Once we got the land this void was completely filled. Thus the second blessing itself can be complete and have an ending invocation.

[365] Section 25.

"Good and Bestower of good" blessing.[366] We see, then, that this blessing is recited whenever [Hashem grants] an abundance of good [and is not limited to situations where wholeness ensues as a result of that good]. Thus this blessing has an opening invocation but not a closing invocation.

This characteristic of the "Good and Bestower of good" blessing is the reason that its inclusion in the after-meals blessings is only Rabbinic, as we stated. That is why the *Gemara* specifies that this blessing, because of its Rabbinic origin, has an opening but not a closing invocation. In other words the blessing is Rabbinic because it is on an abundance of good [and not on completeness] and for the same reason we do not complete it with a closing invocation.

May Hashem be blessed and may the Name of His Glory be blessed for-ever, *omain v'omain!*

ברוך הוא וברוך שם כבודו לעולם, אמן ואמן![367]

Section 32 – *Mayim Acharonim: After-Meal Washing – Part 1*

מים אחרונים שלאחר הסעודה אין עתה נוהגים בהם...

Halacha הלכה

Mayim Acharonim is obligatory.

Shulchan Aruch Orach Chaim 181:1

The after-meal washing ritual is not customarily observed nowadays.[368] The *Tosfos* commentary in chapter *Kol HaBosor*[369] writes that [a possible reason for the neglect of this obligation is that] *mayim acharonim* was originally instituted to forestall the harmful effects of מלח סדומית, *melach sdomis*, Sodomite salt[370] but Sodomite salt is not prevalent in our time [so there is no reason to maintain the practice]. To justify his position [that after-meal washing is not mandatory when there is no health reason to require it] *Tosfos* cites a *Gemara*[371] that states, "['... and be holy':[372] this refers to the after-meal washing.] 'For I am holy': this refers to oil", meaning that

—————————— פירוש בנתיבות לב ——————————

[366] As explained in footnote 125 the Maharal equates the longer "Bestower of good" blessing that appears in the after-meals blessings with the shorter version that is recited when good news is received. The application of this blessing to wine is discussed in *Shulchan Aruch Orach Chaim* 175; refer there for particulars of this ruling.

[367] Paraphrase of *Tehillim* 72:19. In the widely disseminated London edition of the Maharal's *Nesivos Olam* Chapter 18 ends here, however the following sections appear in earlier editions and were apparently omitted from the London edition in error.

[368] Evidently the *mayim acharonim* requirement was widely ignored in the Maharal's time. The Maharal will take strong issue strong issue with this behavior in the remainder of this chapter. In fact the *Shulchan Aruch* is unequivocal about the obligatory nature of *mayim acharonim*.

[369] *Chulin* 105a, *davar hamaschil* "*Mayim*".

[370] Literally, salt from the area of the city of Sodom, located near the Dead Sea and divinely destroyed because of its immoral character. As will emerge in the Maharal's discussion of the after-meal washing obligation and in this commentary, there is a mystical aspect to the detrimental effects of Sodomite salt but the prosaic explanation as provided in the *Gemara* in *Eruvin* 17b is that Sodomite salt is more potent than ordinary salt and can damage the eyes on contact. Since salt commonly accompanies meals – indeed our Sages in *Brachos* 40a recommend taking salt with meals – and since Sodomite salt may also be present, there is a risk that some of it may remain on the hands and enter and damage the eyes through hand contact. Thus our Sages decreed after-meal hand washing to remove the Sodomite salt risk.

From the scientific standpoint Dead Sea salt is indeed chemically different from sea salt, which is more than 95% sodium chloride or NaCl – table salt. Dead Sea salt, though, is less than 20% sodium chloride. Bromine is the primary element, accompanied by magnesium, calcium and other metals. (See Ma'or, Zeev, et al. "Antimicrobial properties of Dead Sea black mineral mud", *International Journal of Dermatology*, Volume 45, Issue 5, May 2006.) So it is certainly plausible that Sodomite salt will act differently on the body than table salt.

[371] *Brachos* 53b. The Maharal will discuss this *Gemara* in greater depth in the next section.

[372] *Vayikra* 20:7.

it was customary to anoint their hands with oil [after a meal].

[Now, one might think that an action described by a verse is unconditionally mandatory] but we do not find, [*Tosfos* continues,] that the custom to hand-anoint was mandatory or even a fulfillment of a command,[373] so the verse-reference is merely an allusion. [Similarly, the reference at the beginning of the verse to after-meal washing must also be an allusion and the practice not mandatory . Thus there is no harm in neglecting it when Sodomite salt is not prevalent].

Now, it is true, [*Tosfos* continues,] that the *Gemara* [in *Brachos*] states that just as a contaminated person is disqualified from Temple service,[374] so also is a person with contaminated hands [because he failed to perform after-meal washing] disqualified from reciting blessings [and this implies that after-meals washing really is mandatory. But, this implication does not prove the point because] the issue of contamination arises only for those [who lived at a time when Sodomite salt was prevalent] and for whom, therefore, after-meals washing was mandatory. For those people failure to wash after meals created a situation of contamination. [But for people living at the time of *Tosfos*, hands were highly unlikely to have Sodomite salt on them and therefore they were not considered contaminated even if after-meals washing was not performed.]

This is the gist of the commentary of *Tosfos* on this matter and the *Rosh*[375] and the *Tur*[376] agree [with their conclusion].

Therefore, since people today generally do not observe the after-meal washing procedure we did not place our discussion of it before our discussion of the after-meals blessing.[377] Nonetheless since the practice does appear in the Talmud, and since the Sages of the time were adamant about its importance , as we have said, we will delve into the reasons for the practice here, for the benefit of those who wish to be informed about it.

Besides, even *Tosfos* [378] writes that fastidious people who customarily wash their hands after meals may not recite the after-meals blessings until they do so, since for

──────────── פירוש בנתיבות לב ────────────

[373] Some commandments are mandatory and carry penalties if not observed in addition to a reward if observed; others carry a reward if observed but are voluntary in the sense that there is no penalty if they are not observed. *Tosfos* is saying that the hand-anointing is neither, it was simply a laudable practice at that time and the verse-reference is a post-facto allusion to the practice, not an imperative.

[374] In the Temple context מזוהם, *mezuham*, "contaminated" refers to a person who emits a foul body odor and the meaning is similar with respect to contaminated hands. However, there is a deeper, mystical meaning to the word. For example, the *Gemara* in *Avodah Zara* 22b states that when the serpent came upon Chava he defiled her with a *zuhama*, which was transmitted to mankind, but when Yisroel stood at Sinai their *zuhama* was eliminated. Clearly *zuhama* refers to a spiritual impurity, not to a physical defilement.

The hand "contamination", or *zuhama*, that requires after-meal washing is also primarily spiritual. That explains why, for example, the *Gemara* in *Chulin* 105a says that warm water may not be used for after-meal washing because it does not remove the *zuhama*. Obviously, if *zuhama* were nothing more than the detritus of a meal, warm water would do a better cleaning job than cold water. Moreover the *Gemara* in *Chulin* 105a says that water that had been used for after-meal washing may not be poured on the ground because a רוח רעה, *ruach ra'ah*, literally an "evil spirit" rests over it. Clearly there is more to the need for after-meal washing than meets the physical eye!

[375] On *Brachos* 53b.

[376] *Orach Chaim* 181.

[377] Where it should by rights appear, since it is done prior to the after-meals blessing.

[378] Who does not view after-meals washing as mandatory.

them, unwashed hands are considered contaminated.[379]

Section 33 – Mayim Acharonim: After-Meal Washing – Part 2

ובפרק אלו דברים, אמר רב יהודה אמר רב...

From chapter *Eilu Devarim*:[380] "'…and you shall sanctify yourselves': this refers to the pre-meal washing. '…and be holy': this refers to the after-meal washing. '…because I am holy':[381] this refers to oil".[382] 'I am Hashem, Your G-d':[383] this refers to the after-meals blessings."

[How are we to understand the association between sanctity and actions pertaining to meals?] It is appropriate that a person's **primary** sustenance, upon which his life depends, should be undertaken in a state of complete purity and sanctity. Only bread requires [pre-meal] hand-washing and not fruit,[384] because bread is man's primary sustenance.[385] Eating bread must therefore be done in a state of purity. At the conclusion of a meal a person must again wash his hands to remove contamination, [in preparation for] the blessings he is about to tender to Hashem for his food. This is the implication of "…and you shall sanctify yourselves and be holy".

Now, while pre- and after-meal washing do away with impurity and contamination they do not provide a complete cleansing. More than just impurity and contamination removal is required – so the verse continues, "'…because I am holy": this is oil, [as the *Gemara* explains] because oil provides a complete hand cleansing. It is not sufficient to merely eliminate impurity; an additional level of total cleansing is required.[386]

In today's day and age, however, in our current exile, it is sufficient to rid ourselves of impurity and contamination. Achieving a level of complete sanctity is impossible. Thus we no longer follow the oil-cleansing custom. We can and should continue to distance ourselves from impurity and we accomplish that with pre- and after-meal

–––––––––––––––––––––––––––– פירוש בנתיבות לב ––––––––––––––––––––––––––––

[379] So since there are circumstances where even *Tosfos* hold that after-meals washing is mandatory, the Maharal feels justified in including an explanation of the practice in *Nesiv HaAvodah* – this work.

[380] *Brachos* 53b. This *Gemara*, which the Maharal referred to briefly in the previous section, dissects the clauses in verses from *Vayikra* 11:44 and 20:7 and associates each one with a with a different observance associated with meals.

[381] The three verse clauses mentioned up to this point are from *Vayikra* 11:44.

[382] As mentioned in the previous section, it was customary to anoint hands with oil after a meal. Interestingly, though using oil to clean skin may sound counterintuitive, current scientific research confirms the efficacy of using oils as a skin cleansing agent. Oil acts as an exfoliator to remove dead skin cells and dirt. The fatty acids in many natural oils also help dissolve the sebum produced by skin, creating cleaner skin and pores. Sebum is a sticky oil that clogs pores with dead skin cells and other debris; dissolving it further helps to clean skin.

As mentioned earlier there is a mystical aspect to the pre- and after-meal hand-washings but the prosaic reasons mentioned in the *Gemara* hold true as well.

[383] *Vayikra* 20:7.

[384] From *Shulchan Aruch Orach Chaim* 158:5. "Washing hands for fruit is a sign of arrogance" because, the *Mishna Brurah* explains, he is putting on a show of piety by doing something that is completely unnecessary.

[385] The *Shaar HaTzion* in 158:1 points out that the washing obligation was limited to bread because people build their regular meals around bread (that is, other meal items are viewed as bread accompaniments and the bread is viewed as the primary meal food).

[386] The desired end result of the washing and oil cleansing is primarily spiritual, as the Maharal said earlier. Since we are physical beings, however, the path to a higher spiritual level is achieved through physical actions in the manner prescribed by our Sages.

washing. But the oil-cleansing was intended to add sanctity [rather than to remove impurity]. This is not something that we need to be meticulous about.

It is important to understand the significance of the three things alluded to in the verse, "…and you shall sanctify yourselves, and be holy because I am holy". They are laden with deep wisdom; we cannot elaborate further.

A question: The *Gemara* in chapter *Kol HaBosor* [387] states that after-meal washing is obligatory and explains that this is so because of Sodomite salt. [388] [How do we reconcile that explanation against that of the just-cited *Gemara* in *Brachos* which teaches that the after-meal washing is intended to remove impurity and contamination?] The answer is that this is an additional and independent reason [for the after-meal washing]. It is required in order to remove the Sodomite salt, in addition to its being required to dispel contamination and impurity.

A similar situation pertains with respect to the pre-meal washing [which also has two independent reasons]. It was also instituted to create sanctity. But additionally, it was instituted for uniformity with *Terumah* as the *Gemara* cited earlier[389] explains.

[Since after-meal washing has two independent reasons] why should it not be in effect today [just as pre-meal washing is]?[390] Even if it is true that Sodomite salt is a rarity in our world that is not the only reason [for after-meal washing]. It is also necessary to remove contamination; we are not permitted to recite the after-meal blessings with contaminated and therefore impure hands. And lest you argue that there are people who are not bothered by contamination of the hands, the response would be that their minority mindset is nullified by the preponderant opposing mindset [which **is** bothered by contamination].[391]

──────────────── פירוש בנתיבות לב ────────────────

[387] *Chulin* 105a-b.

[388] See footnote 370.

[389] *Chulin* 105a-b. סרך תרומה, *serach Terumah*, uniformity with *Terumah*. *Terumah* is a percentage "tax" on certain produce types that Jews are obligated to pay to the *Kohanim*, priests, and only priests were entitled to consume it.

The *Mishna Brurah* in 158:1 explains that since *Terumah* had to be eaten in a state of ritual purity, by priests in a state of ritual purity, and since people continually touch things without paying heed, they therefore might unknowingly touch something ritually impure and, by then touching the *Terumah*, rendering it ritually impure as well, and inedible.

Therefore the Sages decreed that priests must ritually wash their hands prior to eating *Terumah*. The Sages further decreed that in order that this hand-washing become ingrained into the habits of the priests, everyone, including non-priests, must wash their hands prior to eating bread. This is what is meant by "uniformity with *Terumah*".

Today *Terumah* is not consumed at all, even by priests, since almost everyone is in state of ritual impurity that will not be remediable until the Temple is rebuilt. However, the pre-meal hand-washing remains in place in anticipation of the Temple's rebuilding, to assure that the ritual purity of *Terumah* be preserved at that time.

[390] The Maharal is apparently assuming that pre-meal washing is in effect today only because of sanctity and therefore after-meal washing should also remain in effect even if only one of the reasons it was instituted is still applicable today. He is apparently taking issue with the *Mishna Brurah* cited in footnote 390 who seems to be saying that both reasons for pre-meal washing, sanctity and uniformity with *Terumah*, are relevant today.

[391] The concept the Maharal is using here is called בטלה דעתו אצל כל אדם, *batla daato eitzel kol odom*. Some laws are relative to the person – for example pre-meal washing requires that no substance intervene between the hands and the water being poured on them but (in some situations) if the person washing is not bothered by the presence of the substance it is not considered interventionary. If, however, the preponderance of people would be bothered by a particular substance, it would be interventionary even

I am therefore incredulous at the statement of *Tosfos* that, because Sodomite salt is not prevalent today, after-meal washing is no longer performed. [Returning to our analogy with pre-meal washing and its having been instituted for uniformity with *Terumah*,] do we have *Terumah* today? [We do not, yet pre-meal washing is still required for the second reason it was instituted – in order to create sanctity. Similarly, after-meal washing should be required in order to remove contamination, even though the Sodomite salt reason may no longer be applicable.]

You might argue that the reason pre-meal washing is required is [not because the second reason, to create sanctity, is sufficient but] because it is verse-derived in the *Gemara*[392]. But that is not so because *Tosfos* [on that *Gemara*] writes that the verse reference is merely an allusion and not an imperative.[393]

Moreover,[394] it seems that the *Gemara*[395] makes a point of citing Abaye's statement regarding Sodomite salt, that [it is so rare that only] a single grain of it can be found in a *kor* of regular salt, [to teach that we need to take precautions against it harming us despite its rarity]. Consider: a *kor*, which equates to thirty *seah*, has just a single grain of Sodomite salt![396] Why does the Gemara see fit to record this fact if not to teach us that we should never conclude that in places where Sodomite salt "is not found" , after-meal washing is not obligatory? That indeed seems to be the point of Abaye's statement that a *kor* has just a single grain of Sodomite salt – to teach us that after-meal washing is obligatory even though it would be a rare occurrence for that single grain to make an appearance on someone's hands. Even though it would be highly exceptional, since it is theoretically possible, we take that remote possiblity into account.

Now, it might be argued that the purpose of Abaye's statement regarding the ratio

---

— פירוש בנתיבות לב —

to the small minority of people who would not be bothered by it and they too would have to remove it before washing. Their mindset is nullified by the preponderant opposing mindset.

Here as well, the Maharal is saying, if there are a small minority of people who are not bothered by hand contamination, their mindset is nullified by the preponderant contrary mindset and even the minority will have to cleanse their hands from the contamination with after-meal washing.

[392] *Chulin* 106a. The *Gemara* cites the verse in *Vayikra* 15:11, "And whoever the *zav* touches, and the latter did not rinse his hands…". A *zav* is a person with a particular kind of ritual impurity and someone he touches requires a purification process. The verse refers to the purification process as hand-rinsing but in fact the touched person requires full immersion in a *mikva*, a ritual bath, as part of his purification process. Using the *drush* method of exegesis the *Gemara* explains that the reference to hand-washing is an indirect endorsement of the need to pre-wash before meals.

This, then, might be the reason that pre-washing is required nowadays even though the uniformity with *Terumah* reason does not apply, whereas, since there is no biblical imperative for after-meal washing, that may not apply today.

[393] Thus there is no greater reason to preserve pre-washing than post-washing since both have verse allusions and both were originally instituted for two reasons, one of which applies today and one of which does not. If pre-washing is universally viewed as binding today, the same should be true for post-washing.

[394] Up until this point the Maharal has been arguing that the after-meal washing obligation is in effect today for the reasons provided by our Sages, aside from the Sodomite salt reason. Thus, even if one argues that Sodomite salt is no longer a factor nowadays, it does not affect the after-meal washing obligation. Now, however, the Maharal attacks the premise that Sodomite salt is no longer a factor. He will argue that Sodomite salt is as much a danger as it ever was and therefore remains a valid reason (along with the other reasons) for the after-meal washing to remain obligatory.

[395] *Chulin* 105b.

[396] A *seah* is the equivalent in volume of 144 eggs. Therefore a *kor* is the volume equivalent of 4,320 eggs – an extremely large volume – and the ratio of Sodomite salt to regular salt is so extremely low that only a single grain of Sodomite salt will appear in a *kor* of salt!

---

of a grain to a *kor* is to teach us that the presence of Sodomite salt is an unnatural phenomenon.[397] If Sodomite salt were naturally occuring there would be more of it since things that occur naturally, characteristically occur in greater abundance. [Abaye is telling us that it is supernatural because] that is indicative of how powerful it is.[398] But even if that were so, it would still imply that after-meal washing is imperative despite Sodomite salt's rarity, even if that were not Abaye's primary message.[399]

The inescapable conclusion, then, is that Sodomite salt is not common, and is not a natural phenomenon as we see from the extent of its uncommoness, but nonetheless we must [protect ourselves against it by] maintaining the obligatory nature of after-meal washing.

I also see no reason to distinguish between Babylonia, where the *Amoraim* [who authored the *Gemara*] were based and the lands where we are currently, by claiming that Sodomite salt was present there but it is not present where we are now.[400] There is no indication in the *Talmud* that Sodomite salt was common in their time and place.[401]

Therefore we must accept the fact that the concern [about the dangers of Sodomite salt] is independent of probabilities; the mere possiblity of it's presence is sufficient reason to take measures to eliminate it and that is the reason that after-meal washing is mandated.

We must add that our Sages possess deep wisdom and they do not always base their pronouncements on what is common and regular. When their wisdom dictates that it is prudent to take heed of a remote possiblity, not doing so is foolhardy and inappropriate. The issue of speaking during a meal is similar, as we pointed out earlier;[402] the possiblity [of choking in that manner] is remote but our Sages instructed us to take it into account, so we must do so.

An additional factor we must take into account that mitigates toward an after-meal washing obligation is that our Sages instructed[403] us to eat salt after every meal and so salt is, for us, a standard meal component.[404] This makes it more plausible that a

---

פירוש בנתיבות לב

[397] And not, as the Maharal has been maintaining, to teach us that after-meal washing is required despite Sodomite salt's rarity.

[398] That is, it's power to harm is not limited by the laws of nature so it is far more potent than its chemical formulation might indicate. Abaye is thus issuing a warning rather than instructing us about after-meal washing.

[399] After all, what would the purpose of Abaye's warning be if it were not actionable, and what precautions against Sodomite salt are possible other than after-meal washing to remove this potent caustic agent, which might have been introduced to our hands in the course of a meal along with regular salt, from our persons?

[400] This is one of the arguments cited in the commentary of *Tosfos*, *Brachos* 53b. As mentioned earlier, the position of *Tosfos*, which the Maharal takes strong issue with, is that after-meal washing may not be obligatory today.

[401] On the contrary, it is clear from the statement of Abaye that it was very uncommon so there are no grounds to conclude that it is any different outside of Babylonia and in the present time.

[402] Chapter 17, section 8, which discusses the prohibition against speaking while eating, instituted to prevent choking. The Maharal there remarks that the danger is remote but still must be taken into account. See the reference for details.

[403] *Brachos* 40a.

[404] Note that *Tosfos* in *Eruvin* 17b writes that this custom is no longer prevalent either, which accords with

---

person might encounter Sodomite salt during meals, and more understandable, especially in light of its high potency, that we have to deal with the possiblity that he might do so. Add to that the fact that Sodomite salt is not a natural substance, as we said earlier, which makes it [more dangerous and] more demanding of an extremely cautious stance.

Finally, who said that Sodomite salt is the only salt that can potentially cause harm? Ordinary salt is also [caustic and] capable of causing harm! The *Gemara* speaks of the most extreme danger, the salt variety that can blind, but that is not to say that ordinary salt cannot inflict [a lesser degree of] harm.

Thus, after-meal washing is obligatory.[405]

Section 34 – Mayim Acharonim: After-Meal Washing – Part 3

ובפרק כל הבשר, כי אתא רב דמי אמר...

From chapter *Kol HaBasar*:[406] "When Rav Dimi came [from Israel to Babylonia[407]] he reported that a failure to perform pre-meal washing caused someone to eat pig meat, and a failure to perform after-meal washing caused a wife to be divorced from her husband. When Ravin came he reported that a failure to perform pre-meal washing caused someone to eat improperly slaughtered meat and a failure to perform after-meal washing caused a murder."[408]

If we properly understand this *Gemara* we will see that [through these seemingly mundane stories] our Sages are communicating great and weighty concepts regarding pre- and after-meal washing.

Pre-meal washing removes ritual impurity and prevents a person from eating in a

———————————— פירוש בנתיבות לב ————————————

his view that after-meal washing today is not a hard-and-fast obligation.

[405] The *Aruch HaShulchan, Orach Chaim* 181:5 writes strongly that after-meal washing is obligatory and maintains that *Tosfos* holds the same; in arguing to the contrary *Tosfos* was merely trying to excuse people of his time who were neglecting it. He cites a *Zohar* in *Parshas Pinchas* which warns strongly against being lax in this obligation and quotes the *Magen Avraham* who writes that the Kabbalists were very stringent with respect to after-meal washing. He also quotes *Shailos u'Teshuvos min HaShamayim* 57 (an early work by an author who received responses to his questions in a heavenly vision) who writes that in response to his query as to whether or not after-meal blessing was obligatory, he was told that it is, and that if one treats it lightly his days and years are treated lightly as well – that is, they will be shortened.

[406] *Chulin* 106a.

[407] Where the Babylonian Talmud was authored and these events recorded.

[408] *Rashi* writes that Rav Dimi and Ravin were reporting different versions of the same two incidents. The first incident involved a Jewish innkeeper who serviced both a Jewish and non-Jewish clientele. He served the non-Jews less expensive non-kosher meat but served the Jews kosher meat. A Jew once entered his inn and neglected his pre-meal washing obligation. The innkeeper, observing this, assumed he was a non-Jew and served him improperly slaughtered meat (or, according to Rav Dimi, pig meat).

The second incident is recorded in detail in *Yoma* 83b. Rabbi Meir, Rabbi Yehudah and Rabbi Yosi lodged at an inn. They wished to hand the innkeeper their purses for safekeeping but when he told them his name, Kidor, Rabbi Meir, who possessed a power to read character from names, realized that the innkeeper was not to be trusted so held on to his purse while the others proceeded to give him theirs. When they later asked him to return the purses he denied having received them, so they devised a ploy to recover them. They noticed that he had lentil residue on his lip – a result of his failure to perform after-meal washing, which includes washing the mouth area (see the commentary of the *Rif* on *Chulin* 37b). So they quietly went to his home and told his wife that the innkeeper instructed them to hand them the purses and as a sign that the instruction was really coming from the innkeeper, they told her that he had instructed them to tell her that he had just eaten lentils. The sign convinced her and she handed over the purses. When her husband later found out what happened he killed her (or, according to Rav Dimi, he divorced her).

state of ritual impurity. Laxity in pre-meal washing [which reflects an uncaring attitude toward ritual uncleanliness] leads a person to the extreme of ritual uncleanliness, which is the consumption of pig meat[409] or improperly slaughtered meat.[410] Forgoing pre-meal washing is the first step down a slipperly slope that ends with the ultimate in [food-based] ritual uncleanliness. Eating pig. Eating unslaughtered meat.[411]

Failing to observe after-meal washing is failing to distance oneself from contamination, and the human spirit finds this revolting and repulsive. It is therefore debilitating to the spirit. [Following that path to its ultimate conclusion] leads to [a complete destruction of the spirit, or] murder [according to Ravin].[412]

The other point of view,[413] that is causes divorce, holds that divorce partakes of the nature of murder [but not the extent of murder]. This is because a man and his wife together are like one person and when they divorce the unified entity that they personified is diminshed. Rav Dimi holds that contaminated and disgusting hands are not, fundamentally, equivalent to a complete nullification of the spirit [as does Ravin]. Repulsiveness contracts the spirit [but does not snuff it out]. That is why he says that it leads to divorce, which is is similar in that it too attenuates the spirit [represented by the former joint couple] without snuffing it out.[414]

No one would deny that divorce is more of a spirit-suppressor than neglecting after-meal washing, whose effect on the spirit, relative to that of divorce, is mild. But the point is that an act that constitutes a mild diminshment of the spirit, such as neglecting after-meal washing and reciting the after-meal blessing with contaminated hands, will **lead to** the more pronounced spirit diminishment of divorce. The opposing point of view holds that it will continue to spiral downwards until it in fact does lead to murder.

The implications of pre- and after-meal washing are deeper than we have explained

---

———————————————— פירוש בנתיבות לב ————————————————

[409] We know that pig meat is prohibited but how do we know that it is also considered ritually unclean? For the answer to that question see *Devarim* 14:8: "And the pig… it is **ritually unclean** for you".

[410] We know that improperly slaughtered meat is prohibited but how do we know that it is also considered ritually unclean? For the answer to that question see *Vayikra* 17:15: "And any person… who eats improperly slaughtered meat… shall remain **ritually unclean**…".

[411] Presumably the Maharal is implicitly referring to the principle of עבירה גוררת עבירה, *avairo goreres avairo*, one sin leads to another sin, as stated in *Avos* 4:2. The downward progression is commonly in the same area of transgression, so it stands to reason that a person who starts off lax in observance of ritual uncleanliness in relatively "minor" ways, such as pre- or after-meal washing, will end up being lax in observance of ritual uncleanliness in major ways.

[412] Interestingly, the *Kaf HaChaim* on *Shulchan Aruch* 157 cites a *Yalkut Shimoni* who writes that the suffering of *Iyov* was caused by his failure to perform the after-meal washing. He thereby failed to drive away the *sitra achra*, the evil forces of the "dark side" (see footnote 415), who strenuously prosecuted him. The commentary of Rav Chaim Vital in *Shaar HaMitzvos, Parshas Ekev* also says that the after-meal washing is akin to a bone thrown to the *sitra achra* to appease him and get him to leave and not cause harm. We "feed" him the residue of food on our hands as a peace offering of sorts (See the *Ramban* on *Vayikra*, 16,8 where he articulates a similar concept to explain the *sa'eir la'azazel*, the scapegoat of the *Yom Kippur* service.)

Possibly the spirit diminution the *Gemara* here is talking about is a result of the *sitra achra's* vindictive activity after having been deprived of his after-meal washing due.

[413] That of Rav Dimi.

[414] The Maharal in *Nesiv HaTorah* chapter 4 writes that a wife puts the finishing touch on the creation of man since her role is to "complete" him and make him whole.

them here but it is inappropriate to expand over-much on these matters.[415] We entered into this discussion only to make the point that our Sages were extremely meticulous about after-meal washing and the consequence of ignoring it are worse than ignoring pre-meal washing. [416]

Therefore I declare that one must never, under any circumstance, flout the words of our Sages [even if we conjecture that the reasons they were uttered no longer apply].[417]

———————————————————— פירוש בנתיבות לב ————————————————————

[415] Due to their Kabbalistic origins. As an example of what the Maharal is referring to we will cite something said in the name of the *Arizal*, the foremost 16th century Kabbalist, as reported by his primary student, Rav Chaim Vital in *Shaar HaMitzvos, Parshas Ekev*. "The *sitra achra* hovers over the meal table, as stated in the *Zohar, Parshas Terumah*, and can gain power over a person at that time more than at other times... A person must be very stringent with respect to his thought-focus when he performs the after-meal washing to prevent the *sitra achra* from instigating against him."

The *sitra achra* can be viewed as "the dark side" – forces of evil created by Hashem to provide a foil to the forces of good, in order that man have free choice and be able to earn reward by subduing the forces of evil within himself and choosing good. Clearly the after-meal washing plays a role in warding off the *sitra achra*.

[416] In addition to the more severe consequences described here, up to and including murder or divorce, the *Gemara* in *Eruvin* 17b states that while soldiers are exempt from pre-meal washing due to the exigencies of their situation, they are nonetheless required to continue the practice of after-meal washing. Moreover the *Gemara* in *Chulin* 105a says explicitly that while pre-meal washing is laudatory, after-meal washing is obligatory. So it is clear that after-meal washing is more stringent not only in terms of its effects but also in terms of its practice.

[417] In summary, here are the reasons presented by the Maharal for adhering to after-meal washing in modern times: (1) Fastidious people have to wash after-meal even according to the lenient opinions; others are in the minority and should be bound by the majority attitude. (2) We must rid ourselves of contamination and impurity. (3) It is required in order to remove Sodomite salt. (4) Laxity in areas of "low-level" contamination and impurity weakens the spirit and leads to more severe weakened-spirit situations.

Here are the reasons the Maharal disagrees with the idea that the Sodomite salt risk is not a factor today: (1) Abaye records the rarity of Sodomite salt precisely to make the point that we are concerned about its risk despite its rarity, and even if his primary purpose is to inform us that its effect is supernatural, we are also, by the way, being informed of the risk. (2) There is no indication that the risk of Sodomite salt is limited by time or geographic location. (3) Our Sages are aware of factors that others are not aware of that sometimes necessitate protecting against what would otherwise be viewed as remote dangers. (4) Because salt is a recommended meal accompaniment, the risk of Sodomite salt being present on hands after-meal is greater. (5) Regular salt also presents a level of danger even when Sodomite salt is not present.

SUMMARY – נתיב מהיר

1. The significance of sustenance and the challenge of providing it cannot be overstated. That is why it is the exclusive province of Hashem. And it is why the after-meals blessing is so important. A cup of wine – a blessing-cup – is particularly apropos for the after-meals blessings because it is indicative of the extent of the bounty we enjoy from Hashem. When wine, the expression of the abundance of our bounty, is in front of us we are motivated to praise and bless Hashem on the full gamut of blessing we enjoy from Him.

2. The view of the Maharal is that wine for the blessing-cup have a modicum of water, but no more than a modicum in order for it to be suited for that purpose. Wine has a dark side in that it brings lamentation to the world. Adding water to wine dissipates that negative characteristic.

3. The Gemara enumerates ten requirements for a blessing-cup, making a point of stating that there are precisely ten requirements. The point is that these ten correspond to another ten – the ten blessings that Yitzchok bestowed on Yaakov. The Maharal demonstrates how each of the blessing-cup requirements correspond to a blessing in the sequence of Yitzchok's blessings. Fulfilling the blessing-cup requirements evoke the corresponding blessings.

   Interior and exterior cup-washing corresponds to the blessings of "dew from the skies and moisture from the earth". Assuring that the wine is undiluted corresponds to the "abundance of wine" blessing. Filling the cup to capacity corresponds to the blessing for an abundance of grain; it also leads to unbounded blessing in this world and the world-to-come.

4. "Surrounding" the blessing-cup corresponds to the blessing of "nations shall serve you". "Enrobed" corresponds to "and nations shall bow to you".

5. Taking the blessing-cup in both hands signifies power since the hands symbolize power. Transferring it to the right hand shows ascendancy. This corresponds to blessings to be dominant over brothers and ascendant over them. A further implication of this symbolism is that the power of rulership belongs to the people and it is their responsibility to accept the rulership of the king on themselves.

6. Lifting the blessing-cup a *tefach* off the ground signifies the blessing of "Your mother's sons will bow to you". Gazing at it signifies "Those who curse you shall be cursed". The Gemara advises the holder of the blessing-cup to present from it to his wife, children and household members in order to spread the blessing to them as well.

7. The six blessings that correspond to the ascendancy of Yaakov over Esav are omitted today, according to one view in the *Gemara*, since in our present state of exile those blessings are not in effect.

   There is a version of the *Gemara* text that does not count sharing the blessing cup with family members as one of the ten but rather counts picking up with both hands and transferring to the right hand as two separate actions. The Maharal is uncomfortable with this text version since it does not preserve the correspondence between the ten blessing cup actions and the ten blessings that Yitzchok bestowed on Yaakov. He ultimately rejects it since the preponderant text version is the one he originally presented, that counts blessing-cup sharing as one of the ten, and considers picking up with both hands and transferring to the right hand a single action.

8. There are four blessings in the after-meals blessing set. The first three are biblical in origin; the last is Rabbinic. The texts of these blessings were composed at different times and by different individuals. Moshe composed the first blessing, specifically over food, when the miracle of the *mon* started. Yehoshua composed the second blessing, over the land, when he led the nation into the land of Israel. Dovid and Shlomo composed the text of the third blessing, over Yerushalayim and the Temple (although our text was revised to reflect the fact that the Temple was subsequently destroyed). The last, Rabbinic blessing of "the Good and Bestower of good" was instituted in Yavneh in commemoration of those murdered in Beitar.

   The Maharal presents several approaches to understanding the relevance of the four blessings to an after-meal setting. The first views the first three blessings as relating in some fashion to food – either directly, or via the food blessings of the land, or via the enhancements to the quality of our food through the Temple.

9. The second approach to understanding the sequence of blessings is to view them as a progression of completeness. First, man's need for nutritional completeness are satisfied; this is applicable to all mankind. Then Yisroel's homeland needs are satisfied through their inheritance of the land of Israel. Then Yisroel's "no holds barred" completeness was achieved through Yerushalayim and the Temple.

10. The third approach is a progression of sanctity, moving from the mundane, food completeness, to the land, which is physical but has a spiritual component as well, to the Temple, which was completely spiritual.

11. The next approach is again food-centric: the first blessing refers to food itself. The next blessing refers to a receptacle for delivering the blessing of food – that is, the land. The Temple, subject of the third blessing, is the conduit that channels blessing from Above to the physical realm.

The fourth blessing notes Hashem's extreme benevolence toward Yisroel. Even at a time when we were apparently at our lowest point after the destruction of the Temple, the events at Beitar demonstrated that Hashem continues to be benevolent toward us.

12. The Maharal explains why the phrase, "… and through His benevolence" in the introductory responsive *mezuman* portion of the after-meals blessing is preferable to the variant, "'… and from [part of] His benevolence". The latter phrase seem to limit Hashem's capabilities. Similarly the Maharal explains why the phrase "and through His benevolence, He has given **us** life" is preferable to the variant "and through His benevolence, [He has given life]". The latter phrase seems to divorce us, personally, from the blessing. Others hold that to say "us" is again limiting, since Hashem's benevolence is universal but the Maharal nonetheless holds that it is preferable to explicitly include ourselves as blessing recipients.

13. The formula in the responsive introductory portion requires a build-up of praise to Hashem, such that each successive response adds to what was said before it.

14. Hashem utilizes three "conduits" to channel sustenance to His creations . *Chen* is for the few who have actually earned what Hashem bestows upon them. *Chesed,* benevolence, is for those who are need more than they are entitled to. *Rachamim* is for those incapable of earning their sustenance. Everyone, however, gains their life-flow from the benevolence conduit because that is unrestricted and universal – it is an intrinsic property of Hashem and extends even to the world -to-come.

15. The phrase, "nourishment is never withheld from us and will never be withheld from us…" has several variants. The one just cited uses a "soft" grammatical paradigm with the emphasis on the nourishment, which was not and will not be withheld from us. Another variant uses a "hard" grammatical paradigm with is translated, "Hashem has never withheld and will never withhold nourishment from us"; here the emphasis is on Hashem, the provider, rather than on the nourishment, which is provided. Both variants are valid but to change grammatical paradigms in mid-sentence would seem illogical – although an argument can be made that it is also sensible to use the "hard" paradigm first, to establish that we recognize Hashem as the provider, then switch to the more common "soft" paradigm.

16. Hashem created the universe in order that Yisroel have a setting to perpetuate the greatness of His name. He provides sustenance to the world to enable that perpetuation to continue and he does this via his "great name", the *Havaya* name. The blessing enumerates three progressively higher levels of sustenance that Hashem provides mankind, as well as enumerating sustenance for non-human creatures.

17. We declare that Hashem nourishes "everything" to make it clear that Hashem intrinsically yearns and desires to sustain everything, independent of any potential recipient. Hashem will only provide sustenance when it is asked for and thus appreciated. We declare that Hashem nourishes "everything" to make it clear that we do appreciate and request his beneficence.

18. The second blessing, for the land, is bracketed front and back by expressions of gratitude to Hashem for providing us long-term livelihood in the form of the land. In this blessing we thank Hashem for all the benefits that Israel has over other lands, and for its capacity to accommodate all members of Yisroel, no matter how many of us there are.

19. The three attributes of the land of Israel – appealing, good and spacious – came about in the merit of

our forefathers, to whom the land was originally given. "Appealing" is in the merit of Avrohom. "Good" is in the merit of Yaakov. "Spacious" is in the merit of Yitzchok.

20. With *bris*, Torah and statutes Hashem made man complete in every respect – for our bodies he gave us the *bris* covenant which is fulfilled on our physical persons and brings our bodies to a state of perfection, for our intellects he gave us the Torah which brings our minds to a state of perfection and for our animated spirit he gave us the statutes which the spirit fulfills even though they are beyond comprehension, and thereby brings our spirit to a state of perfection. These three items were also given to us in the merit of the forefathers. *Bris* is associated with Avrohom. Statutes are in the merit of Yitzchok. The Torah is in the merit of Yaakov.

21. Life, favor and benevolence is the third triad that is associated with our forefathers. The tenth benefit in this blessing is "for the provision of food…" which is the single most overarching benefit. There is significance in its being, specifically, tenth. Because of its importance it is not associated with any one of the forefathers.

22. Hashem provides our needs whether they are regularly scheduled or intermittent. We thank Him for the set of ten benefits mentioned in the previous section. We thank and bless Him for providing us that which we need for our survival and for that which we enjoy but do not need for our survival.

23. Just as the land of Israel is set apart from other lands in its sanctity so must Yisroel be set apart and sanctified and that is accomplished through *Milah*, which separates us from lowliness. That is why *Milah* appears in the land blessing. The Torah further sets us apart by elevating us to a higher level of sanctity, breaking the bond with physicality entirely. It was because of the spiritual nature of the land that we merited *Bris* and Torah and were thereby transformed into a totally differentiated and G-dly people.

24. The Torah is the more exalted of the covenants between Hashem and Yisroel but because *Milah* is engraved on our bodies it takes precedence in this blessing. Moreover "covenant" is mentioned more times in connection with *Milah* than it is in connection with Torah, for the same reason.

25. One possible reason the second blessing contains a double thanks is because we are thanking Hashem both for our original entry into it and for the second entry when we returned to build the second Temple. The sanctity of the land was different when we re-entered it than it was when we first entered it so a second invocation of thanks is appropriate. Moreover bracketing the blessing with thanks beginning and end indicates a complete thanks, just as the "blessed are You…" formula at the beginning and end of a typical blessing indicates complete blessing.

On a deeper level the double thanks is another way of expressing the fact that we as well as our land are completely under the dominion of Hashem.

26. One must not lump other lands together with Israel in the land blessing, nor may one add additional praises to the prescribed "…He who builds Yerushalayim with mercy". We end with a blessing whose wording indicates that the land of Israel is under the direct supervision of Hashem, with no intermediary.

27. We recite the third blessing for the Temple in the after-meals blessings because the Temple is the ultimate form of completion, as mentioned earlier. We add other apparently unrelated requests to this blessing so that they too might enjoy wholeness and completion. We appeal to Hashem for this wholeness on the basis of his role as our Father and his role as our King. We mention the Davidic dynasty because this is an integral component of our wholeness.

The Maharal concludes this section with a grammatical discussion to determine the proper pronunciation of two of the words in the blessing.

28. Because Shabbos and Yerushalayim are both holy, we pay homage to Shabbos in the Yerushalayim blessing. It is not appropriate to open or close this blessing with requests for mercy because that runs counter to the upbeat spirit of Shabbos. We may and do, however, ask for consolation over the ancient sorrow of the destruction of the Temple in this blessing.

29. In general one may not recite "Omain" at the conclusion of one's own blessing because "Omain" is designed to reinforce the blessing itself; one cannot reinforce what he himself has just uttered. However one may recite "Omain" at the conclusion of one's own Yerushalayim blessing because it represents the

ultimate level of completeness after the prior two blessings. Some, though, understand that one may self-answer "Omain" at the end of any sequence of blessings.

30. The fourth (Good and Bestower of good) blessing mentions Hashem's Kingship three times, once for the sake of that blessing itself, once for the third (Yerushalayim) blessing, which must omit its own Kingship mention, and once for the second (land) blessing. This section discusses why the Kingship mentions are omitted from the second and third blessings, and why, once omitted, compensatory mentions must be added in the fourth blessing.

31. The fourth blessing contains ten praises to Hashem since it depicts Hashem as intrinsically good and as the universal conferrer of good; ten represents "ultimate" in this context. Hashem's attribute of goodness is timeless and we so indicate in this blessing. Hashem's flow of beneficence is without end so, fittingly, this blessing does not have a concluding invocation, signifying its endlessness.

32. The *Tosfos* commentary justifies the then-prevalent custom to ignore the *mayim acharonim* obligation on the basis that the primary reason given for it, the removal of Sodomite salt is (according to Tosfos) not relevant today. However, the Maharal takes strong issue with this omission. He explains why in the forthcoming sections.

33. Blessing Hashem must be undertaken in a state of spiritual purity as well as physical cleanliness. That is why we must wash our hands after meals and prior to reciting the after-meal blessings. The *Gemara* describes a further oil-based cleansing that brings an additional level of purity but we are not on a level where we can be receptive to that additional purity so this custom has been abandoned.

   Removing Sodomite salt is an additional reason for *mayim acharonim* but it is not the only reason. The Maharal explains why even this reason is in effect today and why geography is also not a factor in determining the danger from Sodomite salt.

34. Laxity in performing pre-meal washing, which was instituted to create a state of purity before eating, leads to extremes of ritual uncleanliness, up to and including eating non-kosher meat. Similarly laxity in performing post-meal washing, which was instituted to distance oneself from contamination prior to the after-meal blessing is debilitating to the spirit and can lead to extremes up to and including murder.

End Notes

פירוש בנתיבות לב

ⁱ **On Wine**

Wine – the Bright Side

The Maharal in *Chidushei Aggados* on *Sanhedrin* 70a explains the significance of wine in detail. Wine is a powerful potion, the Maharal writes, because it has strong spiritual as well as physical characteristics. It "gladdens both Hashem and men". This is evident in the process by which wine is derived. It originates from the hidden interior of the grape and is thus more associated with the hidden (spiritual) world than with the open and exposed physical world. In fact, as the Maharal points out in *Drush al HaMitzvos*, the *Gematria* value of wine in Hebrew, יין, *yayin*, is 70, the same value as the word for "secret", סוד, *sod*. Indeed the reward reserved for the righteous in the world-to-come is metaphorically compared to "wine secreted in grapes" to highlight its hidden nature.

Because of its spiritual properties wine should by rights be reserved for spiritual things – the *Gemara* gives as an example, comforting mourners. It is also utilized as an instrument by which to reward the wicked while they are yet in this world for their paltry good deeds, so as to avoid the need for rewarding them in the world-to-come. The reward for good deeds is spiritual so wine, with its spiritual properties, is ideal for this purpose.

Wine – the Deleterious Side

Because wine is spiritual in nature but resides in a physical context it is susceptible to misuse, with generally catastrophic results, up to and including death. This is why the *Gemara* says that wine brings lamentation to the world (see footnote 22). Wine has a beneficial effect on people who are generally spiritual – it attenuates wisdom in those who are wise – but it has a negative effect on people who tend toward the physical, as can be seen in the typical effects of drunkenness on such people.

What is the origin of this negative effect? In *Drush al HaMitzvos*, the Maharal explains that wine is by nature associated with hiddenness but when it is extracted from its hidden state in the grape, bottled and imbibed it is no longer covert, it is exposed, and in the process it become a powerful "exposure agent" that acts upon those who drink it. That is why the *Gemara* in *Eruvin* 65a says, "When wine enters, secrets emerge". The Torah (*Beraishis* 9, beginning at verse 20) relates the unfortunate consequences suffered by Noach when he planted a vineyard after exiting the ark, over-imbibed and allowed his nakedness to be exposed. This too is an instance of the "exposure agent" at work, to disastrous effect.

The *Gemara* says that the Torah portion relating the effects of Noach's encounter with wine has thirteen instances of the letter *vov* (vowelized with the *patach* sound, the Maharal explains) which in combination sounds like a cry of dismay: *vay!* The course of human history was changed detrimentally as a result of those events, justifying cries of dismay. The significance of the number thirteen is that complete good is described by the thirteen attributes of Hashem's mercy listed in *Shmos* 34:6-7. The thirteen instances of the letter *vov* show that the effects of the misuse of wine are completely bad – diametrically opposite the complete good described by Hashem's thirteen attributes.

(Parenthetically, the expression גם זו לטובה, *gam zu l'tova*, "this too shall be for the good", which is commonly said when hearing apparently bad news as a statement of faith in Hashem's ability to turn what appears at first glance to be bad into a blessing, uses the word זו, *zu*, instead of the more common זה, *zeh*, because the numeric value of זו is thirteen. This signifies that even something that appears totally bad, with no redeeming value, can be, and with faith, will be, transformed by Hashem into good! See *Nesiv HaBitachon* Chapter 1 for more on this topic.)

Wine – the Somber Side

In *Gevuros Hashem* Chapter 60 the Maharal explains that wine symbolizes a heavenly decree. As an example (from Chapter 10 of *Gevuros Hashem*), when Yosef revealed himself to his brothers and urged them to go to Israel and return to Egypt with his father Yaakov, Yaakov's extended family and all their possessions (*Beraishis* 45) Yosef sent back with them several items for his father that carried a hidden significance. One of them, says Rashi on verse 23, based on a *Gemara* in *Megillah* 16b) was יין ישן, *yayin yoshon*, aged wine, since "the minds of old people takes delight in aged wine".

The Maharal explains that this wine was an allusion to the heavenly decree communicated to Avrohom that his descendants would find refuge in Egypt but would be enslaved there shortly thereafter. In sending the aged wine to his father Yaakov, Yosef was hinting to Yaakov that he should not fear descending to Egypt because that particular decree, as difficult as though it may be, was part of the divine plan that would ultimately lead to Yisroel's redemption. The *Gematria* value of *yayin yoshon* is 430, the precise number of years that were decreed for the Egyptian exile. Yosef intended that Yaakov, once assured of this, would "take delight" through the message of the "aged wine".

Conclusion

Wine is thus a primarily spiritual substance but it must be handled with care because it can be a two-edged sword, beneficial to some, in the right contexts, but extremely harmful to others, who misuse it.

Rav Boruch Sorotzkin *z"tl* points out a critical difference between the feast that our forefather Yaakov prepared for his father Yitzchok prior to obtaining the blessings (*Beraishis* 27) and the feast that his earthly brother Esav prepared. In verse 25 the Torah reports that Yaakov brought wine to accompany the feast and Yitzchok partook of it. But there is no indication that Esav did the same. The reason is simple. To Yaakov, wine is a spiritual "elevator" and enhances the power of blessing, as

---

explained earlier. It was only natural to bring wine to a feast that was a precursor to blessing. But Esav's wine experience was completely different. To him wine is an exposer of his base and corrupt inner self. It was the last beverage he would think to bring to a feast that would end, he hoped, in his receiving blessing.

It behooves us to remember that as Jews we are primarily spiritual beings but in our weakened *galus* state – especially in the context of the decadent world we live in – it is easy to succumb to physicality. We need to be realistically self-aware and not delude ourselves into imagining that, with our wine-drinking, we are climbing the heights of *ruchnius* while in reality we are over-indulging ourselves into the depths of an animalistic, Esav-like *gashmiusdike* state.

ⁱⁱ **More on the Two-Hand Symbolism**

The Maharal at the beginning of *Derech Chaim*, his work on tractate *Avos*, explains that while deviation to one side or another symbolizes finiteness, a center-line that does not deviate to either side symbolizes infinity. Yisroel, in particular are referred to as "Hashem's handiwork", מעשי ידיו, literally work of his **hands**, with the emphasis on the plural of hands.

Each hand individually represents a deviation to either the left or right side. But when both hands are employed in a balanced fashion they counteract their respective pulls to the side and the result is adherence to a perfect center. That which is created with "hands" in this manner, namely Yisroel, is free of any deviation from the center-line and therefore endures forever.

The concept the Maharal is describing in the context of the blessing-cup is different in that the reference is to both hands of a person, not of Hashem, and the intended result of the symbolism is not eternity as a result of a counterbalancing of extremes but rather universality as a result of inclusion of extremes and the area that spans them. Nonetheless, there is a common theme in that the two-hand symbolism in both usages implies a kind of perfection. In *Derech Hashem* the perfection is in the form of eternity. Here it is in the form of universality.

ⁱⁱⁱ **The Power of Thought and the Evil Eye**

The secular world views thought as an intangible brain activity with no implication beyond micro-current flowing through neurons. It is actions that count, they say, and thoughts that do not lead to actions have no import and are therefore meaningless.

This, however, is not the Jewish perspective on thought. The subject is wide-ranging and is worthy of a book in its own right. In this essay we will summarize the Jewish perspective on thought with a focus on *ayin hora*, or evil eye – one of the better known areas where the reality of thought plays a significant role.

The Reality and Potency of Thought

The 10th of the *Rambam's* 13 principles of faith is that Hashem, "…knows all the deeds of human beings and their thoughts…". This is evident in that there are commandments that are purely thought-based, such as belief in Hashem. There are also prohibitions that are triggered by motivation such as, "Do not… place a stumbling block before the blind" (*Vayikra* 19:14) which encompasses intentionally giving bad advice in order to achieve personal gain. The verse continues, "and you shall fear your G-d". *Rashi* explains that the verse adds this phrase as a wake-up call to the advice-giver. He might want to claim that his advice was well-meant and not intended for his own benefit, so the verse exhorts him to remember that Hashem knows his motivations and thoughts and if they are in fact selfish he will have to face the consequences.

Moreover the prohibition against idolatry, *avodah zara*, can actually be transgressed purely through thought. The Maharal in *Chidushei Aggados, Kiddushin* 40a, explains why. He writes that since Hashem is all-encompassing, he encompasses our thoughts as part of the larger whole; in fact our intellects, being non-physical, are especially connected to Hashem. A person who harbors heretical thoughts is in effect attempting to create an "island" that is not a part of, and isolated from Hashem. He is attempting to disconnect his intellect from Hashem. This is an act of rebellion that is as serious as, if not more serious than, than physically worshiping idols. In his *Drasho l'Shabbos Shuva* the Maharal adds that this behavior is actually destructive to the mind.

It is clear that our thoughts are not ours alone. They are known outside of ourselves and have effects that extend beyond our minds.

Beyond that, thoughts have an effect on the physical world. See *Nefesh HaChaim, Shaar Aleph*, and in particular chapters 4 and 14, where Rav Chaim Volozhiner explains that our actions, words and **thoughts** have the power to affect the celestial worlds, and that since the celestial worlds control the flow of Hashem's beneficence to our own world, improper thoughts and motivations can negatively affect events in our physical world, and proper thoughts and motivations can positively affect events in our physical world. He cites the verse, "He forms their hearts together, He understands all their deeds" (*Tehillim* 33:15) – the same verse cited by the *Rambam* in support of his 10th principle.

Thoughts, then, have both a reality and a potency outside our minds. Not only do they accrue merit or demerit to their "owners" but they also affect the world-at-large as well.

The Power of an Individual's Thoughts and the Evil Eye

It is also possible for an individual's thoughts to have a positive or negative effect even on specific people. In *Michtav MiEliyahu* v.3 pages 96-97 Rav Eliyahu Dessler explains that Hashem created man, as the Torah teaches, "in the image of G-d" (*Beraishis* 9:6) and that means that Hashem gave man capabilities "resembling" His own, as it were. Now, Hashem created the world by willing it into existence (in ten "steps", as discussed by our Sages). We were granted a similar power to affect reality by willing things to happen. Our thoughts actually create an "energy" that triggers events.

From a practical standpoint these events often do not come to fruition because the object of our wish may himself have wishes that run counter to our own and the energy created by his wishes may overpower and negate the energy of our own wishes. Possibly he has merits that shield him from the negative effects of our wishes.

Nonetheless, even if the energy does not come to fruition on its intended object, it remains in existence and must find an "outlet". The Maharal in Chapter 2 of *Beer Hagolah* compares this pent-up energy to throwing a rock with force. If it hits its target the force is expended but if it is blocked it bounces back and rebounds on the person who did the throwing. More on this in footnote 88 in connection with the parameters that govern the penalty for *aidim zomimim* (false witnesses).

Rav Dessler writes that if all humankind joined in willing a common goal it would be in its power to bring it about since there would be no counter for all the common thought-energy created thereby. Because that common goal might not be a good one, Hashem blocked such events from taking place by making it impossible for mankind to unite for an evil common goal – this is the underlying explanation of the events of the tower of *Bavel* (see *Beraishis* 11). Humankind will only be able to join in a common goal at the end of days when all will join in service to Hashem and there will no longer be a motivation toward evil.

Rav Chaim Friedlander, citing Rav Dessler and the *Chazon Ish*, whom we will quote shortly, discusses this as well in *Sifsei Chaim, Pirkei Emunah V'Hashgacha*, page 393 and explains that this concept is the basis behind *ayin horah*, or "evil eye". A very common impetus for willing something negative to happen to another person is jealousy or simply an inability to begrudge someone else their good fortune. The negative energy released is real and dangerous and thus our Sages urge us to be circumspect about our possessions and good fortune and avoid ostentation and braggadocio.

(It is called "evil eye" and not "evil thought" because the process of casting ill-will on a person begins with seeing him or his possessions; see footnote 85. See also *Chidushei Aggados* on *Baba Metziah* 42a where the Maharal writes that the expression "evil **eye**" derives from the fact that the eye is inherently limited. Contrary to the popular expression "as far as they eye can see", the Maharal points out that the eye's range is very constrained and there is far more that the eye **cannot** see. The nature of blessing, on the other hand, is that it is unconstrained. Thus "eye" connotes the opposite of blessing.)

What are the mechanics behind this negative thought energy and its ability to have a harmful effect on others? Rav Dessler, in *Michtav MiEliyahu* 4, p. 6, explains that no man is a spiritual island; we are all interconnected at our spiritual roots and are therefore interdependent. We all derive some degree of spiritual energy from every other being. The Maharal in *Chidushei Aggados* on *Horiyos* 10a expresses a similar concept. He compares Yisroel to an organism with many interdependent parts, each part drawing energy from, and providing energy to, the other parts.

People who do not begrudge others their good fortune, whose very existence bothers them, blot these others out from any of their emanations of positive spiritual energy. Therefore, to the extent that the web of interdependencies that sustains the evil eye victim relies on the evil eye perpetrator, the victim is cut off from a vital life source. He is weakened, vulnerable and susceptible to harm.

In this light we understand that *ayin horah* is very real and not at all a "superstition". It is discussed in *Gemara* and cited as a factor affecting Jewish law – *halacha*. For example, one may not display a lost object, even for its own benefit (air it out, etc.) if visitors are present because it may be damaged, as *Rashi* explains, by *ayin horah* of the visitors (*Baba Metziah* 30a). One may not stand in the field of his fellow when the crop is ripe because, as *Rashi* explains, he may damage it through his *ayin horah* (*Baba Basra* 2b). Two brothers, or a father and son, may not be called consecutively to the Torah because of *ayin horah* (*Shulchan Aruch Orach Chaim* 141:6). And, soberingly, the *Gemara* in *Baba Metziah* 107b says that Rav went to a cemetery, recited incantations over the individual graves to ascertain the cause of death and reported that ninety-nine percent died through *ayin horah*, and only one percent through natural causes.

In fact, the Maharal in *Gur Aryeh Beraishis* 21:14 cites a *R'em* who says that even though the *Gemara* in *Bava Metzia* 87a states that sickness did not come onto the world scene until the time of Yaakov, that applied only to divinely-induced sickness, but sickness as a result of evil eye existed even before the time of Yaakov. The *R'em* says that just as a person could have been injured by a sword prior to the time of Yaakov, so could a person have been injured by evil eye, so potent is its power.

The *Chazon Ish* discusses the power of thought to affect events in *Likutim, Baba Basra* 14, #21. He writes, citing several sources in the *Gemara*, that a person's thoughts can imperceptibly trigger real-world events and that this is one of the enigmatic aspects of creation. A fleeting thought, he says, can wreak serious destruction on substantial physical structures. Therefore when people gossip about a successful venture, they jeopardize it since that can cause jealousy and result in the evil eye.

Evil Eye in the Context of Divine Justice

One must keep in mind, the *Chazon Ish*, cautions, that Hashem's will is behind all events and that if it were not the will of Hashem for damage to occur no evil eye could instigate it. The evil eye in this respect is one of the tools in Hashem's arsenal, so to speak, that He uses to carry out His will. [It is no different from a gun wielded by a criminal – which also appears to cause harm even though it is also only an agent of Hashem in carrying out His will.]

In this light it is clear that one can only suffer from an evil eye as a result of a divine decree. Negative divine decrees are typically the outcome of improper actions. One way a person can bring evil eye vulnerability on himself is by ostentatiously flaunting possessions or attributes in a manner that evokes jealousy in others. While jealousy is improper, a jealous person nonetheless suffers and a person who causes others to be jealous is responsible for their suffering. This can activate the divine attribute of justice and cause a revaluation of his entitlement to the things he was flaunting, in light of the pain he caused to others by making them jealous of him – and to possibly lose those things (from *Michtav MiEliyahu* 3, p. 313).

(It is also plausible, the *Chazon Ish* says, that the greater the person, the greater the potency of his "eye" in both positive and negative senses. There are also factors that affect susceptibility to the evil eye – for example there are times when Hashem's attribute of strict justice is dominant and people are judged more harshly than they would be otherwise. At such times the evil eye is more likely to have its negative effect.)

The *Netziv* in *Ha'emek Dovor* on *Beraishis* 37:13, in *Harchev Dovor* states that to gain divine protection from dangers posed by humans, who have free choice, requires a greater degree of merit than would be required to gain divine protection from non-human dangers. The *Sifsei Chaim* cited abovesays that this applies to evil eye as well.

Evil Eye as a "Klippo"

Rav Shlomo Alkabetz, in his Kabbalah-based work *Shoresh Yishai* on *Rus*, associates the evil eye with a *klippah*, a spiritual entity rooted in impurity. *Klippos*, like all spiritual entities, are agents of Hashem, but these particular agents are enforcers when punishment is called for. The *klippah* associated with the evil eye is named *Ra'ah*, which means "evil". It attaches itself to that which a miserly eye is cast upon, infecting it and using it as a "base" from which to emanate harm.

Why, asks Rav Alkabetz (on *Rus* 2.2), did Boaz warn Rus not to collect harvest leavings from fields other than his own? The answer is that some field owners resented the stricture to permit the poor to collect the leavings. They possessed an *ayin ra'ah*, or evil eye, and thereby invoked the *klippah* named *Ra'ah*, which attached itself to the leavings in their fields. Gathering and using those leavings would thus bring misfortune to the hapless poor person who collected them. Boaz was warning Rus to avoid those harmful leavings and to stick with those in his own field since, unlike some of the other field owners, Boaz had an *ayin tova*, a benevolent eye, and his leavings would thus not be harmful to the leaving-collectors. (See *Mishlei* 23:6-8: "Do not dine upon the bread of a person with evil eye and do not desire his delicacies… He will tell you to eat and drink, but his heart is not with you… You will vomit out your morsel that you ate…".)

The Maharal on Evil Eye

The Maharal devotes *Nesiv Ayin Tov* ("a good eye") of *Nesivos Olam* to discussing this subject. Similar to Rav Alkabetz, but without referencing *Klippos*, he notes, based on a *Gemara* in *Sotah* 38b, that the evil eye has contaminating properties and substances infected with it are outside the pale. Attempting to benefit from these substances is equivalent to attempting to benefit from substances that are *tameh*, spiritually befouled, and is actually (per the *Gemara*) prohibited. Rav Dessler explains this to mean that since benevolence is one of the world's foundations, a person who lacks it – such as a person who possesses an evil eye – shakes the world's very foundations and weakens his own attachment to existence as well as the attachment of those who associate with him, by causing them to benefit from his evil-eye-infected possessions. The prohibition against benefiting from these substances is to safeguard people from this danger.

The Maharal also writes that the negative energy emanated by a person with an *ayin horah* is so palpable that birds can actually sense it and most of them will therefore avoid traps set for them because they can detect the negative energy of the bird-trappers. In discussing the relationship between *ayin horah* and the *egla arufa* ritual he states that *ayin horah* can kill – as borne out by the *Gemara* in *Baba Metziah* cited above – and he labels the person casting the *ayin horah* a murderer.

The Maharal concludes the *Nesiv* with, "A person should take extreme care to protect his possessions from *ayin horah*, as our Sages taught, 'blessing devolves only on items that are hidden from the eye' (*Taanis* 8b) as the verse indicates, 'Hashem will order the blessing to be with you in your granaries' (*Devarim* 28:8). [The blessing takes effect when the produce is hidden in the granaries and not when it is exposed.]

Antidotes for Evil Eye

The first line of defense against the evil eye is circumspection. As noted above, flying below the radar with respect to one's possessions and attributes inoculates them against the evil eye. However we are not hermits and it is not always possible to avoid exposing one's assets to others.

The *Gemara* in *Brachos* 55a prescribes advice for those who wish to protect themselves from the evil eye. It suggests that one should grasp his right thumb in [the palm of] his left hand, and his left thumb in [the palm of] his right hand and say, אנא פלוני בר פלונית מזרעא דיוסף קאתינא דלא שלטא ביה עינא בישא. "I, *Ploni* [his name] son of *Plonis* [his mother's name] am a descendant of Yosef, who was immune to the evil eye". The *Gemara* goes on to explain why Yosef was immune to the evil eye, as we will discuss shortly. The origin of this advice is a *Gemara* in *Brachos* 20a which states that Rabbi Yochanan did, for good reason, something that could cause the evil eye but claimed immunity from it as a descendant of Yosef. The commentators cite verses to explain that all Jews are considered the spiritual descendants of Yosef even if they are not his physical descendants, so we may all use this formula.

Rav Chaim Kanievsky א"שליט, as cited in *Sefer Doleh U'Mashkeh* p. 370 and in *Sefer Segulas Rabboseinu* p. 138 recommends this practice to those who fear the evil eye. He also specified that the mother's name, rather than the father's name (as some versions of the *Gemara* have it) be used in the formula.

The *Ben Ish Chai* in *Sefer Ben Yehoyada* on the *Gemara* in *Brachos* provides a *Kabbalah*-based reason for the grasping of the thumbs. He explains that the thumbs, which are separate from the other fingers, represent Yisroel, who are separate from the other nations. The other four fingers with the palm, in which the opposing thumb is grasped, contain thirteen joints (three on each finger plus the wrist) which is the *Gematria* numeric value of אחד, *echod*, one, and of אהבה, *ahava*, love. Grasping the thumbs in the manner described creates a unity with a value of twenty-six (thirteen doubled) which is the *Gematria* value of Hashem's ineffable name (*yud* followed by *hai* following by *vov* followed by *hai*). Presumably he means that this action envelopes Yisroel (thumbs) in our **love** of Hashem (who is **One**) and places us under the protection of Hashem via invocation of his ineffable name. More information on this intriguing shield against the evil eye can be found in *Sefer Segulas Rabboseinu* by Yishai Mazalmian (5763).

Finally, if we are claiming protection from the evil eye as descendants of Yosef it behooves us to understand why Yosef was immune to the evil eye and attempt to emulate him as best we can. The *Gemaros* in *Brachos* gives two reasons. The first is based on the blessings Yaakov gave the sons of Yosef (*Beraishis* 48:16). In those blessings he compared the descendants of Yosef to fish, who are immune to the evil eye because they are concealed by the water. As explained above, concealment of one's assets is the first line of defense against the evil eye. The second reason is that Yosef steadfastly resisted the blandishments of the wife of Potiphar (*Beraishis* 39) and refused to sin with her – as the *Gemara* puts it, "the eye that refused to sate itself on that which did not belong to him is shielded from the evil eye".

Rav Dessler (*Michtav MiEliyahu* 4 p. 6) explains that both properties derive from fish. Since they live under water, not only are they shielded from the gaze of others, but they live in their own world, isolated from the goings-on in the dry-land world around them. They are not seen by the "outside" and they do not see, and therefore cannot covet, what others have on the outside.

If we inculcate both these properties of Yosef into our own lives – that is, we are circumspect with our possessions and we build walls around ourselves to avoid the temptations of the outside world, and thus do not cast our eye on the possession of others – we will be secure, like Yosef, against *ayin hora*. In that event we can legitimately call ourselves Yosef's descendants and utilize the *Gemara's segulah* with a clean conscience.

May Hashem protect us from the *ayin horah* **of** others and bless us to project only *ayin tov* **onto** others.

iv **The Ashes of Yitzchok**

Vayikra 26:42 relates that when we are in the depths of exile, Hashem "remembers" the merits of the forefathers Avrohom and Yaakov in our favor. But the verse does not utilize "remembers" with respect to our forefather Yitzchok. Why this distinction? Rashi on the cited verse explains that Yitzchok is distinguished because of the *Akeida* (see *Beraishis* 22) – a seminal event in Jewish history wherein Hashem tested Avrohom, Yitzchok's father, by commanding him to offer Yitzchok as a sacrifice and at the last moment, just as Yitzchok was about to be slaughtered, commanded him to desist. Avrohom offered a ram as a sacrifice instead of his son, and, as Rashi, based on a *Medrash Tanchuma* points out in *Beraishis* 22:13, over every sacrificial act that Avrohom performed on the ram, he prayed, "May it be Your will that this should be deemed as if it were being done to my son: as if my son were slaughtered, as if his blood were sprinkled, as if my son were flayed, as if he were burnt and reduced to ashes."

Because Yitzchok was willing to sacrifice his life to fulfill Hashem's command, his signature attribute is *din*, strict, untempered justice. Because of Yitzchok's willingness to make the supreme sacrifice to fulfill Hashem's command, his merit stands in our favor to this day – as Rashi points out on *Vayikra* 26:42, "Yitzchok's ashes [always] appear before Me, gathered up and placed upon the altar". Avrohom envisioned himself actually sacrificing Yitzchok when he sacrificed the ram, so the ram's ashes are a proxy for Yitzchok's ashes. Hashem does not have to "remember" the merit of Yitzchok as he does the merit of Avrohom and Yaakov because the mound of ashes is always present in front of Him, as it were, a constant reminder.

As we explained in footnote 236, from the standpoint of strict justice there are no "entitlements" since no one can measure up to the standard of strict justice. The best we can hope for is that we find favor in Hashem's eyes, as it were, and to be gifted with sustenance that is not conditioned on merit. In effect we are acknowledging that by Hashem's strict standards we are nothing, as the Maharal speaks out in *Gevuros Hashem* Chapter 64. This is Yitzchok's legacy; it is represented by the mound of ashes – the epitome of nothingness, of lack of existence. This is the merit of Yitzchok that continually stands us in good stead. When Hashem sees Yitzchok's mound of ashes it invokes His conduct of unconditional mercy; the conduct that enables us to enjoy his beneficence even though we do not deserve it.

(This is why there is such an emphasis on the *Akeida* on *Rosh HaShana* when our fate is determined for the new year. We appeal to that aspect of Hashem's comportment with us that is not contingent on our measuring up to the strict justice standard.)

v **More on *Milah***

Milah – Enabler of Existence

In addition to removing the barrier to a relationship between Hashem and Yisroel, as detailed in footnote 261, *Milah*, on a general level, enables a relationship between Hashem and mankind. The *Gemara* in *Nedarim* 31b states that, "*Milah* is significant because if not for *Milah* Hashem would not have created His world". The Maharal in *Chidushei Aggados* on that *Gemara* writes that the world would have no basis for existence without *Milah* because *Milah* is the covenant between Hashem and mankind and without it there would be no relationship between Hashem and mankind. Since the world was created for the sake of that relationship there would be no point in the world persisting otherwise. (As we discussed in footnote 261, Yisroel is mankind's "representative" in mankind's relationship with Hashem which is why *Milah* is specifically mandated for Jews. See *Rambam, Mishna Torah, Melachim* 10:7.)

Targum Onkelos translates "*Bris*" as קיימא, *kayama*, a force that maintains. *Bris Milah* is the "maintainer" of the relationship between Hashem and mankind.

Milah Prevents Destruction

The Maharal in *Gur Aryeh* on *Beraishis* 41:55 discusses why Yosef demanded that the Egyptians circumcise themselves prior to his selling them food during the years of famine. The intent was not conversion – we do not encourage non-Jews to convert – but rather, Yosef, with his divine vision, realized that the reason the produce that the Egyptians themselves hoarded for the famine rotted was because the Egyptians were uncircumcised. *Milah* is a "maintainer"; it promotes persistence. Lack of *Milah* – the presence of the foreskin – leads to the opposite: rotting and disintegration. That is why the private produce of the Egyptians rotted and that is why Yosef commanded them to circumcise themselves.

Milah – Our Connection with the Metaphysical

Although *Milah* is a physical act on a physical person it is essentially metaphysical in nature in that it elevates man to a state where he can have a connection with Hashem. In *Chidushei Aggados* on *Nedarim* 31a the Maharal writes that Milah is on the eighth day because eight is step beyond the physical world. The physical world is represented by seven – a central point (1) with arcs extending towards each of the four points of the compass (4), up and down (2). The world, which was created in seven days, is bound by time and space. Eight projects us into a metaphysical world that is not limited by those boundaries.

The Maharal often distinguishes between matter and form. Matter is physical. Form is not. Eight-day *Milah* is in the category of metaphysical form.

The *Gemara* in *Nedarim* 31a declares, "Great is *Milah* in that it did not let pass a delay of even one hour on the part of the righteous Moshe". The reference is to the incident described in *Shmos* 4:25-26 (see the commentary of *Rashi*) where, despite Moshe's greatness, his life was at risk because he briefly tarried before performing *Milah* on his son. Why is this indicative of the greatness of *Milah*? The reason *Milah* is unforgiving of delay is because its origins are in a world that is beyond time – and this is its greatness.

Milah – Our Mark of Servitude to Hashem

As noted, *Milah* enables and establishes a covenantal relationship between Hashem and Yisroel. What is the nature of this relationship? Simply put, it is one of servant to Master. We, Yisroel, are the servants and Hashem is our Master. In his *Drush L'Shabbos Shuva* the Maharal writes that *Milah* "brands" us as servants of Hashem in the same manner that ordinary servants are customarily branded with the insignia of their human masters. Indeed, the Maharal writes in *Tiferes Yisroel* chapter 9 that Avrohom was the first to be commanded to perform *Milah* not simply because he was the first to establish the possibility of a relationship with Hashem, as mentioned earlier, but because he defined that relationship by referring to Hashem as אדון, *adon*, Master. We recognize this aspect of *Milah* in one of the accompanying blessings: וצאצאיו חתם באות ברית קדש, *v'tzeetzaav chasam b'os bris kodeh*, "… [Hashem] branded his [Yitzchok's] offspring with the sign of the holy covenant".

The Maharal in *Gur Aryeh* on *Shmos* 12:6 writes that in preparation for our exodus from Egypt Yisroel was commanded to perform *Milah* and the *Pesach* sacrifice. Since we were exiting servitude to Pharaoh and entering into servitude to Hashem we were required to "rebrand" ourselves accordingly. That *Milah* constituted our formal entry into the service of Hashem. (The purpose of the Pesach sacrifice at that juncture was to initiate us into servitude with our first commanded act of service. This is why a non-circumcised person is forbidden to partake of the *Pesach* sacrifice – he has not entered himself into formal service to Hashem.)

Milah – Arouser of Divine Mercy

In *Gevuros Hashem* chapter 35 the Maharal presents another reason *Milah* was required before the redemption from Egypt and that is that the blood of *Milah* evokes divine mercy. *Tehillim* 44:23 says, "For it is for Your sake that we are killed all the time, [that] we are considered as sheep for the slaughter". The *Gemara* in *Gittin* 57b applies this verse to *Milah* – throughout history Jews sacrificed to the point of death, ignoring the decrees of oppressors, in order to perform *Milah*. *Milah* "reminds" Hashem of our willingness to sacrifice for His sake and causes Hashem to be merciful to us and free us of oppression. It was thus an appropriate precursor to our exodus from Egypt.

May our continued perseverance against today's *Milah* antagonists similarly evoke divine mercy and may we thereby merit a redemption from our current exile.

לשבת רְצֵה וְהַחֲלִיצֵנוּ יְיָ אֱלֹהֵינוּ בְּמִצְוֹתֶיךָ וּבְמִצְוַת יוֹם הַשְּׁבִיעִי הַשַּׁבָּת הַגָּדוֹל וְהַקָּדוֹשׁ הַזֶּה. כִּי יוֹם זֶה גָּדוֹל וְקָדוֹשׁ הוּא לְפָנֶיךָ, לִשְׁבָּת בּוֹ וְלָנוּחַ בּוֹ בְּאַהֲבָה כְּמִצְוַת רְצוֹנֶךָ, וּבִרְצוֹנְךָ הָנִיחַ לָנוּ יְיָ אֱלֹהֵינוּ, שֶׁלֹּא תְהֵא צָרָה וְיָגוֹן וַאֲנָחָה בְּיוֹם מְנוּחָתֵנוּ. וְהַרְאֵנוּ יְיָ אֱלֹהֵינוּ בְּנֶחָמַת צִיּוֹן עִירֶךָ, וּבְבִנְיַן יְרוּשָׁלַיִם עִיר קָדְשֶׁךָ, כִּי אַתָּה הוּא בַּעַל הַיְשׁוּעוֹת וּבַעַל הַנֶּחָמוֹת.

בר"ח ויו"ט וחול המועד וראש השנה אֱלֹהֵינוּ וֵאלֹהֵי אֲבוֹתֵינוּ, יַעֲלֶה וְיָבֹא, וְיַגִּיעַ, וְיֵרָאֶה, וְיֵרָצֶה, וְיִשָּׁמַע, וְיִפָּקֵד, וְיִזָּכֵר זִכְרוֹנֵנוּ וּפִקְדוֹנֵנוּ, וְזִכְרוֹן אֲבוֹתֵינוּ, וְזִכְרוֹן מָשִׁיחַ בֶּן דָּוִד עַבְדֶּךָ, וְזִכְרוֹן יְרוּשָׁלַיִם עִיר קָדְשֶׁךָ, וְזִכְרוֹן כָּל עַמְּךָ בֵּית יִשְׂרָאֵל לְפָנֶיךָ, לִפְלֵיטָה, לְטוֹבָה, לְחֵן וּלְחֶסֶד וּלְרַחֲמִים, לְחַיִּים וּלְשָׁלוֹם, בְּיוֹם
רֹאשׁ הַחֹדֶשׁ | חַג הַמַּצּוֹת | חַג הַשָּׁבוּעוֹת | חַג הַסֻּכּוֹת | הַשְּׁמִינִי חַג הָעֲצֶרֶת | הַזִּכָּרוֹן
הַזֶּה. זָכְרֵנוּ, יְיָ אֱלֹהֵינוּ, בּוֹ לְטוֹבָה, וּפָקְדֵנוּ בוֹ לִבְרָכָה, וְהוֹשִׁיעֵנוּ בוֹ לְחַיִּים. וּבִדְבַר יְשׁוּעָה וְרַחֲמִים, חוּס וְחָנֵּנוּ, וְרַחֵם עָלֵינוּ וְהוֹשִׁיעֵנוּ, כִּי אֵלֶיךָ עֵינֵינוּ, כִּי אֵל מֶלֶךְ חַנּוּן וְרַחוּם אָתָּה.

וּבְנֵה יְרוּשָׁלַיִם עִיר הַקֹּדֶשׁ בִּמְהֵרָה בְּיָמֵינוּ. בָּרוּךְ אַתָּה יְיָ, בּוֹנֵה בְרַחֲמָיו יְרוּשָׁלָיִם. אָמֵן

בָּרוּךְ אַתָּה יְיָ אֱלֹהֵינוּ מֶלֶךְ הָעוֹלָם, הָאֵל, אָבִינוּ, מַלְכֵּנוּ, אַדִּירֵנוּ, בּוֹרְאֵנוּ, גּוֹאֲלֵנוּ, יוֹצְרֵנוּ, קְדוֹשֵׁנוּ קְדוֹשׁ יַעֲקֹב, רוֹעֵנוּ רוֹעֵה יִשְׂרָאֵל, הַמֶּלֶךְ הַטּוֹב וְהַמֵּטִיב לַכֹּל, שֶׁבְּכָל יוֹם וָיוֹם הוּא הֵטִיב, הוּא מֵטִיב, הוּא יֵיטִיב לָנוּ. הוּא גְמָלָנוּ, הוּא גוֹמְלֵנוּ, הוּא יִגְמְלֵנוּ לָעַד, לְחֵן וּלְחֶסֶד וּלְרַחֲמִים וּלְרֶוַח הַצָּלָה וְהַצְלָחָה, בְּרָכָה וִישׁוּעָה, נֶחָמָה, פַּרְנָסָה וְכַלְכָּלָה, וְרַחֲמִים וְחַיִּים וְשָׁלוֹם וְכָל טוֹב, וּמִכָּל טוּב לְעוֹלָם אַל יְחַסְּרֵנוּ.

הָרַחֲמָן, הוּא יִמְלוֹךְ עָלֵינוּ לְעוֹלָם וָעֶד.
הָרַחֲמָן, הוּא יִתְבָּרַךְ בַּשָּׁמַיִם וּבָאָרֶץ.
הָרַחֲמָן, הוּא יִשְׁתַּבַּח לְדוֹר דּוֹרִים, וְיִתְפָּאַר בָּנוּ לָעַד וּלְנֵצַח נְצָחִים, וְיִתְהַדַּר בָּנוּ לָעַד וּלְעוֹלְמֵי עוֹלָמִים.
הָרַחֲמָן, הוּא יְפַרְנְסֵנוּ בְּכָבוֹד.
הָרַחֲמָן, הוּא יִשְׁבּוֹר עֻלֵּנוּ מֵעַל צַוָּארֵנוּ וְהוּא יוֹלִיכֵנוּ קוֹמְמִיּוּת לְאַרְצֵנוּ.
הָרַחֲמָן, הוּא יִשְׁלַח לָנוּ בְּרָכָה מְרֻבָּה בַּבַּיִת הַזֶּה, וְעַל שֻׁלְחָן זֶה שֶׁאָכַלְנוּ עָלָיו.
הָרַחֲמָן, הוּא יִשְׁלַח לָנוּ אֶת אֵלִיָּהוּ הַנָּבִיא זָכוּר לַטּוֹב, וִיבַשֶּׂר לָנוּ בְּשׂוֹרוֹת טוֹבוֹת יְשׁוּעוֹת וְנֶחָמוֹת.

הָרַחֲמָן, הוּא יְבָרֵךְ אֶת (אָבִי מוֹרִי) בַּעַל הַבַּיִת הַזֶּה, וְאֶת (אִמִּי מוֹרָתִי) בַּעֲלַת הַבַּיִת הַזֶּה, אוֹתָם וְאֶת בֵּיתָם וְאֶת זַרְעָם וְאֶת כָּל אֲשֶׁר לָהֶם,

הָרַחֲמָן, הוּא יְבָרֵךְ אוֹתִי (וְאָבִי \ וְאִמִּי \ וְאִשְׁתִּי \וְזַרְעִי \ וְאֶת כָּל אֲשֶׁר לִי)

אוֹתָנוּ וְאֶת כָּל אֲשֶׁר לָנוּ, כְּמוֹ שֶׁנִּתְבָּרְכוּ אֲבוֹתֵינוּ, אַבְרָהָם יִצְחָק וְיַעֲקֹב, בַּכֹּל, מִכֹּל, כֹּל, כֵּן יְבָרֵךְ אוֹתָנוּ כֻּלָּנוּ יַחַד בִּבְרָכָה שְׁלֵמָה, וְנֹאמַר אָמֵן.

בַּמָּרוֹם יְלַמְּדוּ עֲלֵיהֶם וְעָלֵינוּ זְכוּת, שֶׁתְּהֵא לְמִשְׁמֶרֶת שָׁלוֹם, וְנִשָּׂא בְרָכָה מֵאֵת יְיָ, וּצְדָקָה מֵאֱלֹהֵי יִשְׁעֵנוּ, וְנִמְצָא חֵן וְשֵׂכֶל טוֹב בְּעֵינֵי אֱלֹהִים וְאָדָם.

לשבת הָרַחֲמָן, הוּא יַנְחִילֵנוּ יוֹם שֶׁכֻּלּוֹ שַׁבָּת וּמְנוּחָה לְחַיֵּי הָעוֹלָמִים.
לר"ח הָרַחֲמָן, הוּא יְחַדֵּשׁ עָלֵינוּ אֶת הַחֹדֶשׁ הַזֶּה לְטוֹבָה וְלִבְרָכָה.
ליום טוב הָרַחֲמָן, הוּא יַנְחִילֵנוּ יוֹם שֶׁכֻּלּוֹ טוֹב.
לר"ה הָרַחֲמָן, הוּא יְחַדֵּשׁ עָלֵינוּ אֶת הַשָּׁנָה הַזֹּאת לְטוֹבָה וְלִבְרָכָה.
לסוכות הָרַחֲמָן, הוּא יָקִים לָנוּ אֶת סֻכַּת דָּוִד הַנּוֹפָלֶת.

הָרַחֲמָן, הוּא יְזַכֵּנוּ לִימוֹת הַמָּשִׁיחַ וּלְחַיֵּי הָעוֹלָם הַבָּא.
בחול מַגְדִּיל (בשבת ור"ח ויו"ט וחול המועד וראש השנה מִגְדּוֹל) יְשׁוּעוֹת מַלְכּוֹ, וְעֹשֶׂה חֶסֶד לִמְשִׁיחוֹ לְדָוִד וּלְזַרְעוֹ עַד עוֹלָם. עֹשֶׂה שָׁלוֹם בִּמְרוֹמָיו, הוּא יַעֲשֶׂה שָׁלוֹם עָלֵינוּ וְעַל כָּל יִשְׂרָאֵל, וְאִמְרוּ אָמֵן.

יְראוּ אֶת יְיָ קְדוֹשָׁיו, כִּי אֵין מַחְסוֹר לִירֵאָיו. כְּפִירִים רָשׁוּ וְרָעֵבוּ, וְדוֹרְשֵׁי יְיָ לֹא יַחְסְרוּ כָל טוֹב. הוֹדוּ לַיְיָ כִּי טוֹב, כִּי לְעוֹלָם חַסְדּוֹ. פּוֹתֵחַ אֶת יָדֶךָ, וּמַשְׂבִּיעַ לְכָל חַי רָצוֹן. בָּרוּךְ הַגֶּבֶר אֲשֶׁר יִבְטַח בַּיְיָ, וְהָיָה יְיָ מִבְטַחוֹ. נַעַר הָיִיתִי גַם זָקַנְתִּי, וְלֹא רָאִיתִי צַדִּיק נֶעֱזָב, וְזַרְעוֹ מְבַקֶּשׁ לָחֶם. יְיָ עֹז לְעַמּוֹ יִתֵּן, יְיָ יְבָרֵךְ אֶת עַמּוֹ בַשָּׁלוֹם.

ברכת המזון

לחול: עַל נַהֲרוֹת בָּבֶל שָׁם יָשַׁבְנוּ גַּם בָּכִינוּ, בְּזָכְרֵנוּ אֶת צִיּוֹן. עַל עֲרָבִים בְּתוֹכָהּ, תָּלִינוּ כִּנֹּרוֹתֵינוּ. כִּי שָׁם שְׁאֵלוּנוּ שׁוֹבֵינוּ דִּבְרֵי שִׁיר וְתוֹלָלֵינוּ שִׂמְחָה, שִׁירוּ לָנוּ מִשִּׁיר צִיּוֹן. אֵיךְ נָשִׁיר אֶת שִׁיר יְיָ, עַל אַדְמַת נֵכָר. אִם אֶשְׁכָּחֵךְ יְרוּשָׁלָיִם, תִּשְׁכַּח יְמִינִי. תִּדְבַּק לְשׁוֹנִי לְחִכִּי אִם לֹא אֶזְכְּרֵכִי, אִם לֹא אַעֲלֶה אֶת יְרוּשָׁלַיִם עַל רֹאשׁ שִׂמְחָתִי. זְכֹר יְיָ לִבְנֵי אֱדוֹם אֵת יוֹם יְרוּשָׁלָיִם, הָאֹמְרִים עָרוּ עָרוּ עַד הַיְסוֹד בָּהּ. בַּת בָּבֶל הַשְּׁדוּדָה, אַשְׁרֵי שֶׁיְשַׁלֶּם לָךְ אֶת גְּמוּלֵךְ שֶׁגָּמַלְתְּ לָנוּ. אַשְׁרֵי שֶׁיֹּאחֵז וְנִפֵּץ אֶת עֹלָלַיִךְ אֶל הַסָּלַע.

לשבת ויום טוב: שִׁיר הַמַּעֲלוֹת, בְּשׁוּב יְיָ אֶת שִׁיבַת צִיּוֹן, הָיִינוּ כְּחֹלְמִים. אָז יִמָּלֵא שְׂחוֹק פִּינוּ וּלְשׁוֹנֵנוּ רִנָּה, אָז יֹאמְרוּ בַגּוֹיִם, הִגְדִּיל יְיָ לַעֲשׂוֹת עִם אֵלֶּה. הִגְדִּיל יְיָ לַעֲשׂוֹת עִמָּנוּ, הָיִינוּ שְׂמֵחִים. שׁוּבָה יְיָ אֶת שְׁבִיתֵנוּ, כַּאֲפִיקִים בַּנֶּגֶב. הַזֹּרְעִים בְּדִמְעָה, בְּרִנָּה יִקְצֹרוּ. הָלוֹךְ יֵלֵךְ וּבָכֹה נֹשֵׂא מֶשֶׁךְ הַזָּרַע, בֹּא יָבֹא בְרִנָּה נֹשֵׂא אֲלֻמֹּתָיו.

תְּהִלַּת יְיָ יְדַבֶּר פִּי, וִיבָרֵךְ כָּל בָּשָׂר שֵׁם קָדְשׁוֹ לְעוֹלָם וָעֶד. וַאֲנַחְנוּ נְבָרֵךְ יָהּ, מֵעַתָּה וְעַד עוֹלָם, הַלְלוּיָהּ. הוֹדוּ לַיְיָ כִּי טוֹב, כִּי לְעוֹלָם חַסְדּוֹ. מִי יְמַלֵּל גְּבוּרוֹת יְיָ, יַשְׁמִיעַ כָּל תְּהִלָּתוֹ.

הִנְנִי מוּכָן וּמְזֻמָּן לְקַיֵּם מִצְוַת עֲשֵׂה שֶׁל בִּרְכַּת הַמָּזוֹן, שֶׁנֶּאֱמַר: וְאָכַלְתָּ וְשָׂבָעְתָּ, וּבֵרַכְתָּ אֶת יְיָ אֱלֹהֶיךָ, עַל הָאָרֶץ הַטֹּבָה אֲשֶׁר נָתַן לָךְ.

המזמן: רַבּוֹתַי נְבָרֵךְ.

המסובין: יְהִי שֵׁם יְיָ מְבֹרָךְ מֵעַתָּה וְעַד עוֹלָם.

המזמן: יְהִי שֵׁם יְיָ מְבֹרָךְ מֵעַתָּה וְעַד עוֹלָם. בִּרְשׁוּת מָרָנָן וְרַבָּנָן וְרַבּוֹתַי, נְבָרֵךְ (אֱלֹהֵינוּ) שֶׁאָכַלְנוּ מִשֶּׁלּוֹ.

המסובין: בָּרוּךְ (אֱלֹהֵינוּ) שֶׁאָכַלְנוּ מִשֶּׁלּוֹ וּבְטוּבוֹ חָיִינוּ.

המזמן: בָּרוּךְ (אֱלֹהֵינוּ) שֶׁאָכַלְנוּ מִשֶּׁלּוֹ וּבְטוּבוֹ חָיִינוּ. בָּרוּךְ הוּא וּבָרוּךְ שְׁמוֹ.

בָּרוּךְ אַתָּה יְיָ, אֱלֹהֵינוּ מֶלֶךְ הָעוֹלָם, הַזָּן אֶת הָעוֹלָם כֻּלּוֹ בְּטוּבוֹ בְּחֵן בְּחֶסֶד וּבְרַחֲמִים, הוּא נוֹתֵן לֶחֶם לְכָל בָּשָׂר כִּי לְעוֹלָם חַסְדּוֹ. וּבְטוּבוֹ הַגָּדוֹל תָּמִיד לֹא חָסַר לָנוּ, וְאַל יֶחְסַר לָנוּ מָזוֹן לְעוֹלָם וָעֶד. בַּעֲבוּר שְׁמוֹ הַגָּדוֹל, כִּי הוּא אֵל זָן וּמְפַרְנֵס לַכֹּל וּמֵטִיב לַכֹּל, וּמֵכִין מָזוֹן לְכָל בְּרִיּוֹתָיו אֲשֶׁר בָּרָא. בָּרוּךְ אַתָּה יְיָ, הַזָּן אֶת הַכֹּל.

נוֹדֶה לְּךָ, יְיָ אֱלֹהֵינוּ, עַל שֶׁהִנְחַלְתָּ לַאֲבוֹתֵינוּ אֶרֶץ חֶמְדָּה טוֹבָה וּרְחָבָה, וְעַל שֶׁהוֹצֵאתָנוּ, יְיָ אֱלֹהֵינוּ, מֵאֶרֶץ מִצְרַיִם, וּפְדִיתָנוּ מִבֵּית עֲבָדִים, וְעַל בְּרִיתְךָ שֶׁחָתַמְתָּ בִּבְשָׂרֵנוּ, וְעַל תּוֹרָתְךָ שֶׁלִּמַּדְתָּנוּ, וְעַל חֻקֶּיךָ שֶׁהוֹדַעְתָּנוּ, וְעַל חַיִּים חֵן וָחֶסֶד שֶׁחוֹנַנְתָּנוּ, וְעַל אֲכִילַת מָזוֹן שָׁאַתָּה זָן וּמְפַרְנֵס אוֹתָנוּ תָּמִיד, בְּכָל יוֹם וּבְכָל עֵת וּבְכָל שָׁעָה.

לַחֲנֻכָּה וּפוּרִים:

עַל הַנִּסִּים, וְעַל הַפֻּרְקָן, וְעַל הַגְּבוּרוֹת, וְעַל הַתְּשׁוּעוֹת, וְעַל הַמִּלְחָמוֹת, שֶׁעָשִׂיתָ לַאֲבוֹתֵינוּ בַּיָּמִים הָהֵם בַּזְּמַן הַזֶּה.

לַחֲנֻכָּה:

בִּימֵי מַתִּתְיָהוּ בֶּן יוֹחָנָן כֹּהֵן גָּדוֹל, חַשְׁמוֹנַאי וּבָנָיו, כְּשֶׁעָמְדָה מַלְכוּת יָוָן הָרְשָׁעָה עַל עַמְּךָ יִשְׂרָאֵל לְהַשְׁכִּיחָם תּוֹרָתֶךָ, וּלְהַעֲבִירָם מֵחֻקֵּי רְצוֹנֶךָ, וְאַתָּה בְּרַחֲמֶיךָ הָרַבִּים עָמַדְתָּ לָהֶם בְּעֵת צָרָתָם, רַבְתָּ אֶת רִיבָם, דַּנְתָּ אֶת דִּינָם, נָקַמְתָּ אֶת נִקְמָתָם, מָסַרְתָּ גִּבּוֹרִים בְּיַד חַלָּשִׁים, וְרַבִּים בְּיַד מְעַטִּים, וּטְמֵאִים בְּיַד טְהוֹרִים, וּרְשָׁעִים בְּיַד צַדִּיקִים, וְזֵדִים בְּיַד עוֹסְקֵי תוֹרָתֶךָ. וּלְךָ עָשִׂיתָ שֵׁם גָּדוֹל וְקָדוֹשׁ בְּעוֹלָמֶךָ, וּלְעַמְּךָ יִשְׂרָאֵל עָשִׂיתָ תְּשׁוּעָה גְדוֹלָה וּפֻרְקָן כְּהַיּוֹם הַזֶּה. וְאַחַר כֵּן בָּאוּ בָנֶיךָ לִדְבִיר בֵּיתֶךָ, וּפִנּוּ אֶת הֵיכָלֶךָ, וְטִהֲרוּ אֶת מִקְדָּשֶׁךָ, וְהִדְלִיקוּ נֵרוֹת בְּחַצְרוֹת קָדְשֶׁךָ, וְקָבְעוּ שְׁמוֹנַת יְמֵי חֲנֻכָּה אֵלּוּ, לְהוֹדוֹת וּלְהַלֵּל לְשִׁמְךָ הַגָּדוֹל.

לְפוּרִים:

בִּימֵי מָרְדְּכַי וְאֶסְתֵּר בְּשׁוּשַׁן הַבִּירָה, כְּשֶׁעָמַד עֲלֵיהֶם הָמָן הָרָשָׁע, בִּקֵּשׁ לְהַשְׁמִיד לַהֲרֹג וּלְאַבֵּד אֶת כָּל הַיְּהוּדִים, מִנַּעַר וְעַד זָקֵן, טַף וְנָשִׁים, בְּיוֹם אֶחָד, בִּשְׁלוֹשָׁה עָשָׂר לְחֹדֶשׁ שְׁנֵים עָשָׂר, הוּא חֹדֶשׁ אֲדָר, וּשְׁלָלָם לָבוֹז. וְאַתָּה בְּרַחֲמֶיךָ הָרַבִּים הֵפַרְתָּ אֶת עֲצָתוֹ, וְקִלְקַלְתָּ אֶת מַחֲשַׁבְתּוֹ, וַהֲשֵׁבוֹתָ לּוֹ גְּמוּלוֹ בְּרֹאשׁוֹ, וְתָלוּ אוֹתוֹ וְאֶת בָּנָיו עַל הָעֵץ.)

וְעַל הַכֹּל, יְיָ אֱלֹהֵינוּ, אֲנַחְנוּ מוֹדִים לָךְ, וּמְבָרְכִים אוֹתָךְ, יִתְבָּרַךְ שִׁמְךָ בְּפִי כָּל חַי תָּמִיד לְעוֹלָם וָעֶד. כַּכָּתוּב, וְאָכַלְתָּ וְשָׂבָעְתָּ, וּבֵרַכְתָּ אֶת יְיָ אֱלֹהֶיךָ עַל הָאָרֶץ הַטֹּבָה אֲשֶׁר נָתַן לָךְ. בָּרוּךְ אַתָּה יְיָ, עַל הָאָרֶץ וְעַל הַמָּזוֹן.

רַחֵם, יְיָ אֱלֹהֵינוּ, עַל יִשְׂרָאֵל עַמֶּךָ, וְעַל יְרוּשָׁלַיִם עִירֶךָ, וְעַל צִיּוֹן מִשְׁכַּן כְּבוֹדֶךָ, וְעַל מַלְכוּת בֵּית דָּוִד מְשִׁיחֶךָ, וְעַל הַבַּיִת הַגָּדוֹל וְהַקָּדוֹשׁ שֶׁנִּקְרָא שִׁמְךָ עָלָיו. אֱלֹהֵינוּ, אָבִינוּ, רְעֵנוּ, זוּנֵנוּ, פַּרְנְסֵנוּ, וְכַלְכְּלֵנוּ, וְהַרְוִיחֵנוּ, וְהַרְוַח לָנוּ יְיָ אֱלֹהֵינוּ מְהֵרָה מִכָּל צָרוֹתֵינוּ, וְנָא אַל תַּצְרִיכֵנוּ, יְיָ אֱלֹהֵינוּ, לֹא לִידֵי מַתְּנַת בָּשָׂר וָדָם, וְלֹא לִידֵי הַלְוָאָתָם, כִּי אִם לְיָדְךָ הַמְּלֵאָה, הַפְּתוּחָה, הַקְּדוֹשָׁה וְהָרְחָבָה, שֶׁלֹּא נֵבוֹשׁ וְלֹא נִכָּלֵם לְעוֹלָם וָעֶד.

סעיף לד

ובפרק כל הבשר כי אתא רב דימי אמר מים ראשונים האכילו בשר חזיר אחרונים הוציאו אשה מבעלה כי אתא
רבין אמר ראשונים האכילו בשר נבילה אחרונים הרגו הנפש, הנה בדבר זה באו לבאר דברים גדולים בענין מים
ראשונים ובענין מים אחרונים כאשר תבין, כי מים הראשונים מסלק הטומאה שלא תהיה אכילתו בטומאה וכאשר
אין נזהר במים הראשונים הוא בא לדבר שהיא טומאה לגמרי כמו אכילת חזיר ואכילת נבילה שכל זה מה שלא
היה נזהר באכילת טמאה היה גורם אכילה טמאה לגמרי כמו אכילת בשר חזיר או אכילת נבילה, ומים אחרונים
כאשר אינו מטהר ידיו מן הזוהמא הוא שקוץ ומאוס אל הנפש ודבר זה בטול הנפש ולכך אמר שמביא דבר זה
הריגת הנפש לגמרי, ולמ"ד שגרשו אשה מבעלה כי גרושי אשה מבעלה דומה קצת להריגת הנפש, וזה כי איש
ואשה ביחד הם כמו אדם אחד וכאשר מגרש את אשתו הרי זה בטול האדם לפי שהיו ביחד אדם אחד כי סבר
כאשר יש לו ידים מזוהמים ומאוסים אין זה בטול הנפש לגמרי רק הוא קצת בטול הנפש בטול הנפש דבר המאוס, ולכך אמר
כי גרמו גרושי אשה מבעלה שהוא קצת הריגת ובטול האדם, אע"פ כי בודאי כי גרושי אשה היא יותר בטול הנפש
מן דבר שהוא מאוס שזה אין כל כך בטול הנפש אבל בטול נפש זה מן דבר שהוא מאוס היה גורר אחריו גרושי
אשה ולמ"ד הריגת הנפש לגמרי, והדברים האלו עוד עמוקים מה שרמזו כאן בענין מים ראשונים ומים אחרונים,
ואין להאריך בדברים אלו רק באנו לבאר כי החכמי' הרבה הזהירו על מים אחרונים ועונשן יותר מן מים ראשונים,
ולכך אני אומר שאין לבטל דברי חכמים כלל וכלל:

זהו שמן שהיו סכין ידיהם בשמן ולא מצאנו בשום מקום שיהיה שמן לא חובה ולא מצוה אלא על כרחך דהוה אסמכתא בלבד, והא דאמר התם כשם שהמזוהם פסול לעבודה כך ידים מזוהמות פסולין לברכה, היינו להם לפי שהיה עליהם חובה ליטול ידים אחר הסעודה ולפיכך נחשבים כמזוהמות כאשר אינו נוטל, כך כתבו התוספות שם וכך פסקו שם הרא"ש ז"ל והטור, ומפני שאין בני אדם נוהגים בהם לכך לא סדרנו דין מים האחרונים לפני ברכת המזון, מ"מ כיון שנמצא זה בתלמוד ומאוד הזהירו על זה כמו שנתבאר הנה נפרש טעם המצוה הזאת והרוצה לשמוע ישמע, והרי אף התוספות כתבו שהמעונגים שרגילין ליטול ידיהם אחר הסעודה מעכבת הנטילה מלברך ברכת המזון כי זה אצלם כמו מזוהם:

סעיף לג

ובפרק אלו דברים אמר רב יהודה אמר רב והתקדשתם אלו מים ראשונים והייתם קדושים אלו מים אחרונים כי קדוש אני זה שמן אני ה' אלהיכם זו ברכה ע"כ וביאור זה כי האכילה של אדם אשר היא חיותו ראוי שתהיה בטהרה ובקדושה לגמרי ולכך לא צריך נטילה רק ללחם שעליו יחיה האדם ולא צריך נטילה לפירות שכל זה מפני כי הלחם אשר עליו יחיה האדם צריך שיהיה בטהרה לכך צריך שיהיה נטילה לפני המזון ולאחר אכילתו צריך ג"כ נטילה שלא יהיה זוהמא על ידיו בשביל הברכה שמברך השם ית' על מזונו, וזהו פירוש והתקדשתם והייתם קדושים, ואלו שניהם הם סילוק הטומאה והזוהמא ועדיין אין כאן זיכוך גמור והוא צריך יותר מן הסרת הטומאה זיכוך גמור ועל זה אמר כי קדוש אני זה שמן כי השמן הוא זיכוך לידים ודבר זה לא די שיהיה לו הסרת הטומאה רק כי יש לו זיכוך גמור עוד יותר, אבל עתה בגלותנו די לנו להסיר הטומאה והזוהמא אבל שיהיה לנו הקדושה בשלימות דבר זה אין לנו ולכך אין נוהגין בדבר זה, ובלאו הכי כי בודאי מן הטומאה יש להרחיק ודבר זה הוא על ידי מים ראשונים ואחרונים אבל דבר שהוא לתוספת בלבד אין להיות נזהר כ"כ בזה, ויש לך להבין ג' דברים אלו והתקדשתם והייתם קדושים כי קדוש אני כי הם דברי חכמה מאוד ואי אפשר לפרש יותר, ומה שאמרו בפ' כל הבשר דמים אחרונים חובה ומפרש שם מאי חובה משום מלח סדומית דבר זה בפני עצמו שהיא חובה משום מלח סדומית נוסף על מה שצריך להסיר הזוהמא והטומאה, וכן מים ראשונים הם בשביל קדושה וגם הם בשביל סרך תרומה כמו שמפרש שם שני הטעמים וא"כ למה לא יהיו נוהגים גם כן אפילו אם נאמר דמלח סדומית אינו נמצא בינינו מ"מ מלח סדומית בלחוד לא הוי טעם רק כי צריך להסיר גם הזוהמא כי איך נברך בידים מזוהמות שהם נחשבים טומאה ואם בשביל שאין מקפיד האדם על הזוהמא למה לא נאמר כי דעתו בטילה, ותימה על דברי התוס' שכתבו בשביל שאין מלח סדומית מצוי בינינו לכך אין נוהגין במים אחרונים והרי מים ראשונים משום סרך תרומה וכי תרומה יש בינינו אם משום דרש שדרשו וידיו לא שטף במים כדאיתא התם הרי התוספות כתבו שגם זה הוא אסמכתא בעלמא ואינו דרשא גמורה, אבל נראה שבשביל כך קאמר על מלח סדומית אמר אביי ומשתכח כי קורא בי כורא כלו' בכור שהוא שלשים סאה לא נמצא רק קורט אחד ומה הוצרך לדבר זה אם לא שבא לאשמעינן שלא תאמר במקום שלא נמצא מלח סדומית לא אמרו שהוא חובה ולכך אמר שהרי לא נמצא בכור רק כמו קורט א"כ הוי הם חובה אע"ג הכי הוי הם חובה אע"פ וכי הי שלא שכיח לגמרי שיהיה נמצא קורט זה על הידים על כל זה הוא חובה, וכן אף במקום שאינו שכיח לחוש שמא שמא פעם אחת נמצא אף אם אינו רק בדרך רחוק מאוד, ומ"מ יש לפרש הא דאשמעינן שלא נמצא בכור רק קורט אחד שבא לאשמעינן כי המלח סדומית שנמצא אצלנו אינו כמנהגו של עולם שא"כ היה נמצא הרבה שכך כל דבר שהוא כמנהגו של עולם הוא הרבה אבל הוא שלא כמנהגו של עולם וזה מורה על גודל כחו, ומ"מ יש ללמוד ג"כ מזה אע"ג שלא בא לאשמועינן, אף שאינו שכיח עם כל זה זה מים אחרונים חובה, מ"מ סוף סוף המלח הזה אינו שכיח ואינו רגיל שהרי הוא מעט ועם כל זה הוא חובה, ולא ידעתי ג"כ שום חלוק בין מדינה למדינה בבל שהיו האמוראים שם ובין ארצות אלו לומר כי שם היה שם מלח סדומית ובארצות אלו אין מלח סדומית כי לא מצאנו בתלמוד שהיה מלח סדומית רגיל ביניהם, ולכך נראה דלא תליא ברגיל כלל רק בשביל שאפשר שיהיה כאן מלח סדומית צריך להסיר אותו ולכך צריך מים אחרונים, ויראה לומר ג"כ כי יודעי חכמה הם החכמים לא בכל מקום הלכו אחר שכיח ורגיל, רק כי כאשר הדעת נותן לפי החכמה שיש לחוש לדבר אף שהוא רחוק מ"מ אם אינו חש הרי הוא יוצא מן סדר השכלי ואין לעשות כן כמו שפרשנו למעלה אצל אין משיחין בסעודה שאף שהוא רחוק חש היו חושין ועיין למעלה, וכאן מפני שאמרו ז"ל אחר כל אכילתך אכול מלח א"כ המלח שייך לסעודה מצד עצמו ולכך יש לחוש שיקרה לו באכילתו מלח סדומית אחר שהמלח הזה הוא מלח סדומית הוא יותר מליח שהוא חזק ביותר ולכך יש לחוש שיקרה לו, ומכ"ש לפי מה שאמרנו כי אין המלח הזה נמצא כמנהג הטבע ודבר שאין כמנהג הטבע יש לחוש יותר ויותר, ועוד קשה וכי במלח סדומית דוקא תליא מלתא כי שאר מלח גם כן יש לחוש לו רק דבגמרא נקט אשר אשר הוא מזיק יותר והוא מסמא את העינים ושאר מלח לכל הפחות מזיק ולכך הוא חובה:

כפשטיה שהעונה אמן אחר ברכותיו ה"ז משובח היינו ברכת המזון דווקא בברכה אחרונה הזאת היא השלמה על הכל:

סעיף ל

ברכה רביעית הטוב והמטיב, כבר בארנו למעלה ענין הברכה הזאת שנתקנה בבהמ"ז. ובגמרא בפרק שלשה שאכלו (מ"ה ע"ב) א"ר יוחנן הטוב והמטיב צריכה מלכות מאי קמ"ל כל ברכה שאין בה מלכות לא שמה ברכה והאמר ר' יוחנן חדא זימנא אמר ר' זירא לומר שצריכה שתי מלכיות חדא דידה וחדא דבונה ירושלים אי הכי נבעי תלתא חדא דבונה ירושלים וחדא דברכת הארץ כו' ה"ה דאפי' בונה ירושלים נמי לא צריך אלא כיון דאמר מלכות בית דוד לאו אורח ארעא שלא לומר מלכות שמים רב פפא אמר הכי קאמר צריכה שתי מלכיות לבד מדידה. ופירוש זה כיון שאמר מלכות בית דוד, לאו אורח ארעא שלא להזכיר מלכות שמים, ובונה ירושלים אי אפשר להזכיר מלכות שמים דאין להזכיר מלכות שמים עם מלכות בשר ודם ולכך תקנו להזכיר אותו בהטוב והמטיב. ורב פפא סבר כי אף כנגד ברכת הארץ צריך להזכיר מלכות שמים, ומפני שהטוב והמטיב כוללת כל טובה שהוא מן הש"י, ולכך כיון שלא הזכיר מלכות בבונה ירושלי' משום דלאו אורח ארעא להזכיר מלכות שמים עם מלכות בשר ודם, לכך יש להזכיר כנגד זה מלכות שמים בהטוב והמטיב, אשר הטוב והמטיב כוללת כל טובה, ולכך מה שחסר מן ברכת בונה ירושלים ומן ברכת הארץ כולל אותו בהטוב והמטיב שהיא כוללת הכל, ותקנו שתי מלכיות בר מדידה עד שהם שלש מלכיות, ואלו הן ג' מלכיות ברוך אתה ה"א מלך העולם זה א', אבינו מלכנו ב', המלך הטוב ג'. ומקשין על נוסח שלנו בברכת רחם שאנו אומרים האל אבינו מלכנו רענו וכו' ואם כן כבר נזכר בברכת רחם מלכות שמים, ואם כן למה יש להזכיר מלכות שמים בברכת הטוב והמטיב לומר אבינו מלכנו אדירנו וכו'. ואין זה קשיא דבברכת רחם לא נזכר אבינו מלכנו לשבח הש"י ולומר שהוא יתב' שזהו נקרא הזכרת מלכות, רק שאנו אומרים כיון שאתה מלכנו ראוי על המלך שיהיה רענו זוננו פרנסנו ובשביל רענו זוננו בקשת רענו זוננו הזכיר מלכנו ואין זה נקרא מלכות. אבל בברכת הטוב והמטיב שאמר אבינו מלכנו אדירנו בוראנו גואלנו יוצרנו קדושנו קדוש יעקב רוענו רועה ישראל הטוב והמטיב לכל) לא הזכיר שום בקשה, וכן המלך הטוב והמטיב לכל לא הזכיר שום בקשה רק שאומר שהוא יתברך מלך, וזה נקרא מלכות שבא לשבח השם יתברך שאתה מלך, רק אח"כ אמר אל שבכל יום ויום הוא הטיב וכו', וזה סמך על מה שהזכיר שם אל ולכך לא קשה מידי:

סעיף לא

ובברכה זאת הזכיר עשרה שבחים שבהם האל א', אבינו ב', מלכנו ג', אדירנו ד', בוראנו ה', גואלנו ו', יוצרנו ז', קדושנו ח', רוענו רועה ישראל ט', המלך הטוב הוא עשירי. כי כבר אמרנו כי הברכה שהוא הטוב והמטיב היא ברכה עליונה על הכל במה שהוא יתברך טוב ומטיב לכל, ולכך עולה עשרה מדריגו' עד העשירי שהוא קודש לגמרי כי כל עשירי הוא קודש ומצד מדריגה זאת שהוא העשירי הוא טוב ומטיב לכל, והבן הדברים האלו מאד. ומפני שברכה זאת נתקנה על רבוי הטוב וכמו שאמר הטוב והמטיב שר"ל שהוא מטיב ברבוי טוב עד שהוא מטיב אל הכל, לכך מזכיר ג"כ שהטיב מן תמידית הטוב שהוא מטיב בעבר ובהוה ובעתיד. ושלש גמולות הם החסדים שגומל הש"י עם העולם, וכל דבר שהש"י עושה טובה נקרא זה שהטיב להם, וכאשר מציל את האדם מן הדבר שהוא צרה נקרא שגמל חסד אתו כמו (שם נ"ד ע"ב) ד' חייבין להודות. וברכה זאת אין לה חתימה כלל וקאמר בגמרא שאין חותמין בברכה זאת לפי שהיא מדרבנן. ועיקר הטעם כי אין חותמין בברכה זאת, שאין חותמין בברכה רק היכא שהברכה היא דבר שלם ומסיים כמו ברכת הזן שהוא דבר מסוים שהמזון הוא השלמת האדם שהוא חסר והמזון משלים אותו, ומפני שהברכה היא על דבר שהוא הקרקע. ולפיכך הוא מגביה כוס של ברכה מן השלמה לגמרי ולכך יש על זה ברכה שלימה שמשלים הברכה בברוך אתה וכו'. וכן ברכת הארץ על ידי הארץ האדם יושלם, ובה"מ הוא שלימות לכל העולם, ולכך יש לברכה זאת שלימות גם כן שמשלים הברכה בברוך כמו שפרשנו למעלה אצל ברכת הארץ שצריך שיאמר בה הודא' תחלה וסוף. אבל ברכת הטוב והמטיב שנתקנה על כל הטוב שהטיב השם יתברך, והרי אף כשמביאין לו שנוי יין צריך לברך הטוב והמטיב אין זה רק רבוי טוב ומברך על זה הטוב והמטיב ולכך פותח בברוך ואין חותם בברוך, ובשביל זה ג"כ כי ברכה זאת היא מדרבנן כמו שפרשנו. ולכך קאמר בגמרא בשביל שהיא מדרבנן פותחת בברוך ואינה חותמת בברוך, ור"ל שברכה זאת היא מדרבנן לפי שהברכה הזאת על רבוי תוספת טובה בלבד ולכך גם כן אין חותם ומשלים בברוך, ברוך הוא וברוך שם כבודו לעולם אמן ואמן:

סעיף לב

מים אחרונים שלאחר הסעודה אין עתה נוהגין בהם, וכתבו התוספות בפ' כל הבשר אין נוהגין בהם מפני שתקנו מים אחרונים מפני מלח סדומית ואין מלח סדומית מצוי בינינו וראיה לזה שהרי דריש ג"כ כי קדוש אני

סעיף כז

ברכה ג' רחם ה' וכו', כבר אמרנו מפני מה תקנו ברכה זאת בברכת המזון, מפני כי ברכה זאת היא השלמה אחרונה דהיינו בנין ירושלים וב"ה והיא שביעה והשלמה לגמרי, ולכך היא האחרונה בברכות שהם מן התורה. ומפני כך מזכיר בברכה זאת אבינו מלכנו וכו', ואף כי אין אלו דברים שייכים לברכת בונה ירושלים, רק מפני כי ברכה זאת שהיא בנין ירושלים היא השלמה שביעה לגמרי עד שאינם חסרים כמו שהתבאר, ולכך אנו מבקשים שלא נהיה בשום דבר חסר. ואל תצריכנו לא לידי מתנת בשר ודם ולא לידי הלואתם כלומר שלא נהיה חסרים משום דבר בעולם. ולכך זכר כאן ז' דברים, רענו א', זוננו ב', פרנסנו ג', וכלכלנו ד', והרויחנו והרוח לנו מצרותינו ה', ונא אל תצריכנו ו', ובנה ירושלים ז', הרי שבעה, כי במספר שבעה יש השלמה ושביעה כמו שבארנו במקום אחר, ולכך בא על מספר זה לשון שבעה מלשון שביעה והשלמה. ומה שאמר אבינו מלכנו אתה שאתה הוא אבינו שהוצאתנו לעולם כמו האב שהביא את הבן לעולם, וגם אחר שהוצאתנו אל העולם אתה מלכנו שהמלך נותן קיום לעם, לכך מצד אלו ב' דברים אין ראוי שנהיה חסרים דבר שאם נהיה חסרים יאמרו על מעשה ידיך שהם חסרים, כי אתה אבינו וכן מצד שאתה מלכנו אם נהיה חסרים יאמרו כי המלך ראוי להשלים ולקיים העם ולכך רענו וכו'. ותקנו להזכיר מלכות בית דוד בבונה ירושלים כמו שאמרו בגמרא, וזה כמו שאמרנו כי ברכה זאת היא השלמה אחרונה לישראל, ומלכות בית דוד בפרט היא השלמה ישראל. ודבר זה ידוע כי מלכות בית דוד היא השלמה ישראל, כי גם שאר מלכות הוא השלמה לעם כמו שהוא ידוע, וע"י השלמה הזאת של מלכות בית דוד מקבלים ישראל השלמה על השלמה עד שהשכינה הוא מלכא שוכן ביניהם ולכך צריך להזכיר מלכות בית דוד בבונה ירושלי'. ומה שאנו אומרים רענו זננו הזי"ן בחטף על דבר זה קרא הראב"ע ז"ל תגר מאוד והאריך בדבריו בפירוש שלו לקהלת, ואמר כי עשו המלה הזאת כאלו היה שורש המלה זנה, וכמו שאומרים ענני העי"ן בחטף ף מן ענה כך הם אומרים זננו בחט"ף הזי"ן, ושורש המלה אינו כך רק שורש המלה זו"ן מנחי העי"ן וכמו שוב שהוא שוב כן מנחי עי"ן, ויאמר שובנו אלקי ישענו (תהלים פ"ה) מן שוב, לכך צריך לומר זוננו בנקודה שקוראים האשכנזים מלאפו"ם. ובאמת כאשר עמדתי על דקדוק הלשון נהגתי לומר זוננו, אמנם אם היה נמצא בנוסחאות ישנות הזי"ן בחט"ף אני אומר שאין לשנות אם נמצא כך בנוסחאות ישנות, שכך קרא תגר על הפיוט ג"כ שנתבאר למעלה באריכות וע"ש.

סעיף כח

ובשבת פותח בנחמה ומסיים בנחמה ואומר קדושת היום באמצע. ומה שתקנו להזכיר את השבת בברכת רחם, לפי שירושלים וב"ה הוא קדוש והשבת הוא קדוש לכך הזכרת שבת בברכה זאת דוקא. ופותח בנחמה ומסיים בנחמה שמתחיל נחמנו בירושלים עירך ובציון משכן כבודך ומסיים מנחם עמו בבנין ירושלים, ולא יאמר רחם כי ל' רחם שייך על אחד שהוא אחד שהוא בצרה ויאמר רחם עלי בצרה זאת, ואין ראוי שיאמר בשבת שהוא יום מנוחה שהוא בצרה. ואף שאומר והרוח לנו מכל צרותינו אין זה רק כי יהיה להם צרה שירויח להם מצרתם, אבל לחתום בזה שהחתימה היא עיקר בברכה אין לחתום כך וכיון שאין לחתום בזה גם אל יהיה פותח בו. אבל נחמנו לא נאמר על מי שהוא בצרה, רק על אבילות ישנה שהוא אבלות ירושלים ודבר זה יש לומר בשבת, אבל רחם אשר הלשון הזה משמע על מי שהוא בצרה דבר זה אין להזכיר בשבת כלל. ואותם שאומרים רחם בשבת וסומכים על אותם הדעות שאומרים כי אין חלוק בין רחם ובין נחם, אין זה ראוי כי יש חלוק גדול בין רחם ובין נחם למבין.

סעיף כט

וחותם בונה ירושלים ואומר המברך אמן על ברכת עצמו, אע"ג שאין עונין אמן אחר ברכת עצמו כבר אמרנו למעלה כי בסוף הברכות יש לומר אמן. ובגמרא (שם מ"ה ע"ב) אמרינן העונה אמן אחר ברכותיו הרי זה מגונה ומקשה והא אמרינן העונה אמן אחר ברכותיו ה"ז משובח ומתרץ לא קשיא הא בברכת בונה ירושלים הא בשאר ברכות, והנראה מפי' רש"י ז"ל כי הא דאמר הרי זה משובח היא כאשר הוא סוף כל הברכות שהוא מברך זו אחר זו ובברכה שהיא בסוף יאמר אמן על ברכת עצמו, ומשמע לפי זה הא דאמר בבונה ירושלים לאו דוקא בונה ירושלים, אלא כאשר אומר איזה ברכות ביחד צריך לומר בברכה שהיא בסוף אמן, אלא דנקט בונה ירושלים לאשמועינן דברכת בונה ירושלים יש לומר בסוף אמן, אע"ג דהטוב והמטיב אחריה מ"מ כיון שאינה רק דרבנן צריך לומר אמן אחר בונה ירושלים. ופרשנו למעלה כי בשביל שאמרו (שם נ"ז ע"ב) גדול העונה אמן יותר מן המברך, ולפיכך דוקא אחר ברכת עצמו כי העונה הוא תמיד מוסיף על הראשון כמו שהתבאר למעלה אבל לא המברך עצמו, והעונה אמן אחר ברכת עצמו הרי הוא בור, אבל כאשר הוא סוף הברכות הסוף במה שהוא סוף הוא דבר לעצמו, ולכך כאשר עונה שם אמן הוא ג"כ דבר בפני עצמו והוא יותר ממה שברך, כן צריך לפרש. אבל לפי מה שאמרנו למעלה כי ג' ברכות של ברכת המזון והברכה האחרונה שהוא בונה ירושלים היא השלמה אחרונ' שהשלים את ישראל, והשלמה הזאת מגיע עד מדריגת אמן אשר אמרו עליו גדול העונה אמן יותר מן המברך ולפיכך המברך עצמו יש לו לענות אמן, ופירוש ברור הוא כאשר תבין דבר זה. לפי זה יהיה פירוש הגמ'

לברכת הארץ, ופי' זה כי כמו שהארץ היא קדושה נבדלת משאר ארצות לכך צוה שיהיו נמולים, כי צריך לארץ אומה נבדלת משאר אומות כמו שהארץ נבדלת משאר ארצות, ואין דבר שנבדלים בו ישראל לגמרי משאר אומות רק המילה והיא קדושה, מפני שהמילה היא הסרת הערלה שהיא גנות וגנאי גשמי חמרי לכך סלוק הערלה היא קדושה, לכך אנו אומרים אשר קדש ידיד מבטן. ועוד צריך להזכיר התורה בברכת הארץ וזה עוד יותר מעלה של קדושה, כי המילה קדושה והיא סלוק הערלה שהיא גנות וגנאי גשמי, ואילו התור' היא קדושה והיא הסרת גשמי לגמרי. ושניהם שייכים אל הארץ דהיינו סלוק גנות וגנאי הגשמי היא הערלה ועוד על זה היא התורה שהוא סלוק הגשמי לגמרי. כי כאשר יש להם הארץ שהיא נבדלת בקדושה מכל הארצות, זכו ועלו ג"כ למילה שבה ישראל נבדלים מכל האומות מצד שאין בהם פחיתות הערלה שהיא גנות גשמי, ועוד הם נבדלים יותר במה שיש להם התורה השכלית הנבדלת מכל חכמה. ומפני שיש לחשוב כי הארץ שנתן הש"י לישראל היא בתחתונים ואין לה המעלה אלקית, ועל זה אמר שצריך להזכיר בברכ' הארץ ברית ותורה, כי בשביל הארץ זוכים ישראל אל שני דברים אלו דהיינו המילה והתורה ועל ידם ישראל נבדלים אלקיים לגמרי. המילה בה נבדלים מן פחיתות הגשמי שהיא הערלה, ובתורה יש להם המעלה הנבדלת לגמרי. וכל זה זכו בשביל הארץ כי הארץ נבדלת מכל שאר ארצות בקדושה, ובשביל זה זכו לקנות עוד מעלה היא המילה, ועוד יותר על זה התורה והכל מצד זכות ארץ ישראל כי שם ראוי להיות התורה כי אוירא דא"י מחכים, ולכך אמר שצריך להזכיר בברכת הארץ ברית ותורה והבן הדברים האלו מאד.

סעיף כד

צריך להקדים ברית בתורה שזה נתן בג' בריתות וזה נתן בי"ג בריתות, וכל זה קשה למה נתנה המילה בי"ג בריתות והתורה נתנה בג' בריתות. ודבר זה מפני כי הברית הוא החבור שיש בין שני דברים, והמילה שהיא בגופו ובעצמו של אדם הוא ברית וחבור עם הש"י יותר מן התורה, ולכך על המילה נכרתו י"ג בריתות שזהו בשביל הברית של המילה שהיא בבשר שהוא ברית גמור, ועל ידו זכו להיות להם ג"כ ברית התורה שהיא מעלה עליונה שכלית, ומ"מ ברית המילה היא קודמת שהוא ברית גמור בגופו של אדם ולכך ברית המילה יש עליה י"ג בריתות והיא קודמת. ומה שדוקא ג' בריתות נכרתו על התורה וי"ג על המילה אין כאן מקומו. וכל הפוחת לא יפחות מאחד, כי גם ע"י אחד נזכר בזה מעלת הארץ גם כן, שזכו ישראל להיות נבדלים מכל האומות כאשר יש להם הארץ שהיא נבדלת מכל הארצות.

סעיף כה

וצריך שיאמר בברכת הארץ נודה לך תחלה וסוף, בתחלה אומר נודה לך ואח"כ אומר ועל הכל אנו מודים לך וזהו בסוף. ויש לפרש כי זה כנגד ביאה ראשונה שנתן להם הארץ וכנגד ביאה שניה, כי קדושה ראשונה קדשה לשעתה ולא קדשה לעתיד לבא ועל זה לכך צריך שיאמר להזכיר הודא' תחלה וסוף כי ברכה זאת שייך בה הודאה כמו שאמרנו, כי הודאה שייך דוקא בברכת הארץ, ולכך כמו כל ברכה שאינה סמוכה לחברתה צריך שיאמר בה ברכה תחלה וסוף, ובברכה זאת שייך הודאה לכך יזכר בה הודאה תחלה וסוף וזהו מורה על ההודאה שלימה, כמו כאשר אומר ברכה תחלה וסוף היא ברכה שלימה. אך כי יש עוד דבר מופלג בחכמה מה שצריך להזכיר בברכת הארץ הודאה, כי כאשר מזכיר בכל מקום הודאה הוא מוסר עצמו אל הש"י בשביל הטובה שעשה עמו, כי זהו ענין ההודאה כמו שיתבאר עוד במקומו ענין זה שכל הודאה מוסר עצמו אל השם יתברך. ומפני כי נתן לאדם הארץ אם כן יחשוב השמים שמים לה' והארץ נתן לבני אדם וכאלו האדם ח"ו יוצא מרשות הש"י, ולכך צריך לומר הודאה תחלה וסוף ובהודאה זאת מוסר עצמו ונפשו אל הש"י שעשה אתו הטובה הזאת, ובשביל כך האדם והארץ הכל אל הש"י ולא יצא דבר מרשותו ית', וכדי שיהיה כאן הודאה שלימה צריך שיאמר הודאה תחלה וסוף וזהו הודאה שלימה ודבר זה הוא דבר מופלג, ולכך יאמר הודאה תחלה וסוף אע"ג שהיא ברכה הסמוכה לחברתה הרי לא נזכר הודאה בברכה שלפניה.

סעיף כו

החותם מנחיל ארצות הרי זה מגונה, כי הברכה היא דוקא על ארץ ישראל, ואם מברך ברוך מנחיל ארצות היתה הארץ משותפת לשאר ארצות ואין לארץ שיתוף בשאר ארצות כלל ולפיכך הרי זה בור. וכן האומר ומושיע את ישראל בבונה ירושלים הרי זה בור, מפני שהוא חותם בשתים ואין לחתום בשתים. וכל שאינו אומר ברית ותורה בברכת הארץ ומלכות בית דוד בבונה ירושלים לא יצא ידי חובתו, כבר אמרנו דבר זה למה זה צריך ברית ותורה כי דבר זה הוא שבח אל הארץ. והחתימה על הארץ ועל המזון לא נחשב שהוא חותם בשתים כי פירושו הארץ שהיא מוציאה המזון כך מפרש בגמרא, ומה שצריך לומר מלכות בית דוד בבונה ירושלים עוד יתבאר בסמוך. וחותם על הארץ ועל המזון, ויש לשאול כי למה לא חותם בארץ בלבד. אבל דבר זה כי החתימה לעולם הוא יותר כמו שפרשנו בחתימת ברכת הזן, ולכך חותם על הארץ שהיא מוציאה המזון כי מה שמוציאה המזון אשר המזון הוא מן הש"י בזה תדע מעלת הארץ, כאשר הארץ מיוחדת למזון שהש"י משפיע בעצמו ולא נתן פעל זה לשום מלאך ולשום שליח לכך הארץ ג"כ היא אל הש"י וכדכתיב (שמות י"ט) כי לי כל הארץ:

ולכך ארץ חמדה היה בשביל זכות אברהם. ובשביל יעקב היה ארץ טובה, כי הטוב הוא שאין בו פסולת ולכך יעקב נקרא טוב לפי שלא היה בזרעו פסולת ולכך בזכותו היה הארץ טובה בכל ואין בה פסולת. ורחבה מצד יצחק אבינו שראוי לו הרחבה ביותר, כמו שאמר יצחק (שם כ"ו) כי עתה הרחיב ה' לנו ופרינו בארץ. ומה שהרחבה ראוי ליצחק דבר זה יש לך להבין מאוד, ואלו דברים הם מופלגים בחכמה מאוד, ולכך הזכיר אלו שלשה דברים.

סעיף כ

ואומר ועל בריתך שחתמת בבשרנו ועל תורתך שלמדתנו ועל חקיך שהודעתנו, הזכיר ג' דברים הברית שהוא בגופו, ועל תורתך היא התורה שהיא אל השכל, והחוק הוא מה שאין השכל יכול להשיג אותו אבל הוא גזירת דין בלבד, וזה שייך לנפש כאשר אין השגה בזה אל השכל ונפש האדם פועל המצוה אף כי אינו יודע ומשיג בשכל. כי השלים את האדם בכל, נתן אל הגוף המילה שהיא בבשר, ונתן אל השכל התורה, ואל הנפש שהיא העושה החקים אף שאין השגה בהם, וכל פעולה אשר יפעול אדם מתיחס אל הנפש שהוא כח פועל כאשר ידוע, ולכך החקים שעיקר שלהם לעשות המצוה שהם חקים ואין לאדם השגה בהם מתיחסים מעשה המצות אל הנפש הפועלת. ולכך אצל התורה אמר שלמדתנו ואצל החקים אמר שהודעתנו כי הוא מבלי לימוד שהלימוד הוא שייך אל השכל. וגם מה שאמר על בריתך שחתמת בבשרנו ועל תורתך שלמדתנו ועל חקיך שהודעתנו ג"כ זכו בשביל זכות האבות כאשר תבין, כי המילה הוא לאברהם, ותורתך בשביל זכות יעקב כדכתיב (תהלים פ"א) ויקם עדות ביעקב וגו' ובארנו זה באריכות בפרק משה קבל תורה (אבות פ"א) ע"ש, ועל חקיך וכו' והחוק הוא גזירה מן הש"י מצד מדת הדין ואל זה זכו מצד יצחק, הרי לך ג' דברים אלו שהם ג"כ נגד האבות.

סעיף כא

ועל חיים חן וחסד גם אלו שלשה הם מן זכות ג' אבות ג"כ כאשר תבין הדברים על אמתתם. ולכך מזכיר שלש שלש ארץ חמדה טובה ורחבה, ועוד מזכיר שלש ועל בריתך וכו', ועוד מזכיר שלש ועל חיים חן וחסד. כי ברכה זאת היא ברכת הודאה ומודה לפני הש"י כי מה שעשה להם מן הטוב לא בזכות עצמם רק בשביל זכות האבות. ותשעה דברים שנותן זכר שנותן על זה הודאה אל הש"י, ובעשירי אמר ועל אכילת מזון וכו' ודבר זה הוא עשירי מפני כי אכילת מזון יותר על הכל מפני שקשים של אדם מזונותיו הם מזונותיו כמו שהתבאר למעלה ולכך ראוי שיתן הודאה על זה בעשירי.

סעיף כב

ואמר שאתה זן ומפרנס כו' בכל יום ובכל עת ובכל שעה, פירוש זה כי כי האדם צריך לפרנסה כפי מה שמתחדש לו, כי היום הוא צריך לזה ומחר כפי מה שמתחדש לו לאחר הכל כפי שמתחדש לו הזמן צריך האדם לפרנסה. והעת ג"כ לפני עצמו, כי היום יש לו עתות מיוחדים דהיינו רגע זו או רגע זו מן היום וזה נקרא בכל עת, ואין לעת המשך זמן כלל, ואינה כמו שעה כי יש לכל שעה מן היום המשך זמן, אבל העת שהיא הרגע מן היום אין לה המשך זמן ואין עת זו כמו זו ומתחדש לו דבר בעת מיוחד. ופירוש בכל שעה, כי השעה חלק מן היום כי היום נחלק לשעות, ובשעה זו צריך לדבר זה ובשעה זו צריך לדבר אחר. כלל הדבר כי האדם הוא בעל שנוי וצריך לפרנסה כפי מה שמתחדש, והש"י נותן לו פרנסתו בכל יום כפי מה שהתחדש לו היום, וכן העת מן היום שהוא רגע מן היום או שעה מן היום לכך כפי שהוא שהיא חלק מן היום וזה מבואר. ומפני כי שייך לומר רגע על היום וג"כ שייך לומר רגע על חצי יום או שליש היום לכך אמר בכל עת ובכל יום. ואמר ועל הכל אנו מודים לך וכו' כי על כל אלו העשרה אנו נותנין הודאה אל הש"י, כי כשם שההודאה היא בעשרה כך ראוי שתהיה ההודאה על עשרה וזהו הודאה שלימה, וכך לחמי תודה הוא ד' מינים תודה ודי בזה למבין. ועל הכל אנו מודים לך ומברכין אותך, כבר אמרנו כי ההודאה היא על דבר שאם לא היה הש"י נותן לו לא היה לו קיום, שכל הודאה כאשר הציל אותו מן הסכנה ומברכין הברכה היא על הטוב. והש"י נתן לאדם פרנסה ואם לא נתן לו לא היה לו קיום ולכך נתן אל הש"י הודאה על זה, ולא די שנתן לו קיום רק אף השביע את נפשו עד שהוא שבע וטוב והוא שייך ברכה:

סעיף כג

ובגמרא פרק שלשה שאכלו (מ"ח ע"ב) תניא ר' אליעזר אומר כל שלא אמר ארץ חמדה טובה ורחבה בברכת הארץ ומלכות בית דוד בבונה ירושלים לא יצא ידי חובתו נחום הזקן אומר צריך שיזכור בה ברית פלימו אומר צריך שיקדים ברית לתורה שזה נתן בג' בריתות וזו נתנה בי"ג בריתות והודאה תחלה וסוף והפוחת לא יפחות ואל יוסיף מאחד וכל הפוחת מאחד הרי זה מגונה וכל החותם מנחיל ארצות בברכת הארץ ומושיע את ישראל בבונה ירושלים הרי זה בור וכל שאינו אומר ברית ותורה בברכת הארץ ומלכות בית דוד בבונה ירושלים לא יצא ידי חובתו מסייע ליה לרבי אלעאי דאמר ר' אלעאי אמר רבי יעקב בר אחא משום רבינו כל שלא אמר ברית ותורה בברכת הארץ ומלכות בית דוד בבונה ירושלים לא יצא ידי חובתו ע"כ. כבר בארנו פי' ארץ חמדה טובה ורחבה, כי אלו ג' הם עיקר ושבח הארץ. ומה שאמר שצריך שיזכור בה ברית ותורה ומה ענין ברית ותורה

טעם. ויש לומר כי דבר זה חכמה, כי יותר קל שאל יחסר אח"כ כיון שכבר עשה הש"י זה ונתן לנו המזון ומכאן ואילך הוא קל שלא יחסר, לכך הראשון שהוא עבר מפעל הדגש קשה והעתיד מפעל הקל שאינו קשה. גם י"ל כי מתחלה צריך לומר לא חסר מפעל הדגש שר"ל שהש"י לא חסר לנו וצריך לתלות הדבר בו ית' שהוא לא החסיר לנו, ומכיון שכבר הזכיר הש"י בלשון לא חסר שוב אין צריך לומר אל יחסר היו"ד בסגול מן הקל וקאי על המזון שלא יהיה חסר לנו ויתן לנו הש"י המזון

סעיף טז

בעבור שמו הגדול, ר"ל כי הש"י מפרנס לכל כדי שיהיה אל העולם קיום, וזה בעבור שמו הגדול שאם לא יהיה לעולם קיום על מי יהיה נקרא שמו הגדול, כמו שאמר, יהושע על ישראל שאם חס ושלום יעשה כליה בישראל ומה תעשה לשמך הגדול, וכי יהא נקרא שמו הגדול על עצים ואבנים ולכך אמר בעבור שמו הגדול כי הוא זן וכו'. ועוד כי הפרנסה הוא קיום האדם ושם הויה הוא שנתתן הויה וקיום לעולם, ולכך אחר שברא העולם והעולם צריך לקיום מיד זכר זה השם הזה ביום עשות ה' אלקים ארץ ושמים וגו', ומפני כך זכר דוד המלך במזמור הודו לה' כי טוב וגו' כ"ו פעמים לעולם חסדו, ובאחרונה שהשלים מספר כ"ו כנגד מספרו של שם הגדול זכר נותן לחם לכל בשר כי לעולם חסדו, כי זה הוא על הכל מה שהוא ית' נותן לחם לכל כי הוא נזכר באחרונה ובו יושלם מספר כ"ו לעולם חסדו שהם כנגד מספר השם המיוחד. ועוד כי המזונות הם על ידי השם ית' בעצמו ולא על ידי מלאך ולכך הפרנסה מתיחס לשם המיוחד בפרט ואין להאריך בזה. וזכר ד' דברים כי הוא זן מה שצריך אל אכילתם והוא חיותו, פרנסה הוא שאר צרכיו וזה נקרא פרנסה, ומטיב לכל הוא הטובה שעושה עם הבריות לבד מצרכיו והוא תוספת טובה כמו שאמרנו למעלה, ומכין מזון לכל בריותיו וכו' וזה נאמר על שאר הנבראים, ושייך בזה ומכין מזון ולא לשון נתינה כי האדם שהוא שייך נותן לו וזוכה בו האדם אבל בשאר נבראים לא שייך לומר רק ומכין מזון לכל בריותיו:

סעיף יז

ברכה זאת פותחת הזן את העולם ומסיים הזן את הכל והחתימה יותר מן הפתיחה, וזה כי תחלה אמר הזן את העולם, ור"ל מצד כי העולם הוא צריך לפרנסה הש"י מפרנס אותו ונותן לו קיום וזהו מצד העולם עצמו, אבל החתימה הזן את הכל זה הוא מצד הש"י אשר הוא חפץ ורוצה לפרנס את הכל וזהו מצד העלה בלבד. וכמו שאמרו ז"ל הקדוש ברוך הוא מתאוה לתפלתן של צדיקים ופירושו מפני כי הש"י הוא חפץ להשפיע הטוב מצד עצמו, ולכך הוא מתאוה לתפלתן של צדיקים עד שיכול להשפיע כי בלא תפלה כאשר הוא עצמו אינו חפץ למה ישפיע הש"י להם, ולכך הוא מתאוה תפלתן עד שישפיע הטוב, ולכך חתם הזן את הכל שהכל מצד חפץ הוא עצמו ית' לפרנס את הכל והבן הדברים האלו מאד:

סעיף יח

ברכה שניה נודה לך, ברכה זאת התחלתה נודה לך וכן בסוף ועל הכל אנו מודים לך ולא כן הראשונה ולא השלישית. כי מה שנתן להם הארץ אשר מן הארץ חיי האדם, ולא כן ברכת המזון שהוא ית' מפרנס אותו כל שעה ולא נקרא נותן לו חיים שנתן לו חיים כאשר מפרנס את האדם שעה אחת כי אין זה כל חייו, אבל הארץ נתן להם למתנת עולמים אשר מן הארץ הם חיים כל ימיהם, ולכך כמו שכל הודאה כאשר נתן לו החיות ועל זה שייך הודאה כך נותן הודאה על הארץ, לכך אנו מתחילין בברכה זאת נודה לך ומסיים בנודה לך. אבל בנין בהמ"ק דבר זה אינו חיות האדם כמו שהוא הארץ שהוא חיות האדם ושייך בזה הודאה גמורה, וכן תמצא בכל הודאה שההודאה תמיד הודאה על חיינו המסורים בידך ועל נשמותינו הפקודות לך, מפני שנתן לנו החיים כאשר נתן לנו הארץ וכמו שאנו אומרים ברכה ועל חיינו וכו', לכך תקנו הודאה תחלה וסוף. ותקנו לומר נודה לך שהנחלת לאבותינו ארץ חמדה טובה ורחבה פירוש זה, ארץ חמדה כי הדברים שבארץ נחמדים הם כמו שאמר הכתוב (דברים ח') ארץ נחלי מים עינות ותהומות יוצאים בבקעה ובהר, ויש בה גנות ופרדסים נאים והפירות וכל אשר בה נחמדי' לאדם. ומפני כי יש דברים שהאדם חומד אותם ואינם טובים בעצמם לבריאות גופו ולתת כח אליו, ועל זה אמר ארץ טובה שהיא טובה בעצמה שהמאכלים שבה הם טובים ומבריאים את האדם ומחזקים אותו וזהו טובה. ואח"כ אמר ורחבה כמשמעו וגם זה מעלה עליונה, וכמו שאמרו ז"ל בפרק הניזקין (גיטין נ"ז ע"א) שנקראת ארץ צבי בשביל שהיא מחזקת כל יושביה ואין להם דוחק הישוב ולכך נזכר זה אחריו.

סעיף יט

ויש לך להבין כי אלו ג' דברים חמדה טובה ורחבה היו בארץ בשביל זכות האבות שאליהם נתנה הארץ ולכך היו בארץ אלו ג' דברי'. כי אברהם היה נחמד בעיני הכל כי עשה טוב עם הכל, כמו שהיתה מדתו של אברהם לעשות חסד וטוב עם הבריות, ואדם כמו זה אין ספק שהוא נחמד בעיני הבריות כאשר הוא מקובל על הבריות. ולכך אמרו לו (בראשית כ"ג) נשיא אלקים אתה בתוכנו וגו' ואמרו עמק שוה הוא עמק המלך שהשוו כל העולם והמליכו אברהם למלך ולא בכח ובחזקה מלך עליהם רק שהיה נחמד ומקובל על הבריות מצד הנהגתו,

סעיף יב

ובפרק שלשה שאכלו (נ' ע"א) ר' אומר ובטובו הרי זה תלמיד חכם ומטובו ה"ז בור רבי אומר ובטובו חיינו הרי זה ת"ח ובטובו חיים ה"ז בור ונהרבלאי מתני איפכא ולית הלכתא כנהרבלאי ע"כ. פי' זה כשאומר מטובו חיינו משמע מקצת טובו, לכך לא יאמר מטובו רק בטובו, וכן אם אמר בטובו חיים משמע כי יש חיים בטובו אבל אינו נותן השבח שהוא היה מקבל החיים מן הש"י, לכך לא יאמר ובטובו חיים רק ובטובו חיינו. וקצת היו אומרים ובטובו חיים ולא ובטובו חיינו דמשמע חיים של כל הבראים וזהו בזה נהרבלאי דס"ל דאין ה"נ נשיאמר ובטובו חיים דוקא דמשמע דכל חי בטובו. ולית הלכתא כך כי לא יאמר כך משמע שהמברך קבל החיים ולכך יאמר ובטובו חיינו, ואי משום דאין דמשמע הכלל א"צ להזכיר כי שהוא היה מקבל החיים:

סעיף יג

ברכת הזימון המברך אומר נברך שאכלנו משלו, והשנים אומרים ברוך שאכלנו משלו ובטובו חיינו, והמברך חוזר ואומר ברוך שאכלנו משלו ובטובו חיינו ומוסיף ברוך הוא וברוך שמו. וכן נכון כי תמיד העונה הוא מוסיף על שלפניו, כמו שהשליח צבור אומר ברכו את ה' המבורך וענין אחריו ברוך ה' המבורך לעולם ועד. וכן המברך אומר נברך שאכלנו משלו ואומרי' השנים אחריו ברוך שאכלנו משלו ובטובו חיינו והמברך אומר ברוך שאכלנו משלו וטובו חיינו ברוך הוא וברוך שמו, הרי כל אחד מוסיף מה שלא אמר שלפניו:

סעיף יד

הזן את העולם כלו בטובו, ר"ל הש"י מצד טובו טובו מפרנס את הכל. ואח"כ אמר כי פרנסת הש"י את העולם הוא מצד ג' פנים, כי יש שראוי לו הפרנסה מצד הדין והם הצדיקים שהם בעולם, וזהו שאמר הזן את העולם בחן ר"ל שהוא מפרנסו מפני שהוא נושא חן בעיני הש"י כמו שאצל נח דכתיב (בראשי' ו') ונח מצא חן וגו', ויש שמפרנסו הש"י מצד החסד והם בני אדם שהם כמו בהמות ואין להם דעת ופרנסתם מצד החסד, ויש אשר פרנסתם מצד הרחמים והם הקטנים אשר לא ידעו מאומה ויש לרחם עליהם, כמו אלו פרנסתם מצד הרחמים. ואח"כ הוא נותן לחם לכל בשר, וזה הוא נאמר על שהוא ית' נותן ומשפיע קיום כל הנמצאו' כאחד. וזה שאמר ונתן לחם לכל בשר כי הלחם סועד הלב ומחזקו, ולכך הקיום שנותן קיום ומשפיע לכל נקרא לחם לפי שהוא סועד ומקים הלב שבו חיות האדם, ודבר זה הוא מצד חסדו ית', ובדבר זה משותפים כל הבראים כאחד שהוא ית' נותן קיום אל הכל בשוה, רק כי הם מחולקים בפרנסתם, כי אשר מפרנס אותו בחן פרנסתו מחולק מן זה שפרנסתו הוא בחסד, וכן זה שפרנסה שלו בחסד מחולק פרנסתו מן אשר פרנסתו ברחמים שכל אחד פרנסתו כפי שהוא ראוי. אבל הקיום הוא אל הכל בשוה והוא מצד החסד כי חסדי הש"י מתפשט אל הכל והכל ראוים אל החסד, ולפיכך דבר זה שהוא נותן קיום אל הכל בשוה אין זה רק מצד מדת החסד אשר מדת החסד הוא מתפשט ומשותף אל הכל, וזה כי לעולם חסדו כלומר חסדו ית' אין לו גבול ושיעור, ואם הש"י עושה חסד אל תאמר כי יש לזה תכלית וגבול כי לעולם חסדו שאין קץ וגבול לחסדו ית'. ויש לך לשאול מפני מה נאמר דבר זה על חסד הש"י בפרט, וכן נאמר במזמור הודו (תמיד) כי לעולם חסדו, וכן בהלל הודו לה' כי טוב כי לעולם חסדו. וזה יש להבין כי כל הדברים הם מצד המקבל, כי המשפט הוא מגיע מצד המקבל שיש עליו המשפט, ואף הרחמים מצד המקבל כאשר מרחם על אחד, חוץ מן החסד כי החסד הוא מצד עצמו שהוא ית' משפיע הטוב והחסד מצד עצמו ואין עושה זה מצד המקבל רק מצד עצמו שהוא טוב. ודבר שהוא מצד עצמו בלתי בלתי תכלית וכך החסד שהוא עושה אל עולם בלתי בלתי תכלית רק הוא לעולם. ולא כן המשפט והרחמים כיון שהם מצד המקבל כי המקבל גורם שהמשפט בא עליו וכן הרחמים ג"כ מצד המקבל, וכמו שהמקבל הוא בעל תכלית כן המשפט והרחמים יש לו תכלית. וזה שאמר הודו לה' כי טוב כי לעולם חסדו ר"ל שיש לשבח הקב"ה כי הוא טוב לכך כל ח"ו כמו שהוא ית' אין קץ וסוף אליו כך חסדי הש"י אין קץ וסוף אליו, אבל שאר דברים שהוא מקבל מצד המקבל יש להם קץ ותכלית. ועוד פי' כי חסדי הש"י הם לעולם ולא יפסוק, כי אף לעוה"ב שלא יהיה המשפט על חוטאים וכן לא יהיה צריך לרחמים, אבל החסד לא יפסוק כלל אף לעוה"ב לא יפסוק החסד והטוב שהוא עושה וזהו כי לעולם חסדו לעולם הבא, ודבר זה ג"כ הוא מטעם אשר התבאר כי חסדי הש"י מצד עצמו לכך כמו שהוא ית' אין תכלית אליו כך חסדי הש"י הם לעולם בלי קץ ותכלית והבן זה:

סעיף טו

ובטובו הגדול לא חסר לנו כו', המלה של חסר הוא מן הקל וכן אל יחסר לנו הקל ה"ד בסגול והוא מן הקל וקאי על המזון, כלומר כי המזון לא היה חסר לנו מפני שהש"י היה נותן לנו תמיד המזון ולכך לא חסר לנו מזון, ואל יחסר לנו מזון לעולם ועד שיתן לנו הש"י מזון שלא נהיה חסרים מן המזון. ויש אומרים לא חסר לנו החי"ת בחיר"ק מפעל הדגש, וצריך לפרש כי לא חסר לנו הש"י מזון רק היה נותן תמיד המזון, וכן אל יחסר היו ה"ד בשוא והחי"ת בפתח מפעל הדגש כלומר שאל יחסר מליתן לנו מזון. אבל אותם שאומרים לא חסר החי"ת בחיר"ק מפעל הדגש, ואחר כך אומרים ולא יחסר היו ה"ד בסגול שהוא מן הקל וא"כ אחד שהוא מן הקל ואחד מן הדגש, אין זה

מצד הש"י אשר הוא טוב ומשפיע הטוב. לכך אמר הטוב והמטיב כלומר הש"י מצד עצמו טוב ומטיב מבלי הכנת המקבל, כי אין לומר שהמקבל מוכן לתוספת טוב שאין הכנה הזאת במקבל, אבל רבוי הטוב הוא מן הש"י שמשפיע ממנו רבוי הטוב והוא לעתים בלבד ואינו דבר תמידי. ולפיכך אין מברכין הטוב והמטיב רק אם אחר ג"כ נהנה עמו שזהו רבוי הטוב ועל זה נתקנה ברכת הטוב והמטיב, וכיון שהיא תוספת טובה אינה מן התורה רק מדרבנן.

סעיף ט

ועוד יש לך לדעת ולהבין כי הברכה הזאת שהיא ברכ' המזון תקנו על שהש"י השלים את ישראל בכל השלמה שאפשר ועל זה יש לברך את הש"י, וכדכתיב ואכלת ושבעת וברכת את ה' אלקיך וגו' וכל שביעה היא השלמה ועל זה יש לברך את הש"י, ומאחר שמברך הש"י אשר השלים את ישראל מברך ג"כ מה שהשלים אותם הש"י והם שבעים ושלמים מכל. ומתחלה מברך שנתן להם מזון ובזה משותפים כל הנבראים שיש להם מזון, ואח"כ זכר מה שהשלים ישראל יותר שנתן להם השלמה זאת ארץ מיוחדת ארץ קדושה נבדלת מכל ארצות ובזה הם נבדלים מכל האומות, ולכך צריך להזכיר בברכה זאת ברית ותורה כמו שיתבאר בסמוך, וברכה ג' תקנו שהשלים הש"י את ישראל בבנין בהמ"ק, ודבר זה השלמה אחרונה שאין עליה עוד שהש"י היה שם ששכינתו ביניהם בירושלים ובבהמ"ק ואין זה כברכת הארץ. ואף כי הש"י השלים את ישראל בהשלמה יתירה ונתן להם הארץ שהיא ארץ מיוחדת ובזה יש לישראל השלמה מיוחדת, מ"מ עדיין לא ידענו כי נתן לישראל השלמה שאין עליה השלמה ובזה נתן להם ירושלים ובהמ"ק והשלמה הזאת היא על הכל. ולכך בהגדה של פסח אמרו כמה מעלות טובות וכו' זכר באחרונה ובנה לנו בהמ"ק והוא השלמה אחרונה. וכל אלו ג' דברים הם השלמה שיושלם האדם עד שהוא שלם בתכלית היותר, אבל ברכת הטוב והמטיב הוא על רבוי הטוב ושהוא טוב ומטיב ואין זה רק תוספת טובה ולפיכך הטוב והמטיב הוא דרבנן בלבד.

סעיף י

ועוד אלו ג' ברכות ברכת הזן הוא השלמת הטבע שהאדם בטבע צריך לאכיל', והארץ אינה השלמת טבעו בלבד רק היא השלמה רוחנית אלקית ג"כ, וזה ידוע כי אוירא דא"י מחכים (ב"ב קנ"ח ע"א), וכמה דברים שנאמרו במעלת א"י ודבר זה א"צ לבאר. אמנם אף כי השלמה הזאת שנתן להם את הארץ היא השלמה אלקית, אין זה דבר אלקי לגמרי כמו ירושלים ובהמ"ק, כי ירושלים עיר הקודש ובהמ"ק שהוא בית קדוש אלקיי הוא השלמת אלקית לגמרי, ולכך אמרו (אבות פ"ה) עשרה נסים נעשו בבהמ"ק כי כל בהמ"ק מעלתו אלקית לגמרי עד כי מושלמים ישראל בתכלית ההשלמה אלקית, ופי' זה הוא כמו פי' שלפני זה. וכל זה יש להזכיר בברכת המזון שתקנו על השביעה שהשלים האדם עד שאין האדם חסר, ובאלו ג' ברכות נעשו ישראל שבעים ושלמים לגמרי.

סעיף יא

ועוד יש לפרש כי כל אלו ג' ברכות הכל הם השלמה אחת לגמרי, כי מפני שתקנו ברכת המזון על שהש"י השלים את ישראל במזון, ותחלה תקנו ברכת הזן שהש"י משפיע מן השמים להם מזון, וצריך אל ברכה זאת מקבל מוכן שהוא מוכן לקבל שפע הברכה ולזה נתן להם הארץ שהיא מקבל מוכן לזה בברכה, ומפני כי הברכה באה ממלמעלה למטה אשר המעלה והמטה הם נבדלים זה מזה, וצריך שיהיה כאן אמצעי אשר הוא שייך למעלה ושייך למטה שעל ידו הברכה באה למטה וזה בהמ"ק, כי בהמ"ק הוא מחבר עליונים ותחתונים ולכך על ידו באים הברכות לעולם מעליונים לתחתונים. וכן תמצא במדרש שדרשו על והנה סולם מוצב ארצה וראשו מגיע השמימה על בית המקדש, שהוא כמו סולם שיורדים בו מלמעלה ועולים בו מלמטה שמחבר עליונים ותחתונים. אמנם הטוב והמטיב אין זה שהוא השלמה רק הוא בא על תוספת טובה ורבוי טובה ואין זה השלמת האדם ולכך הוא מדרבנן. ועוד מצד אחר ברכת הטוב והמטיב דרבנן, כי ג' ברכות הראשונות הם תמידיות אע"ג שבהמ"ק הוא חרב הרי העון היה גורם ומתחלה נבנה שיהיה קיים תמיד, אבל הברכה הרביעית הטוב והמטיב דבר זה אינו תמידי רק לשעה ולעתים וכמו שדרשו את אשר אחון עת אשר אחון, ולפיכך ברכה זו מדרבנן בלבד ולכך קבעו אלו הדברים בברכת המזון, והבן אלו דברים כי כלם הם ברורים. ומה שתקנו הטוב והמטיב בינה על הרוגי ביתר הטוב שלא הסריחו והמטיב שנתנו לקבורה, פי' זה כי ראוי הוא שיהיה מתקנין הטוב והמטיב בינה, כי אחר שנחרבה ביתר ברכת מדת הדין בישראל בשביל חטא ובא העונש עליהם עם כל זה נהג הש"י עמהם בטוב, ודבר זה הוא יותר על כל הטובות שהש"י נוהג כאשר מתוך מדת הדין בא הטוב הזה שלא הסריחו ונתנו לקבורה כי הוא מורה על מדת טובו לגמרי. ולכך כמו שכל אחד תקן הברכה הראוי לו לתקן, כי משה תקן ברכת הזן כשבא להם המן ויהושע תקן ברכת הארץ כשבאו לארץ ודוד תקן בונה ירושלים, כמו כן תקנו ביבנה הטוב והמטיב אחר שבא עליהם פורעניות בשביל חטא שלהם ומתוך הדין הקשה והחושך שהיו יושבים הטיב הש"י עמהם מצד מדת טובו זהו הטוב והמטיב. ופירשו הטוב שלא הסריחו ומטיב שנתנו לקבורה כי טובה על טובה כמו זה שלא הסריחו ונוסף על זה שנתנו לקבורה, שנקרא זה הטוב והמטיב כאשר יש טובה על טובה בפעם אחד:

סעיף ו

ואמר ומגביה מן הקרקע טפח, זה כנגד וישתחוו לך בני אמך. וביאור זה, כי כל השתחויה הוא פשוט ידים ורגלים לגמרי כמו שחה לעפר נפשנו (תהלים מ"ד), וההשתחוה על הקרקע הוא כמו הארץ, ואשר משתחוה אליו הוא נבדל מן הקרקע, כי הקרקע מורה על המשתחוה שהוא על הקרקע ואשר משתחוים לו גבוה מן הקרקע, ולכך מגביהו מן הקרקע טפח נגד וישתחוו לך בני אמך. ואמר ונותן עיניו בו, כי מה שנותן עיניו בו ע"י העין הכל נמצא בפועל, ולכך העין שנותן בכוס של ברכה הוא שנמצא הברכה בפעל ומורה זה כי ישראל הם בעלי ברכה לגמרי, וא"כ אין האחד ראוי לקלל את אשר הוא ברוך בפעל כי כאשר הוא ברוך בפעל הקללה נהפך על עצמו. ודבר זה בארנו בכמה מקומות שעל כן אמרו חכמים לעולם תהא מן ליטא ואל תהא מן לייטא, פי' שיותר טוב אליו שיהיה מקולל מן אחרים מן אשר יקלל את אחרים, כי כאשר מקלל אחר והמקבל אינו מקבל הקללה אותה הקללה נהפכה עליו. ועוד כאשר נותן עיניו בו מורה שנתברך בכל ואין רואה לפניו רק ברכה ולכך ונותן עיניו הוא כנגד אורריך ארור. ואמר ומשגר לאשתו ולבניו ולביתו וזהו כנגד מברכיך ברוך, כי אשתו ובניו ובני ביתו בודאי מברכין את בעל הבית שהרי מקבלים טובה הימנו ובודאי הם מברכין למי שעשה להם טובה, ולכך גם הם מקבלים מן הברכה של בעל הבית כדכתיב מברכיך ברוך ולכך ישגר כוס של ברכה מן לאשתו ולבניו ולבני ביתו.

סעיף ז

הרי לך מבואר ומפורש כי עשרה דברים שנאמרו בכוס הם כנגד עשרה ברכות של ויתן לך, וכאשר תשכיל אז תבין הדברים האלו על אמתן. והעד הנאמן על פי' זה שאמר ר' יוחנן ואנו אין לנו אלא ד' שהם חי מלא שטיפה הדחה, ולמה אין לנו אלא ד' ואין הפירוש שא"צ רק לעשות ד' שהם חי מלא שטיפה הדחה שהרי אמוראים היו עושים עיטור ועיטוף ג"כ. אבל פי' זה, כי עתה כאשר אנו בגלות אין לנו שנעבדוך וכן וישתחוו לך לאומים הוי גביר לאחיך וישתחוו לך בני אמך אוררייך ארור ומברכיך ברוך, כי כל אלי הברכות אינם לישראל כאשר הם יורדים ושפלים בגלות והשכינה אין עמהם. אבל ד' ברכות הראשונות והם מטל השמים ומשמני הארץ ורוב דגן ותירוש שהם תלוים בארץ לא בישראל ואלו הם עדיין בארץ, דודאי אע"ג שאין הברכה כ"כ בארץ כמו שהיה קודם מ"מ הברכה ישנה עדיין בכמה מקומות וכדמוכח ולכך אמר ואנו אין לנו אלא ד'. ומצאתי בנוסחאות שלנו ויש אומרי' ומשגרו לאשתו ולבניו ולבני ביתו, ולנוסח' זו משמע שיש עשרה דברים בכוס של ברכה חוץ מן משגר לאשתו ולבניו ולבני ביתו. והנוסחא הזאת סוברת בודאי מפני כי מקבלו בשתי ידיו ונותנו לימינו נחשבים כשתים ויהיו לפי זה אחד עשר, והרי אמר עשרה דברים נאמרו בכוס של ברכה ולכך גורסין ויש אומרים אחד עשר. ותמהתי על זאת הגירסא כי לנוסחא זאת לא יתכן הפירוש של מעלה שהוא ברור. ואח"כ עייניתי בדברי הרא"ש ז"ל ומצאתי דלא גרס ויש אומרים כלל וכן בטור וכן בכמה פוסקים ג"כ דלא גרסי כך, ובודאי זאת הגירסא היא נכונה כאשר פירשנו כי מקבלו בשתי ידיו ונותנו לימינו הוא דבר אחד:

סעיף ח

ובפרק שלשה שאכלו (מ"ח ע"ב) ת"ר משה תקן לישראל ברכת הזן בשעה שירד להם המן יהושע תקן להם ברכת הארץ כיון שנכנסו לארץ דוד ושלמה תקנו להם בונה ירושלים דוד תקן על ישראל ועל ירושלים עירך ושלמה תקן על הבית הגדול והקדוש הטוב והמטיב ביבנה תקנו כנגד הרוגי ביתר דאמר רב מתנא יום שנתנו הרוגי ביתר לקבורה תקנו ביבנה הטוב והמטיב הטוב שלא הסריחו והמטיב שנתנו לקבורה ת"ר ברכת המזון כך היא ברכה ראשונה ברכת הזן שניה ברכת הארץ שלישית בונה ירושלים רביעית הטוב והמטיב ובשבת מתחיל בנחמה ומסיים בנחמה ואומר קדושת היום באמצע ע"כ. ומה שאמר משה תקן וכו', אע"ג דברכת המזון דאורייתא כדאמר בתר הכי מנין לברכת המזון מן התורה שנאמר ואכלת ושבעת וברכת את ה' אלקיך, רק שר"ל כי משה תקן נוסח הברכה. ומה שיש לברך אלו ג' ברכות ומה ענין ברכת בונה ירושלים אל ברכת המזון. וזה מפני כי הש"י נתן אל האדם ג' דברים, האחד שנתן לאדם ההכרחי אליו כמו המזון שא"א שיהיה האדם בלא מזון, והשני נוסף על זה שנתן לאדם ההכרחי כך נתן להם הארץ הטובה והיא מבורכת בכל עד כי יש להם אף דבר שאינו הכרחי, ועוד יותר מזה שנתן לאדם עד שאין למעלה מזה כלל והוא תכלית השלמה הוא בהמ"ק. כי ע"י בהמ"ק היה להם הברכה בעולם בשלימות לגמרי, וע"י בהמ"ק היה העולם מקבל הברכה בשלימות לגמרי. ואחר שהוא חרב בעונינו יש לבקש רחמים רחם ה' אלקינו וכו' כלומר שיהיה נבנה בהמ"ק במהרה בימינו ואז תהיה הברכה בעולם בשלימות כמו שהיה. ועוד בארנו אלו ג' דברים בנתיב החסד ע"ש, ולכך תקנו אלו ג' ברכות כי כל שלשתן שייכין למזונות. ברכה רביעית הטוב והמטיב, כי ג' ברכות הראשונות הם דברי' שהאדם מוכן אליו, כי האדם בודאי מוכן לקבל המזון שהוא דבר ההכרחי להיות, ואף הארץ בודאי ישראל ראוים שיהיה להם שלימות הזה שהרי הארץ נתנה להם הארץ ירושה, ואף בהמ"ק ראוים ישראל אל זה שיהיה להם הברכה שהוא יותר, אבל הטוב והמטיב אין זה רק מצד הש"י שהוא טוב ומטיב ונתן טובה על טובה וזהו אינו מצד המקבל כלל רק

להו אנן ניעבד לחומרא ומגביהו מן הקרקע טפח אמר רב אחא בר חנינא מאי קרא כוס ישועות אשא ובשם ה'
אקרא ונותן עיניו בו כי היכי דלא ניסח דעתיה מניה ומשגרו לאנשי ביתו במתנה כי היכי דתתברך. ואין ספק כי
מה שיש בכוס של ברכה דוקא עשרה דברים אין זה דבר מקרה שכך אירע המספר, אבל אלו עשרה דברים הם
נגד עשר ברכות שבירך יצחק את יעקב ויתן לך האלקים מטל השמים וכו'. וזה כי כנגד מטל השמי' ומשמני
הארץ הוא שטיפה והדחה, כי הטל מדיח הקרקע מבחוץ עד שהוא מלא טל של ברכה ולכך צריך שטיפה מבחוץ,
והדחה מבפנים כנגד ומשמני הארץ שהוא ג"כ לחלוחית של שמן והוא בפנים הארץ שאין הארץ ארץ יבישה,
הרי השטיפה והדחה הוא כנגד מטל השמים וכנגד ומשמני הארץ. חי כנגד ותירוש כי חי הוא שהיין הוא בכחו
ואינו מזוג, כי כאשר היין הוא חי הוא מורה על הברכה שנתברכו בתירוש ואם אין היין חי רק מים מזוג במים אין זה
ברכה של תירוש כי מזוג אינו תירוש כמו שאמרנו, ולפיכך צריך שיהיה היין חי. מלא כנגד דגן ולא כתיב
ורוב תירוש, מפני כי עיקר הברכה של ותירוש הוא שהיין הוא בכח גדול כאשר הוא יין של א"י, אבל מלא שייך
דוקא בדגן ולכן כנגד זה צריך שיהיה כוס של ברכה מלא על כל גדותיו. ושייך מלוי בגרנות כדכתיב ומלאו
הגרנות בר והדגן הוא משביע האדם עד שהוא מלא ולכך שייך בדגן מלוי, וכאשר יש רוב דגן בעולם אז העולם
הוא שבע ומלא. והיה לו לסדר ולומר מלא חי כדכתיב בקרא ורוב דגן ותירוש, רק כי חי קודם כאשר נתן היין
בכוס צריך שיהיה חי וממלא את הכוס ממנו ולכך אין לומר מלא חי. ומ"ש שנותנים לו נחלה בלי מצרים, כי
כאשר מברך על כוס מלא עד שהכוס הוא כוס של ברכה והברכה בשלימות אין לה גבול. וכן מה
שאמר שזוכה לעוה"ז ועוה"ב כי הברכה הוא מגיע עד בלי גבול אף עד עוה"ב ולכך זוכה לעוה"ז ולעוה"ב כאשר
הברכה היא בשלימות:

סעיף ד

עיטור ועיטוף, עיטור כמו ויהיו עוטרים את דוד ר"ל מסבבים את דוד, וקאמר רבי יהודה מעטרהו בתלמידים
ופי' רש"י תלמידיו סובבים אותו כשהיה מברך, רב חסדא מעטר ליה בנטלי. פי' זה כי העיטור הוא כנגד יעבדוך
עמים, והעבדים הולכים אחר האדון ומסבבים אותו מכל צד והולכים לאחריו ולפניו, ולכך היה מעטר אותו
בתלמידים אשר משמשין לרבם, ודבר זה כי יקבלו ברכה שיהיו העכו"ם עובדים אותו, והנטלי שהם הכוסות
שמסבבים אותו הוא דמיון אל העכו"ם שמסבבים לישראל כמו עבדים לאדוניהם. ומה שאמר רב חנן ובחי פי'
כיון שהיה מעטר אותו בכוסו כמו שכוס של ברכת המזון הוא חי וכך אלו כוסות שהם לעיטור ג"כ היין חי, שלא
יהיה נראה שמברך על כוס שאינו חי. ומה שאמר רב ששת ובברכת הארץ, היינו שאם יהיה מעטר אותו בכוסות
מתחלת ברכת המזון היה נראה כאלו הוא מברך על כוסות הרבה. ואפשר שיש רמז במה שאמר ובחי, כי זה
שהיה מעטר אותו בכוסות הוא כנגד יעבדוך עמים והעמים במספר שבעים והוא מספר יין, ואם לא היה אלא
מזוג לא נקרא יין אשר מספרו שבעים ולכך כנגד יעבדוך עמים הוא העיטור. וכנגד וישתחוו לך לאומים הוא
העיטוף, כי כאשר האדם מעוטף בבגדו הוא דרך כבוד כמו החשוב שיושב מעוטף בבגדו דרך כבוד והבריות
משתחוים לו, וכדקריא ר' יוחנן למאני מכבדותא ודבר זה א"צ לפרש, ולכך העיטוף הוא כנגד והשתחוו לך לאומים
כי השתחויה הוא הכבוד שחולקין לאשר הוא מכובד.

סעיף ה

ואמר ומקבלו בשתי ידיו ומגביהו מן הקרקע טפח זה כנגד הוי גביר לאחיך. וזה שכאשר מקבלו בשתי ידיו זה
מורה שיש לו ברכה של כח, כי הידים הם מושלים כמו ידו בכל, ובכל מקום היד מורה על הממשלה והכח, לכך
מקבלו בשתי ידיו שהיד שבה הכח מקבלת ברכה עד שהוא גביר. ונתנו לימינו זה מורה על התרוממות,
לומר כי הברכה הוא שיהיה גובר על אחיו ומתרומם עליהם, כי הימין מורה על התרוממות כמו שאמר (תהלים
קי"ח) ימין ה' רוממה, ולכך מה שמקבלו בשתי ידיו ונתנו לימינו מורה שיהיה גבור ומושל על אחיו ומתנשא
עליה'. ועוד כי אם מקבלו בידו הימינית לבד היה זה מורה חסרון כי היד היא אחת, ובודאי שנים הם יותר מאחד
ולכך מקבלו בשתי ידיו וזה מורה על כי כחו על כן וידו הוא בכל, שכל אשר הוא גובר הוא מושל בכל וכח שלו כח
כללי. ומה שהוא נותנו לימינו זה מורה שהוא מתנשא במעלה עליונה מאד. ונמצא כי אלו שני דברים מקבלו
בשתי ידיו מורה כי כחו מתפשט בכל ולכך מקבלו בשתי ידיו, ונתנו לימינו מורה שזה מורה התרוממות והנה יש כאן
החשיבות היותר. והבן זה כי הם דברי חכמה. ועוד תדע כי מה שמקבלו בשתי ידיו כי כחו יהיה בכל כן מורה מה
שנתנו לימינו שיהיה גדול ומתרומם למעלה. ועוד תדע כי מה שמקבלו בשתי ידיו ונתנו לימינו דבר זה מורה כי
הכח של הממשלה הוא אל הכלל, שנתנו לישראל כח המלכות והכלל מקבלים את המלך להיות מלך מושל,
ולכך מקבל כוס של ברכה בשתי ידים כי הידים הם כל ידי הם נחשבים מקבלי הברכה שהוא הכח הכח של מלכות,
ונתנו לימינו זה המלך הוא המלך שמקבל הכח והממשלה מן הכלל וכתיב (דברים י"ז) שום תשים עליך מלך מקרב אחיך,
ופירוש זה ברור.

נתיבות עולם, נתיב העבודה פרק יח

סעיף א

הברכה שהוא עיקר בברכות הוא ברכת המזון שיהיה נזהר שיהיה מברך הש"י אשר נתן לו מזונות שלו שהוא דבר גדול על הכל. וכמו שאמרו בפרק ערבי פסחים (פסחים קי"ח ע"א) קשים מזונותיו של אדם יותר מן הגאולה דאלו גאולה כתיב המלאך הגואל אותי מכל רע ואלו כמזונותיו של אדם כתיב האלקים הרועה אותי מעודי. פי' זה כי הגאולה היא כאשר אחד הוא תחת רשותו של אחר, והוא יוצא מרשות אחר לחירות. ולכך המלאך יכול להוציא אותו ולגאול אותו, כי המלאך אין נמצא דבר זה בו שיהיה המלאך תחת רשותו של אדם רק הוא תחת רשות הקב"ה, וזה לא נקרא שהוא תחת אחר כי הוא ית' הכל תחתיו וכך מחייב שיהיה ואין זה חסרון רק כך הוא בריאתו. לכך כאשר אחד הוא תחת רשותו של אחר הוא צריך לגאולה. ולא שייך שעבוד במלאך שיהיה צריך לגאולה, ולכך אפשר שיהיה המלאך גואל אותו מאחר שלא נמצא בו החסרון הזה הוא השעבוד במלאך. אבל הפרנסה שהוא קיום של אדם כי אחר שנברא האדם צריך לקיום, הפרנסה מקיימת האדם, והנה העליונים ג"כ צריכים אל הקיום מן הש"י שהוא ית' מקיים אותם ואיך יהיה דבר זה על ידי מלאך מאחר כי גם המלאך צריך לקיום, כי מאחר שגם המלאך צריך לזה אינו יכול להשלים אחר, ולפיכך הפרנס' היא על ידי הש"י בעצמו. וזהו האלקים הרועה אותי מעודי, ואלו בגאולה כתיב המלאך הגואל אותי. והנה תראה ותבין כי הלב מפרנס כל האיברים בעצמם וכולם מקבלים חיות ממנו, וכן כל הנבראים מקבלים קיום מן השם ית'. וזה אמרם בפ"ק דברכות (י' ע"א) מה הקב"ה זן את כל העולם אף הנשמה זנה את כל האיברים, הרי מדמה הנשמה בזה להקב"ה בענין המזונות, וע"י נזכרו שם הרבה דברים על המזונות שהם קשים ואין כאן מקום זה, ולכך הדעת נותן והשכל מחייב שלפי גודל הדבר הזה שמקבל האדם הפרנסה, צריך לברך את השם ית' על זה ברכה שלימה וכמו שיתבאר עוד דבר זה בברכת המזון. ומאוד דקדקו חכמים ז"ל על ברכת המזון שתהא הברכה בשלימות הגמור כמו שהש"י השלים את האדם במזונותיו. וצריך שיהיה מברך על כוס של יין, ואף האומרים כי ברכת המזון אין צריך כוס מכל מקום מצוה איכא כאשר יש לו כוס של ברכה. וכוס של יין הוא ביותר ראוי לברכה כי הוא מורה על הברכה שהוא מן השם ית' ולכך נקרא כוס של ברכה, ודבר זה הוא ראשון והתחלה לברך הש"י על הטוב שהוא משפיע, וכאשר יש לפניו שפע ברכה הוא היין הוא משבח ומברך ג"כ על שאר ברכה שהוא מקבל מן הש"י ולכך מברך ברכת מזונו על כוס של יין:

סעיף ב

ובפרק שלשה שאכלו (ברכות ג' ע"א) אין מברכין על היין עד שיתן לתוכו מים דברי ר"א וחכמים אומרים מברכין. ובגמ' אמר ר' יוסי בר' חנינא מודים חכמים לר"א בכוס של ברכה שאין מברכין עליו עד שיתן לתוכו מים מאי טעמא אמר ר' אושעי' בעינן מצוה מן המובחר ע"א. ונראה כי אין חלוק בין יין של ארץ ישראל לשאר יינות שבמדינות אלו וצריך שיתן לתוכו מים, כי מאחר שהיין של ארץ ישראל הוא עיקר היין א"כ טבע היין שאין ראוי לברכה בלא מים ולכך יש ליתן בתוכו מים. ומ"מ אין צריך שיתן לתוכו מים עד שיהיה מזוג לגמרי, דהרי משמע כל שהוא נותן לתוכו מים הן הרבה הן מעט, דלא אמר רק שצריך שיתן לתוכו מים ולא אמרו שיהיה מזוג. ועוד אדרבה הרי צריך שיהיה חי והוא אחד מעשרה דברים שנאמרו בכוס של ברכה, אלא בודאי צריך שיהיה חי ולא יהיה מזוג. ואין צריך רק שיתן בו מים כי המים מתקן היין ודי אם יתן בתוכו מעט מים, אבל שיהיה מזוג אדרבא דבר זה אינו כי מזוג אין עליו שם יין גמור רק כיון שהמים הם תקון היין כאשר הוא חי היין, כי היין כאשר הוא בלבד אין זה מן המובחר שהרי היין הביא ילילה לעולם וכמה דברים שאמרו על היין שהוא הפך הברכה, ואמרו י"ג וי"ן כתובין בנח אצל היין כדאיתא בפרק בן סורר ומורה (סנהדרין ע' ע"א), ולפיכך אין מברכין על היין עד שיתן לתוכו מים ואז הוא ראוי לברכה, כי כאשר מחבר היין אל המים עוד אל היין מוכן אל הילילה כאשר יש לו חבור אל המים והוא ראוי לברכה וכך יש לנהוג ולא וג יש בענין אחר:

סעיף ג

ובפרק שלשה שאכלו (ברכות נ"א ע"א) תנא עשרה דברים נאמרו בכוס של ברכה טעון הדחה ושטיפה ומלא עטור ועיטוף ונוטלו בשתי ידיו ונותנו בימינו ומגביהו מן הקרקע טפח ונותן עיניו בו ומשגרו לאשתו ולבניו ולאנשי ביתו אמר ר' יוחנן אנו אין לנו אלא ארבעה בלבד תנא הדחה שטיפה חי מלא הדחה מבפנים ושטיפה מבחוץ א"ר יוחנן כל המברך על כוס מלא נותנים לו נחלה בלי מצרים שנאמר ברכת ה' ים ודרום ירשה רבי יוסי ב"ח אומר זוכה ונוחל שני עולמים העוה"ז והעוה"ב עטור ר' יהודה מעטרהו בתלמידים רב חסדא מעטר ליה בנטלי אמר ר' יוחנן א"ר ששת ובברכת הארץ עטוף רב פפא מעטף ויתיב רב אסי פריס סודרא על רישיה נוטל בשתי ידיו א"ר חנינא בר פפא מאי קרא שאו ידיכם קודש וברכו את ה' ונותנו לימין א"ר חייא בר אבא א"ר יוחנן ראשונים שאלו שמאל מהו שתסייע לימין אמר רב אשי הואיל וראשונים איבעיא להו ולא איפשט

Made in the USA
Coppell, TX
07 January 2025

44069376R00063